'This new edition does not simply update a classic resource for teachers and [...] questions of comparative political science from the dual perspective of democrat[...] and declining trust on the part of the people, it compels us to consider those que[...]'

— **Ben Stanley**, *SWPS University of Social Sciences and Humanities, Poland*

'*Comparative Government and Politics* stands out in a market saturated with introductory textbooks. The tone and style of the text are very accessible and lend themselves well to both those majoring in the field, and those not familiar with it at all.'

— **Johannes van Gorp**, *American University of Sharjah, UAE*

'This book continues to be the leading introductory text in the field, and for good reason. Comprehensive, well-structured, and incorporating analysis of the latest trends and developments, it provides a highly accessible resource for both students and teachers the world over. Its thematic approach and extensive range of country case studies ensure that it is truly international in scope and relevance.'

— **Monique Emser**, *University of KwaZulu-Natal, South Africa*

'I have used this book for the last ten years, and this is the best version I have seen so far. To put it simply, this edition will allow me to teach my introductory course on comparative politics in the way I want to teach it.'

— **Mariely Lopez-Santana**, *George Mason University, USA*

'In my experience, *Comparative Government and Politics* is by far the best stand-alone text in this area. It is thorough, and unlike the many other texts in the field it focuses in an interesting and engaging way on the dynamics of a broad range of comparative political phenomena as they apply to real-world politics. Coupled with McCormick's forthcoming country case studies volume, this will constitute the most comprehensive, and yet interesting and very readable approach to the teaching of this key subject at the undergraduate level.'

— **Daniel Zirker**, *University of Waikato, New Zealand*

'The addition of John McCormick in this classic title for comparative politics has made a significant impact in this edition. Full of new features, captivating graphs and images, this has become an important resource for students of comparative politics as well as an excellent reference point for those teaching the subject. Users of the book will particularly enjoy the spotlights on specific countries and cases, as well as the abundance of interesting data that inspire further research.'

— **Theofanis Exadaktylos**, *University of Surrey, UK*

'This enriched version of a classic textbook remains the first choice of textbook for my introductory comparative politics courses.'

— **Bec Strating**, *La Trobe University, Australia*

'This edition is a substantive enhancement of the previous editions, with more comprehensive coverage of politics in authoritarian regimes, which is of tremendous added value. This is a text on which students and teachers of comparative politics can count.'

— **James Wong**, *The Hong Kong University of Science and Technology, Hong Kong*

'An excellent and comprehensive introduction to comparative government and politics which helps students to understand basic concepts, theoretical and methodological approaches, and key institutions and developments in the field across democratic and autocratic states.'

— **Rosalind Shorrocks**, *University of Manchester, UK*

'The 11th edition of *Comparative Government and Politics* continues to provide a comprehensive introduction to the field of comparative politics, equipping students with the basic knowledge and methods to compare various forms of political organization across geographical and cultural boundaries.'

— **Karsten Schulz**, *University of Groningen, the Netherlands*

COMPARATIVE GOVERNMENT AND POLITICS SERIES

Published

Maura Adshead and Jonathan Tonge
Politics in Ireland

Rudy Andeweg and Galen A. Irwin
Governance and Politics of the Netherlands (4th edition)

Tim Bale
European Politics: A Comparative Introduction (4th edition)

Nigel Bowles and Robert K. McMahon
Government and Politics of the United States (3rd edition)

Paul Brooker
Non-Democratic Regimes (3rd edition)

Kris Deschouwer
The Politics of Belgium: Governing a Divided Society (2nd edition)

Robert Elgie
Political Leadership in Liberal Democracies

Rod Hague, Martin Harrop and John McCormick
Comparative Government and Politics: An Introduction (11th edition)

Paul Heywood
The Government and Politics of Spain

Xiaoming Huang and Jason Young
Politics in Pacific Asia (2nd edition)

Robert Leonardi
Government and Politics of Italy

John McCormick
Cases in Comparative Government and Politics

B. Guy Peters
Comparative Politics: Theories and Methods
[Rights: World excluding North America]

Tony Saich
Governance and Politics of China (4th edition)

Eric Shiraev
Russian Government and Politics (2nd edition)

Anne Stevens
Government and Politics of France (3rd edition)

Ramesh Thakur
The Government and Politics of India

COMPARATIVE GOVERNMENT AND POLITICS

AN INTRODUCTION

11TH EDITION

ROD HAGUE   **MARTIN HARROP**   **JOHN McCORMICK**

Eleventh edition 2019 by
RED GLOBE PRESS

Previous ten editions published by
PALGRAVE

Red Globe Press in the UK is an imprint of Macmillan Education Limited, registered in England, company number 01755588, of 4 Crinan Street, London, N1 9XW.

Red Globe Press® is a registered trademark in the United States, the United Kingdom, Europe and other countries.

ISBN 978–1–352–00504–2 hardback
ISBN 978–1–352–00505–9 paperback

This book is printed on paper suitable for recycling and made from fully managed and sustained forest sources. Logging, pulping and manufacturing processes are expected to conform to the environmental regulations of the country of origin.

A catalogue record for this book is available from the British Library.

A catalog record for this book is available from the Library of Congress.

BRIEF CONTENTS

DETAILED CONTENTS

ILLUSTRATIONS AND FEATURES

SPOTLIGHTS

FOCUS

FIGURES

TABLES

MAPS

PREFACE

In North Korea, the ruling regime carries out a nuclear test. In Zimbabwe, the military removes the leader from power. In India, the one-time dominant ruling party records its worst ever election defeat. In Britain, the government struggles to negotiate its country's exit from the European Union. In Russia, Vladimir Putin is re-elected for a new term as president. Across the northern hemisphere, millions of people experience record heat. In the United States, the president opens a trade war with his country's major trading partners, while baulking at an investigation into Russian interference with the presidential election.

Why is all this happening, and what does it mean? To provide an answer, we must first locate specific developments within a broader framework. Why do different political systems operate on different rules, how do the powers of different governments explain their actions, and how do their citizens feel about the changes they see? Why are some countries ruled by presidents and others by prime ministers? Why do some countries have a single dominant political party while others have dozens? And what is the difference between a supreme court and a constitutional court?

These are the kinds of questions addressed by comparative politics. As well as helping us identify the rules of government and politics, comparative analysis also helps us make sense of political news from around the world. Keeping up with that news is one thing, but being able to understand it and place it in context is quite another. And as advances in technology, trade, and science bring us all closer together, so developments in one part of the world can have effects on many others, making it more important that we understand the changes we see. By studying different governments and political systems, we can better understand not just the country in which we live, but also other countries, their governments, their political decisions, and their people.

This is a book designed to introduce you to the study of comparative government and politics. The goal of the chapters that follow is to provide a wide-ranging and accessible guide for courses and modules in this fascinating and essential sub-field of political science. We will look at the methods and theories of comparison, at the differences between democracies and authoritarian systems, at the many different forms in which the institutions of government exist, and at the ways in which ordinary people take part – or are prevented from taking part – in government and in shaping the decisions that affect their lives.

As with the last edition, the book takes a thematic approach to comparison, with chapters divided into three groups.

◆ The first group (Chapters 1–6) provides the foundations, with a review of the key concepts in comparative politics, followed by chapters on the theories and methods of comparison, on the meaning and the reach of the state, and on the features of democracies and authoritarian systems.
◆ The second group (Chapters 7–12) focuses on institutions, which constitute the core subject matter of political science. It opens with a chapter on constitutions that assesses the power maps that help us make sense of how institutions work and relate to one another. This is followed by chapters on executives, legislatures, bureaucracies, and government at the sub-national and local level, before closing with a chapter on political culture that helps us understand the broader context within which government and politics works.
◆ The third group (Chapters 13–20) looks at political processes, beginning with a survey of political participation, then looking at political communication, parties, elections, voters, and interest groups. The book ends with chapters on public policy and political economy.

The book is designed to meet the needs of students in different countries, approaching the study of government and politics from different perspectives. You may be using it as part of the first (and perhaps only) course or module you are taking on government and politics, as part of a course you are required to take outside your major subject, as part of a course you are taking simply because you are interested in politics, or as part of a course you are taking in your major course of study. Whatever your background and motivation, the chapters that follow are designed to help you find your way through the many different forms in which politics and government exists around the world.

TWO KEY THEMES: DEMOCRATIC REVERSAL, DECLINING TRUST

Politics is always full of drama, and rarely stands still. There is a ceaseless jockeying for power and influence, a constantly changing set of needs and demands, and a cast of heroes and villains whose efforts to govern can sometimes inspire and at other times infuriate. At few times in recent history have the changes been as intense and as rapidly moving as they are today, producing numerous possibilities as new pressures and opportunities take countries in different directions.

Among all the changes we are witnessing, two in particular stand out:

◆ *The reversal of democracy.* Not long ago, democrats were encouraged by the end of the Soviet Union and its control over Eastern Europe, by the end of military governments in Latin America and then in sub-Saharan Africa, and by the democracy movements in North Africa and the Middle East that gave rise to the Arab Spring. One scholar (see Chapter 5) was even inspired to declare the triumph of liberal democracy and the 'end of history'. More recently, though, democracy appears to have been struggling, with challenges to political rights and civil liberties even in countries with strong democratic credentials, including the United States, Britain, France, and Japan. Meanwhile, in many countries that were once democratizing, such as China, Russia, and Turkey, there has been a reversal in trends as authoritarian leaders and political parties have become more powerful.

◆ *Declining trust in government.* The citizens of countries in many parts of the world have expressed new levels of discontent with the performance of their governments, and have shown less trust in their leaders while feeling more politically and economically marginalized. Many worry about what they see as threats to the political, economic, and social values they once thought they could take for granted. Those threats may be real, or they may be imagined, but the result in many cases has been a rising tide of populism as new political leaders point fingers of blame at the political and economic elite. Political and economic divisions have come to the fore, there have been demands for a return of power to 'the people', and new appeals have been made to nationalism as opposition to immigration and globalization grows, along with support for the creation of walls and barriers, whether in a physical or legal sense.

These two themes run through the chapters that follow. We will examine not just the structure of political systems and the ways that citizens relate to them, but we will look also at the ebb and flow of democracy and authoritarianism, and of populism, nationalism, and globalization. In so doing, we will gain more insights into some of the broader and more universal questions of comparative politics: who has power, who does not, how do power relationships evolve, and how do political systems work.

ACKNOWLEDGEMENTS

Writing and producing a book is a team project, dependent on the encouragement of the publisher (writing can be a solitary undertaking) and the professionalism of the production team. In both regards, Red Globe Press is perfection to work with. The authors would like to thank Lloyd Langman for his always thorough, focused, and reassuring leadership on this project, Peter Atkinson for his detailed and creative work on helping bring the project to completion, Anne Halliday for her excellent input as copy-editor, and Amy Brownbridge for her sterling work on the production of the book.

The authors would also like to thank the 15 anonymous reviewers – four from the UK, three from the United States, two from the Netherlands, and one each from Australia, Hong Kong, New Zealand, Poland, Sweden, and the United Arab Emirates – who made many useful suggestions that added strongly to the new edition. They would also like to thank the many other scholars who provided more informal feedback to Red Globe Press, much of which found its way into the new edition.

Finally, John McCormick sends his love to Leanne, Ian, and Stuart for everything they bring to his life.

ABOUT THE AUTHORS

Rod Hague and Martin Harrop were senior lecturers in politics at the University of Newcastle, UK. John McCormick is professor of political science at the Indianapolis campus of Indiana University in the United States. Among his publications are *Cases in Comparative Government and Politics* (2019), *Understanding the European Union* (7th edition, 2017), and *Environmental Politics and Policy* (2017).

GUIDE TO SPOTLIGHT FEATURES

These focus on the 18 country cases from which examples are most often quoted in the body of the text. They in-clude a brief profile of each country (or regional organization, in the case of the European Union), brief descriptions of their political features, some key demographic and economic data, and a short case study of each country in the context of the topic of the chapter in which the Spotlight appears.

Form of government	A general description of the form of a government, including dates on state formation and the adoption of the most recent constitution.
Executive	Form and structure of the executive.
Legislature	Form and structure of the legislature.
Judiciary	Form and structure of the judicial system.
Electoral system	Form and structure of the electoral system.
Parties	Outline of the party system and the major parties at work in the country.
Population	Data for 2017 from World Bank (2018).
Gross Domestic Product	Total value of goods and services produced by a country, in US dollars. Data for 2017 from World Bank (2018).
Per capita Gross Domestic Product	Total value of goods and services produced per head by a country, in US dollars. Data for 2017 from World Bank (2018).
Democracy Index rating	From the Economist Intelligence Unit (2017), which divides states into full democracies, flawed democracies, hybrid regimes, and authoritarian regimes.
Freedom House rating	From Freedom House (2018), which divides states into groups rated Free, Partly Free, or Not Free.
Human Development Index rating	From the United Nations Development Programme (2017), which divides states into groups rated Very High, High, Medium and Low.

GUIDE TO THE ELEVENTH EDITION

It has only been three years since the last edition of *Comparative Government and Politics* was published, and yet much has changed in the world during that time. This new edition is an opportunity to reflect on those changes, but it also remains true to the core purpose and personality of earlier editions: to provide an introductory survey of comparative politics, while integrating some fresh perspectives to the study of the topic.

Structure and features. There are five key structural changes to the new edition:

◆ The two chapters on theories and methods have been moved up so that they are more closely connected to the opening chapter on concepts.
◆ The chapter on executives has been moved ahead of the chapter on legislatures so that the parliamentary system can be explained in more depth ahead of the discussion on legislatures.
◆ The chapter on political economy has been rewritten and restored in response to requests from several instructors.
◆ The coverage of authoritarian states has been greatly expanded, with more examples inserted throughout the text and the chapter sections on authoritarian rule expanded by two-thirds or more.
◆ For the first time, *Comparative Government and Politics* appears in full colour, allowing improvements to the reproduction of figures and tables, with supporting photographs added to illustrate key political phenomena.

All the new features introduced in the last edition have been kept and developed, including the Focus features, the Previews to each chapter, and the closing sets of Key Arguments. Also, the Spotlight features have been redesigned, along with new maps and new sets of further reading.

Length. The phenomenon of textbooks that expand with each edition is well known, but *Comparative Government and Politics* remains one of the notable exceptions. Even with the addition of a new chapter on political economy, the eleventh edition remains only slightly longer than the tenth edition.

Classification of political systems. The last edition saw the introduction of the Democracy Index and the Freedom House ranking *Freedom in the World*. This dual system of classification has been expanded in this edition, with more examples used in the body of the text to illustrate the features of both systems.

Country cases. As with the last edition, this one focuses on a selection of case study countries, enhanced in the new edition so as to provide political, economic, social, and geographical variety, with Turkey added as an example of a hybrid political system. The cases are as follows:

Full democracies	Flawed democracies	Hybrid regimes	Authoritarian regimes
Germany	Brazil	Nigeria	China
Sweden	France	Turkey	Egypt
UK	India		Iran
	Japan		Russia
	Mexico		Venezuela
	South Africa		
	USA		

Note: This classification is drawn from the Democracy Index. The European Union is not classified separately in the index, but all its member states are either full or flawed democracies.

Sources. As always, great care has been taken to use the most recent scholarship and the strongest possible range of sources. The vast majority of the research in political science is published in English by publishers based in Europe and the United States, which has the effect of producing a somewhat lop-sided view of the world. As well as working to include a wide variety of case examples, additional efforts have been made with this edition to seek out scholarship (published in English) from as great a variety of scholars and countries as possible.

MAJOR CHANGES TO THIS EDITION

Throughout the book, arguments have been developed, definitions have been tightened, links have been made to different theories, a wider range of country examples has been added, and the results of new research have been integrated.

	Theme	Key changes
Chapter 1	Key concepts	More country examples injected, new terms defined, and the sections on politics and power have been combined.
Chapter 2	Theoretical approaches	Moved up from its previous position, new details added on the range of political theories, and a new section added on cultural approaches.
Chapter 3	Comparative methods	Moved up from its previous position, details expanded on different methodologies, and expanded sections on nationalism and globalization.
Chapter 4	The state	Expanded section on political authority, new maps added, more discussion of the effects of nationalism on the state.
Chapter 5	Democratic rule	Expanded discussion on democracy and modernization, and rewritten section on the prospects for democracy.
Chapter 6	Authoritarian rule	Expanded explanation of the features and effects of authoritarianism, with new sections on despotism and coercion, and a wider range of country examples.
Chapter 7	Constitutions and courts	New coverage of codified and uncodified constitutions, and considerably expanded section on authoritarian states.
Chapter 8	Executives	Moved up from its previous position, expanded section on heads of state and government, and a new category of unlimited presidential executive.
Chapter 9	Legislatures	Moved back from its previous position, new coverage of models of representation, new discussion of levels of trust, and expanded section on authoritarian states.
Chapter 10	Bureaucracies	Coverage clarified, more detail on new public management and e-government, and considerably expanded section on authoritarian states.

	Theme	Key changes
Chapter 11	Sub-national governments	Expanded coverage of local government, new maps, a greater variety of country examples, and additional depth on authoritarian states.
Chapter 12	Political culture	New clarity to the discussion of political culture, new sections on multiculturalism and identity politics, more depth on political trust.
Chapter 13	Political participation	Expanded discussion of who participates and why, and new coverage of women in government and politics.
Chapter 14	Political communication	Updated to take account of developments with social media and to account for the problem of fake news, and considerably expanded section on authoritarian states.
Chapter 15	Elections	Many new country examples integrated into the chapter, with a considerably expanded section on authoritarian states and the dynamics of their party systems.
Chapter 16	Political parties	New details on legislative elections, updated election results, and considerably expanded coverage of the dynamics and purposes of elections in authoritarian states.
Chapter 17	Voters	Reduced detail on discussion of how voters choose, more detail added on voter turnout, and new detail added on voters in authoritarian states.
Chapter 18	Interest groups	Expanded section on lobbying, new examples of the work of interest groups, more country examples, and new detail on the work of groups in authoritarian states.
Chapter 19	Public policy	More comparison injected into the discussion, new emphasis on issues designed to illustrate the dynamics of policy, and authoritarian section largely rewritten.
Chapter 20	Political economy	New chapter restored from earlier editions, but almost entirely rewritten, with coverage of all major approaches and a new section on authoritarian states.

GUIDE TO LEARNING FEATURES

Key arguments
Each chapter begins with six key arguments, chosen to underline some of the more important points made in the chapter.

KEY ARGUMENTS

- ◆ Interest groups come in many shapes and sizes, with a wide variety of objectives, methods, and levels of influence.
- ◆ Much like political parties, interest groups are a relatively recent addition to the formal processes of government.
- ◆ Interest groups use a combination of direct and indirect channels of influence. Where ties with government are particularly strong, the danger arises of the emergence of sub-governments enjoying preferred access.
- ◆ Pluralism is closely associated with studies of interest groups, but there are reasons to question whether it describes how groups operate in practice.
- ◆ Interest groups are often complemented by wider social movements, whose activities challenge conventional channels of participation.
- ◆ Where the governments of democracies may be too heavily influenced by powerful groups, the problem can be reversed in authoritarian states.

Overview
Each chapter includes an overview of the subject of the chapter, placing it within its broader context and introducing some of the key themes.

INTEREST GROUPS: AN OVERVIEW

Interest groups are bodies which seek to influence public policy from outside the formal structures of government. They do this through a combination of direct pressure on government and the bureaucracy, and indirect pressure via the media and public opinion. They come in many different forms, including employer organizations, consumer groups, professional bodies, labour unions, and single-issue groups. They work primarily at the national level, but can also be found in local and international arenas. Like political parties, interest groups are a crucial channel of communication between society and government, especially in democracies. Unlike parties, they pursue specialized concerns, working to influence government without becoming the government. They are not election-fighting organizations; instead, they typically adopt a pragmatic approach in dealing with whatever power structure confronts them, using whatever channels are legally (and sometimes illegally)

Interest group
A body that works outside government to influence public policy. Also known as a non-governmental organization (NGO).

PREVIEW

Where most of the institutions of government are listed in a national constitution, interest groups (like political parties) are mainly founded and operate outside these formal structures. They have evolved separately, their core purpose being to influence the shaping of policy without becoming part of government; another example of governance at work. They come in several types, and use different methods – both direct and indirect – to achieve their goals. A vibrant interest group community is generally a sign of a healthy civil society, but where the influence of different interests and the groups that support those interests is unbalanced, it can also become a barrier to the impleme elections.

Preview
Each chapter begins with a 250-word outline of the contents of the chapter, designed as a preview of what to expect in the pages that follow.

Concepts
The first time a key term is used it appears in boldface and is separately defined. The definitions are kept as brief and clear as possible, and each term is listed at the end of the chapter in which it is defined.

Protective group
An interest group that seeks selective benefits for its members and insider status with relevant government departments.

moting the rights of women and ethnic minorities, and campaigning on behalf of issues such as human rights and the environment.

Interest groups today come in many shapes and sizes, with a wide range of objectives, methods, and levels of influence. Many have been founded for practical or charitable purposes rather than for political action, but have developed a political dimension as they have worked either to modify public policy or to resist unfavourable changes. Some will have a few hundred members focusing on a short-term local issue and working with local government, while others will have millions of members and work in many different countries, targeting national governments or international organizations. Their variety, in fact, is so great, their methods so varied, and their overlap so considerable that it is not easy to develop a list of discrete types (Figure 18.1).

Type	Focus of interest
Economic	Groups of people with material economic interests, such as business, industry, producers, trades, and workers.
Public	Public concerns, such as consumer, public health, human rights, and environmental interests.
Professional	Specific professions, such as lawyers, doctors, and university professors.
Single-issue	Distinct and narrow issues, such as animal rights or domestic violence.
Religious	Causes and issues tied to particular religions, often with a significant moral element.
Government	Represent the interests of city, local and regional governments to the national administration.
Institutional	Public organizations that influence government even though they are not organized as interest groups. Examples include hospitals, universities, and the armed forces.

Figures
A wide range of figures is used throughout the book to provide visual support to topics covered in the body of the text.

Figure 18.1 Types of interest group

Tables

These display statistics or key features of a topic in the nearby text, or summarize lists of subjects covered in the text.

Table 18.1 Comparing protective and promotional interest groups

	Protective	Promotional
Aims	Defends an interest	Promotes a cause
Membership	Closed: membership is restricted	Open: anyone can join
Status	Insider: frequently consulted by government and actively seeks this role	Outsider: consulted less often by government; targets public opinion and the media
Benefits	Selective: only group members benefit	Collective: benefits go to both members and non-members
Focus	Aim to influence national government on specific issues affecting members	Also seek to influence national and global bodies on broad policy matters

Focus 18.1
Lobbying

Even though it has moved far beyond its origins in the lobby of the British Parliament, lobbying remains the key means by which groups try to influence law-makers (see Godwin, *et al.*, 2013, and Bitonti and Harris, 2018). Lobbyists are usually professionals, often working for corporations or even for lobbying firms consisting of hired guns in the business of interest group communication. Such services are offered not only by specialist government relations companies, but also by divisions within law firms and management consultancies. These operations are growing in number in democracies, with some companies even operating internationally.

Lobbying is on the rise for three main reasons:

◆ Government regulation continues to grow. A specialist lobbying firm working for several interest groups can often monitor proposed laws and regulations more efficiently than would be the case if each interest group undertook the task separately.
◆ Public relations campaigns are becoming increasingly sophisticated, often seeking to influence interest group members, public opinion, and the government in one integrated project. Professional agencies come into their own in planning and delivering multifaceted campaigns, which can be too complex for an interest group client to manage directly.
◆ Many corporations now approach government directly, rather than working through their trade association. Companies, both large and small, find that using a lobbying company to help them contact a government agency or a sympathetic legislator can yield results more quickly than working through an industry body.

Revolving door
The phenomenon in which personnel move between roles as law-makers or bureaucrats and as members of industries impacted by laws and regulations.

The central feature of the lobbying business is its intensely personal character, reaching its most troubling degree in the United States where the **revolving door** is well established. Lobbying is about who you know, and a legislator is most likely to return a call from a lobbyist if the caller is a former colleague. One study of the revolving door phenomenon, however, suggests that rather than seeking privileged insider access, special interests are more focused on how lobbyists with personal experience of the political process can act as a form of insurance for their clients against a political system that is increasingly dysfunctional and unpredictable (LaPira and Thomas, 2017).

Focus

Each chapter includes two Focus features that provide in-depth treatment of a topic related to the subject of the chapter.

Spotlights

Each chapter includes a spotlight case study that covers a nation's background and other statistical data.

SPOTLIGHT EGYPT

Brief profile

Egypt has long been a major player in Middle East politics, thanks not only to its pioneering role in the promotion of Arab nationalism but also to its strategic significance in the Cold War and in the Arab–Israeli conflict. It was also at the heart of the Arab Spring, with pro-democracy demonstrations leading to the fall from power of Hosni Mubarak in 2011. Democratic elections brought Mohammed Morsi to power in 2012, but he was removed in a military coup the following year. Egyptians now face uncertainties that resulted in its recent downgrading in the Democracy Index from hybrid to authoritarian. Egypt has the second biggest economy in the Arab world, after Saudi Arabia, but is resource-poor. It relies heavily on tourism, agriculture, and remittances from Egyptian workers abroad and struggles to meet the needs of its rapidly growing population while seeking to offset the potential threat of Islamic militancy.

Form of government	Unitary semi-presidential republic. Modern state formed 1952, and most recent constitution adopted 2014.
Executive	Semi-presidential. A president directly elected for no more than two four-year terms, governing with a prime minister who leads a Cabinet accountable to the People's Assembly. There is no vice-president.
Legislature	Unicameral People's Assembly (Majlis el-Shaab) with 567 members, of whom 540 are elected for renewable four-year terms and 27 can be appointed by the president.
Judiciary	Egyptian law is based on a combination of British, Italian, and Napoleonic codes. The Supreme Constitutional Court has been close to recent political changes in Egypt; it has 21 members appointed for life by the president, with mandatory retirement at age 70.
Electoral system	A two-round system is used for presidential elections, with a majority vote needed for victory in the first round, while a mixed member majoritarian system is used for People's Assembly elections: two-thirds of members are elected using party list proportional representation, and one-third in an unusual multi-member plurality system in two large districts.
Parties	Multi-party, but unsettled because of recent instability. Parties represent a wide range of positions and ideologies.

95.7m **Population**

$135bn **Gross Domestic Product**

$2,412 **Per capita GDP**

Democracy Index rating	Freedom House rating	Human Development Index rating
✗ Full Democracy	✗ Free	✗ Very High
✗ Flawed Democracy	✗ Partly Free	✗ High
✗ Hybrid Regime	✓ Not Free	✓ Medium
✓ Authoritarian	✗ Not Rated	✗ Low
✗ Not Rated		✗ Not Rated

DISCUSSION QUESTIONS

◆ What do interest groups add to democracy, and what do they subtract?
◆ Is there a hierarchy of interests, giving some groups advantages over others, or does the sheer number and variety of groups result in a balancing of interests?
◆ To what extent do special interests limit the functioning of the market of political ideas?
◆ Is lobbying a natural and inevitable part of the democratic process?
◆ Does pluralism exist, or is it just a theoretical possibility that has been undermined by the unequal influence of different interests?
◆ To what extent is corporatism found in democracies as well as authoritarian regimes?

KEY CONCEPTS

◆ Civil society
◆ Corporatism
◆ Density
◆ Interest group
◆ Iron triangle
◆ Issue network
◆ Lobbying
◆ Nimby
◆ Peak association
◆ Pluralism
◆ Promotional group
◆ Protective group
◆ Revolving door
◆ Social movement
◆ Think-tank

FURTHER READING

Bitonti, Alberto, and Phil Harris (eds) (2018) *Lobbying in Europe: Public Affairs and the Lobbying Industry in 28 EU Countries* (Palgrave Macmillan). An assessment of lobbying in the European Union, including short chapters on each of its member states.
Cavatorta, Francesco (ed.) (2012) *Civil Society Activism under Authoritarian Rule: A Comparative Perspective* (Routledge). One of the few recent studies of the activities of interest groups in authoritarian settings.
Edwards, Michael (ed.) (2011) *The Oxford Handbook of Civil Society* (Oxford University Press). An edited collection of studies on civil society, including chapters on different sectors and on different parts of the world.
Staggenborg, Suzanne (2016) *Social Movements*, 2nd edn (Oxford University Press). A textbook survey of social movements, their methods, and their effects, with cases including the women's, the LGBTQ+, and the environmental movements.

Discussion questions

Each chapter closes with a set of six open-ended discussion questions, designed to consolidate knowledge by highlighting major issues and to spark classroom discussions and research projects.

Key concepts

Designed to help reflect upon and memorise key concepts, a complete list of the main terms defined in boxes across the preceding pages is included at the end of each chapter.

Further reading

An annotated list of six suggested readings is included at the end of each chapter, representing some of the most recent, important and helpful surveys of the topics covered in that chapter.

KEY CONCEPTS

CONTENTS

PREVIEW

The best place to begin the study of any topic is with an exploration of key concepts. Most of the political terms which interest us are embedded in ordinary language; *government*, *politics*, *power*, and *authority* are all familiar terms. But – as we will see – this does not mean that they are easily defined, or that political scientists are agreed on how best to understand or apply them.

This opening chapter begins with a discussion about the meaning of *government* and *governance*, which are related terms but quite different in the ideas they convey: the first focuses on institutions while the second focuses on processes. We then go on to look at *politics*, whose core features are relatively easy to identify, but whose boundaries are not so clear: does it imply a search for a decision, or a competitive struggle for power? This is followed by a review of the meaning of *power*, *authority*, *legitimacy*, and *ideology*, all of which lie at the heart of our understanding of how government and politics work.

The chapter then looks at some of the core purposes of comparative politics, whose value – above all – lies in helping us broaden and deepen our understanding of politics and government, taking us beyond the limitations inherent in studying a single political system. The chapter ends with a review of the challenges involved in classifying political systems, and looks at some of the typologies available to help us make better sense of a complex, diverse, and changing political world.

KEY ARGUMENTS

- Like all fields of study, political science uses concepts whose definitions – while often disputed – are important to understand.

- While *government* describes the institutions and offices through which societies are governed, *governance* describes the process of collective decision-making.

- An exact definition of *politics* is difficult, because the term has multiple nuances. But it is clearly a collective activity, occurring between or among people.

- *Power* is the capacity to bring about intended effects, and is central to understanding both government and politics. *Authority* and *legitimacy* are key related concepts.

- *Ideology* may have lost its original meaning as the science of ideas, but it remains useful as a way of packaging different views about the role of government and the goals of public policy.

- *Typologies* help us compare, imposing order on the variety of the world's political systems, and helping us develop explanations and rules.

KEY CONCEPTS: AN OVERVIEW

Concept
An idea, term, or category.

Political science
The study of the theory and practice of government and politics, focusing on the structure and dynamics of institutions, political processes, and political behaviour.

Social science
The study of human society and of the structured interactions among people within society.

Every field of study is built on a specialized vocabulary made up of terms or **concepts** that need to be understood and defined in order to provide us with our points of reference. **Political science** is no exception. In trying to understand the features which a political system (see later in this chapter) must possess in order to qualify as a democracy, for example, we can agree that some measure of popular control over the rulers is essential; if there were no ways of holding the government to account, there could be no democracy. A good definition of a democracy as a concept, then, is a political system in which government is based on a fair and open mandate from all qualified citizens of a state. As we will see in Chapter 5, though, there are many facets to the discussion of what should – at first glance – be an idea that we can all understand without too much trouble.

This opening chapter reviews several of the most important concepts involved in comparative government and politics, providing the foundations for understanding the chapters that follow. We will start with *government* and *politics*, two concepts that are routinely used interchangeably, but not necessarily applied correctly. We will then look at *power*, a concept that comes in several different forms. We also begin looking at the meaning of the state (covered in much more depth in Chapter 4), and how it relates to *authority*, *legitimacy*, and *ideology*.

These concepts are all central to an understanding of the manner in which governments are organized and the way in which politics unfolds. We will find, though, that their precise meanings are routinely contested. This is a problem found not just in political science, but throughout the social sciences; there is even some dispute about the meaning of the term **social science**. It is used here in the context of studying and better understanding the organized relations and inter-action of people within society. Social scientists study the institutions we build, the rules we agree, the processes we use, our underlying motives, and the outcomes of our interactions.

Ultimately, we need to understand these concepts in order to constructively make comparisons. In turn, we need to make those comparisons in order to better understand human behaviour. Comparison is one of the most basic of all human activities, lying at the heart of almost every choice we make in our lives. No surprise, then, that it should be central to research in the social sciences as a whole, and political science in particular. We can study government and political processes in isolation, but without comparing different cases, examples, and situations, we can never really hope to fully comprehend them, to draw general conclusions about what drives people to act the way they do, or to be sure that we have considered all the explanatory options. Only by looking at government and politics across place and time can we build the context to be able to gain a broader and more complete understanding of how they work.

GOVERNMENT AND GOVERNANCE

Since this is a book about comparative government and politics, the logical place to begin is with a review of the term **government**. Small groups of people can reach collective decisions without any special procedures; a family or sports team can reach an understanding by informal discussion, and these agreements can be self-executing in the sense that those who make the decision carry it out themselves. However, such simple mechanisms are

Government
The institutions and structures through which societies are governed.

Institution
A formal organization or practice with a political purpose or effect, marked by durability and internal complexity.

impractical for larger units such as towns, cities, or states, which must develop procedures and **institutions** for making and enforcing collective decisions. By doing so, they give themselves a government.

The term *government* is usually used to describe the highest level of political offices in a society: presidents, prime ministers, legislatures, governors, mayors, and others at the apex of power. But government actually consists of all organizations charged with reaching and executing decisions for a community. By this definition, the police, the military, bureaucrats, and judges are all part of government, even if they do not come to office through the methods usually associated with government, such as elections. In this broader conception, government is the entire community of institutions endowed with public authority. The term *government* can also apply to the group of people who govern (as in the Japanese government), a specific administration (the Putin government), the form of the system of rule (centralized government), and the character of the administration of a community (good government).

The classic case for the institution of government was made in the seventeenth century by the English philosopher Thomas Hobbes (see Focus 1.1). He argued that government provides

Focus 1.1
Hobbes's case for government

The case for government was well made by Thomas Hobbes (1588–1679) in his famous treatise *Leviathan*, published in 1651. His starting point was the fundamental equality in our ability to inflict harm on others:

> For as to the strength of body, the weakest has strength enough to kill the strongest, either by secret machination, or by confederacy with others.

So arises a clash of ambition and fear of attack:

> From this equality of ability, arises equality of hope in the attaining of our ends. And therefore if any two men desire the same thing, which nevertheless they cannot both enjoy, they become enemies; and in the way to their end, which is principally their own conservation, and sometimes their own delectation, endeavour to destroy or subdue one another.

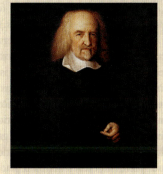

Thomas Hobbes.
Source: Getty Images/De Agostini Picture Library

Without a ruler to keep us in check, the situation becomes grim:

> Hereby it is manifest, that during the time men live without a common power to keep them all in awe, they are in that condition which is called war; and such a war, as is of every man, against every man.

People therefore agree (by means unclear) to set up an absolute government to avoid a life that would otherwise be 'solitary, poor, nasty, brutish and short':

> The only way to erect such a common power, as may be able to defend them from the invasion of foreigners, and the injuries of one another … is, to confer all their power and strength upon one man, or one assembly of men, that may reduce all their wills, by plurality of voices, unto one will … This done, the multitude so united is called a COMMONWEALTH.

Source: Hobbes (1651).

us with protection from the harm that we would otherwise inflict on each other in our quest for gain and glory. By granting a monopoly of the sword to a government, we transform anarchy into order, securing peace and the opportunity for mutually beneficial cooperation.

In a democracy, government supposedly provides security and predictability to those who live under its jurisdiction (see Chapter 5). Citizens and businesses can plan for the long term, knowing that laws are developed in a standardized fashion, take into account competing opinions, and are consistently applied. Of course, nothing is ever that simple, because governments create their own dangers. The risk of Hobbes's commonwealth is that it will abuse its own authority, creating more problems than it solves. As John Locke – one of Hobbes's critics – pointed out, there is no profit in avoiding the dangers of foxes if the outcome is simply to be devoured by lions (Locke, 1690). A key aim in studying government, then, is to discover how to secure its benefits while also limiting its inherent dangers.

In democracies, government is influenced by wider forces, such as interest groups, political parties, the media, corporations, and public opinion. In authoritarian systems, meanwhile, the government may lack much autonomy, and effectively becomes the property of a dominant individual or clan. In both cases, the forces and influences surrounding government come together to form a **political system**. This concept takes us beyond mere institutions and helps us pin down all the factors involved in the political life of a given state or community. It has a hard edge, as reflected in the adverb *authoritatively* in the famous definition of a political system offered by the political scientist David Easton (1965):

> **Political system**
> The interactions and organizations through which a society reaches and successfully enforces collective decisions. See also discussion in Chapter 4 about **regimes**.

A political system can be designated as the interactions through which values are authoritatively allocated for a society; that is what distinguishes a political system from other systems lying in its environment.

SPOTLIGHT NIGERIA

Brief profile

Although Nigeria has been independent since 1960, it was not until 2015 that it experienced a presidential election in which the incumbent was defeated by an opposition opponent. This makes an important point about the challenges faced by Africa's largest country by population, and one of the continent's major regional powers, in developing a stable political form. Nigeria is currently enjoying its longest spell of civilian government since independence, but the military continues to play an important role, the economy is dominated by oil, corruption is rife at every level of society, security concerns and poor infrastructure discourage foreign investment, and a combination of ethnic and religious divisions pose worrying threats to stability. Incursions and attacks since 2002 by the Islamist group Boko Haram, have added to the country's problems, but it has still – nonetheless – been recently upgraded from authoritarian to a hybrid on the Democracy Index.

Form of government	Federal presidential republic consisting of 36 states and a Federal Capital Territory. State formed 1960, and most recent constitution adopted 1999.
Executive	Presidential. A president elected for a maximum of two four-year terms, supported by a vice-president and cabinet of ministers, with one from each of Nigeria's states.
Legislature	Bicameral National Assembly: lower House of Representatives (360 members) and upper Senate (109 members), both elected for fixed and renewable four-year terms.
Judiciary	Federal Supreme Court, with 14 members nominated by the president, and either confirmed by the Senate or approved by a judicial commission.
Electoral system	President elected in national contest, and must win a majority of all votes cast and at least 25 per cent of the vote in at least two-thirds of Nigeria's states. Possibility of two runoffs. National Assembly elected using single-member plurality.
Parties	Multi-party, led by the centrist People's Democratic Party and the conservative All Nigeria People's Party.

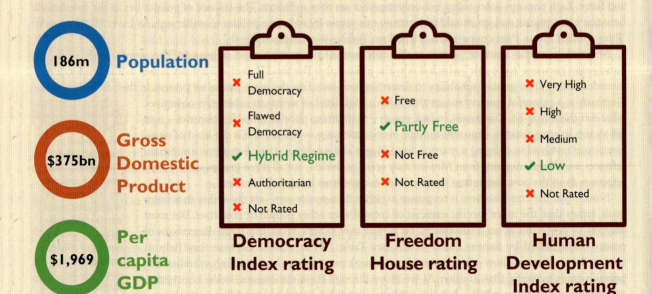

Government and politics in Nigeria

Many of the facets of the debate about government, politics, power, and authority are on show in Nigeria, a country that is still struggling to develop a workable political form and national identity in the face of multiple internal divisions.

Understanding Nigeria is complicated by the lack of durable governmental patterns. Since independence in 1960, Nigerians have lived through three periods of civilian government, five successful and several attempted military coups, a civil war, and nearly 30 years of military rule. The first civilian government (1960–66) was based on the parliamentary model, but the second and third (1979–83, and

President Muhammadu Buhari addresses members of the Nigerian National Assembly in Abuja after submitting his annual federal budget.
Source: Getty Images/Sunday Aghaeze/Stringer.

1999–present) were based on the presidential form. Since 2007, Nigeria has twice made the transition from one civilian government to another, and the long-term political prognosis has improved. Still, considerable uncertainties remain.

Political doubts reflect economic drift, and vice versa. The country's growing population is expected to double in the next 25 years, straining an infrastructure that is already woefully inadequate to support a modern economy. Nigeria's core economic problem is its heavy reliance on oil, which leaves the size and health of the economy – as well as government revenues – dependent on the fluctuating price of oil. To make matters worse, much of the oil wealth has been squandered and stolen, feeding into the corruption that is rife in Nigeria, and there have been bitter political arguments over how best to spend the balance.

Nigeria's problems are more than just economic. In social terms, Nigeria is divided by ethnicity, handicapping efforts to build a sense of national identity. It is also separated by religion, with a mainly Muslim north, a non-Muslim south, and controversial pressures from the north to expand the reach of sharia, or Islamic law. Regional disparities are fundamental, with a north that is dry and poor and a south that is better endowed in resources and basic services. Regional tensions have been made worse by oil, most of which lies either in the southeast or off the coast, but with much of the profit distributed to political elites in other parts of the country.

Further reading

Bourne, Richard (2015) *Nigeria: A New History of a Turbulent Century* (Zed Books).

Campbell, John (2013) *Nigeria: Dancing on the Brink* (Rowman & Littlefield).

Campbell, John, and Matthew T. Page (2018) *Nigeria: What Everyone Needs to Know* (Oxford University Press).

Table 1.1 Lukes's three dimensions of power

Dimension	Core question	Core quality
First	Who prevails when preferences conflict?	Decisions are made on issues over which there is an observable conflict of interests.
Second	Who controls whether preferences are expressed?	Decisions are prevented from being taken on potential issues over which there is an observable conflict of interests.
Third	Who shapes preferences?	Potential issues are kept out of politics, whether through social forces, institutional practices, or the decisions of individuals.

Source: Lukes (2005).

The first dimension is straightforward: power should be judged by identifying whose views prevail when the actors involved possess conflicting views on what should be done. The greater the correspondence between a person's views and decisions reached, the greater is that person's influence: more wins indicate more power. This decision-making approach, as it is called, was pioneered by the political scientist Robert Dahl (1961a) in his classic study of democracy and power in the city of New Haven, Connecticut. In the United States, for example, and in spite of repeated mass shootings, the successful lobbying of the gun lobby has meant that most leaders of the two major political parties have refused to impose meaningful limits on gun ownership, forming what amounts to an elite conspiracy to make sure that guns remain widely available. So far, at least, the gun lobby has prevailed; it has the power (see Chapter 18). The approach is relatively clear and concrete, based on identifying preferences and observing decisions, and connecting directly with the concept of politics as the resolution of conflict within groups.

The second dimension focuses on the capacity to keep issues off the political agenda by preventing the emergence of topics which would threaten the values or interests of decision-makers. As Bachrach and Baratz (1962) once put it, 'to the extent that a person or group – consciously or unconsciously – creates or reinforces barriers to the public airing of policy conflicts, that person or group has power'. In China, for example, fear of government reprisals currently discourages many people from expressing their support for a transition to democracy. By narrowing the public agenda in this way, the ruling communist party renders democracy a non-issue. In order to address the problem of control over the agenda, we need to both study the groups that gain the most from political decisions or the status quo, and those whose views are not heard.

The third dimension broadens our conception of power by extending it to cover the formation, rather than merely the expression, of preferences. Where the first and second dimensions assume conflicting preferences, the third dimension addresses the idea of a manipulated consensus. In war time, for example, governments often seek to sustain public morale by preventing news of military defeats or high casualties from seeping into the public domain. In this and similar cases, agenda control is achieved by manipulating the flow of information so as to prevent any conflict from arising in the first place. So this third dimension of power focuses on manipulating preferences rather than just preventing their expression.

The implication of these examples is that the most efficient form of power is one that allows us to shape people's information and preferences, thus preventing the first and second dimensions from coming into play. Denying people access to information is one way of achieving this, as in the example of the selective briefings initially provided by the power company responsible for operating the Japanese nuclear power station which leaked radiation after the 2011 earthquake. Power, then, is not just about whose preferences win out; we must also consider whose opinions are kept out of the debate and also the wider context in which those preferences are formed.

THE STATE, AUTHORITY, AND LEGITIMACY

We will look at the state in more detail in Chapter 4, but a brief preview is needed here so that we can grasp two other concepts that lie at the heart of our understanding of government and politics: *authority* and *legitimacy*. The world is divided into nearly 200 states (the exact number, as we will see, is debatable – see Focus 4.1), each containing a population living within a defined territory, and each recognized by its residents and by other states as having the right to rule that territory. States provide the legal mandate for the work of governments, allowing them to use the authority inherent in the state. We can compare government and politics at multiple levels, from the national to the local, but it is the state that provides us with our most important point of reference as we work through the complexities of comparison, and states need both authority and legitimacy in order to function effectively.

Authority is a concept that is broader than power and, in some ways, more fundamental to comparative politics. Where power is the capacity to act, authority is the acknowledged right to do so. It exists when subordinates accept the capacity of superiors to give legitimate orders, so that while Russia may exercise some *power* over Russians living in neighbouring countries such as Ukraine, the Baltic States, and Kazakh-stan, its formal *authority* stops at the Russian border. The German sociologist Max Weber (1922) suggested that, in a relationship of authority, the ruled implement the command as if they had adopted it spontaneously, for its own sake. For this reason, authority is a more efficient form of control than brute power. Yet, authority is more than voluntary compliance. To acknowledge the authority of your state does not mean you always agree with its decisions; it means only that you accept its right to make them and your own duty to obey. In this way, authority provides the foundation for the state.

> **Authority**
> The right to rule. Authority creates its own power, so long as people accept that the person in authority has the right to make decisions.

Just as there are different sources of power, so too can authority be built on a range of foundations. Weber distinguished three ways of validating political power:

◆ By tradition, or the accepted way of doing things.
◆ By charisma, or intense commitment to a leader and his or her message.
◆ By appeal to legal–rational norms, based on the rule-governed powers of an office, rather than a person.

This classification remains useful today, even in democracies where we might think that legal–rational authority is the dominant form. We can also add to Weber's ideas: much of what a leader can or cannot achieve, for example, comes down to competence – or at least, to the perception that a leader actually knows what they are doing – and to the extent to which leaders are able to represent the moral values and ideological goals of their followers.

Legitimacy builds on, but is broader than, authority. When a state is widely accepted by its citizens, and by other states with which it deals, we describe it as legitimate. Thus, we speak of the *authority* of an official but the *legitimacy* of a state. Although the word *legitimacy* comes from the Latin *legitimare*, meaning 'to declare lawful', legitimacy is much more than mere legality: where legality is a technical matter, referring to whether a rule is made correctly by following regular procedures, legitimacy is a more political concept, referring to whether people accept the authority of a state, without which its very existence is in question.

> **Legitimacy**
> The condition of being legitimate. A legitimate system of government is one based on authority, and those subject to its rule recognize its right to make decisions.

Legality is a topic for lawyers; political scientists are more interested in issues of legitimacy: how a political system wins, keeps, and sometimes loses public faith in its right to function. A flourishing economy, international success, and a popular governing party will boost the legitimacy of a political system, even though legitimacy is more than any of these things. In fact, we can think of legitimacy as the credit a political system has built up from its past successes, a reserve that can be drawn down in bad times. In any event, public opinion – not a law court – is the test of legitimacy. And it is legitimacy, rather than force alone, which provides the most stable foundation for rule.

> **Ideology**
> A system of connected beliefs, a shared view of the world, or a blueprint for how politics, economics, and society should be structured.

IDEOLOGY

The concepts reviewed so far have mainly been *about* politics, but ideas also play a role *in* politics: political action is motivated by the ideas people hold about it. One way to understand this is via the notion of **ideology**. This is a term that was coined by the French philosopher Antoine Destutt de Tracy during the 1790s, in the aftermath of the French Revolution, to describe the science of ideas. Its meaning has long since changed, and it now denotes packages of ideas related to different views about the role of government and the goals of public policy. An ideology is today understood as any system of thought expressing a view on human nature, the proper relationship between state and society, and the individual's position within this order.

Which specific political outlooks should be regarded as ideologies is a matter of judgement, but Figure 1.1 offers a selection. In any case, the era of explicit ideology beginning with the French Revolution ended in the twentieth century with the defeat of fascism in 1945 and the collapse of communism at the end of the 1980s. Ideology seemed

Focus 1.2
Two options for classifying political systems

With political scientists unable to develop and agree a means of classifying political systems, it has been left to the non-academic world to step into the breach. The two most compelling typologies (used in this book) are the following:

◆ The UK-based Economist Intelligence Unit (EIU, related to *The Economist*, a British weekly news magazine) maintains a Democracy Index based on 60 different measures. These include such factors as the protection of basic political freedoms, the fairness of elections, the security of voters, election turnout rates, the freedom of political parties to operate, the independence of the judiciary and the media, and arrangements for the transfer of power. It then gives states a score out of ten, and divides them into four groups: full democracies, flawed democracies, hybrid regimes, and authoritarian regimes. In the 2017 index, Norway ranked highest with a score of 9.87 and North Korea lowest with a score of 1.08.

◆ The *Freedom in the World* index has been published annually since 1972 by Freedom House, a US-based research institute. It looks at the records of states in the areas of political rights (the ability of people to participate in the political process) and civil liberties (including freedom of expression, the independence of the judiciary, personal autonomy, and economic rights), and gives each state a score out of 100, rating them as Free, Partly Free, or Not Free. Several countries – including Syria and North Korea – have sometimes been ranked in the index as the 'Worst of the Worst'.

Table 1.3 combines the results of these two typologies, focusing on the 18 cases used in this book, while also including examples of countries with the highest and lowest scores on each index. In both indices there have been worrying declines in recent years, the authors of both reports commenting on the kind of reversals of democracy we will examine in other parts of this book. Among the more notable changes of recent years were the downgrading by the EIU of the United States, Japan, and France from full democracies to flawed democracies.

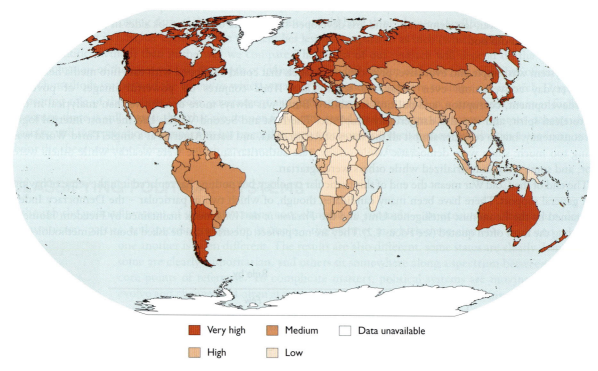

Very high   Medium   Data unavailable

High   Low

Map 1.1 The Human Development Index
Source: United Nations Development Programme (2017).

Table 1.3 Comparative political ratings

	Democracy Index		Freedom in the World	
	Score	Category	Score	Freedom rating
Norway	9.87	Full democracy	100	Free
Sweden*	9.39	Full democracy	100	Free
Canada	9.15	Full democracy	99	Free
New Zealand	9.26	Full democracy	98	Free
Germany*	8.61	Full democracy	94	Free
UK*	8.53	Full democracy	94	Free
USA*	7.98	Flawed democracy	86	Free
Japan*	7.88	Flawed democracy	96	Free
France*	7.80	Flawed democracy	90	Free
South Africa*	7.24	Flawed democracy	78	Free
India *	7.23	Flawed democracy	77	Free
Brazil*	6.86	Flawed democracy	78	Free
Mexico*	6.41	Flawed democracy	62	Partly Free
Nigeria*	4.44	Hybrid	50	Partly Free
Bangladesh	5.43	Hybrid	45	Partly Free
Kenya	5.11	Hybrid	48	Partly Free
Turkey*	4.88	Hybrid	32	Not Free
Thailand	4.63	Hybrid	31	Not Free
Venezuela*	3.87	Authoritarian	26	Not Free
Egypt*	3.36	Authoritarian	26	Not Free
Russia*	3.17	Authoritarian	20	Not Free
China*	3.10	Authoritarian	14	Not Free
Iran*	2.45	Authoritarian	18	Not Free
Saudi Arabia	1.93	Authoritarian	7	Not Free
North Korea	1.08	Authoritarian	3	Not Free

Source: Economist Intelligence Unit (2017) and Freedom House (2018).
*Note: * Cases used in this book. European Union is not rated.*

upon which they are based, we should take into consideration the agendas and values of the EIU and Freedom House, and we should beware the danger of taking classifications and rankings too literally; government and politics are too complex to be reduced to a single table. Nonetheless, these rankings give us a useful point of reference and a guide through an otherwise confusing world, and we will use them in the chapters that follow.

We will go further and also use some economic and social data to help us find our way through the maze. The relationship between politics and economics in particular is so intimate that – as we will see in Chapter 20 – there is an entire field of study devoted to its examination, called political economy. This involves looking not just at the structure and wealth of economies, but also at the influences on economic performance: good governance is more likely to produce a successful economy, and bad governance less so.

Gross domestic product
The core measure of the size of economies, calculated by giving a monetary value to all goods and services produced within a country in a given year, regardless of who owns the different means of production.

The core measure of economic activity is output. There are various ways of measuring this, the most popular today being **gross domestic product** (GDP) (see Table 1.4). This is the sum of the value of the domestic and foreign economic output of the residents of a country in a given year, and is usually converted to US dollars to allow comparison. Although the accuracy of the data itself varies by country, and the conversion to dollars raises additional questions about the appropriate exchange rate, such measures are routinely used by governments and international organizations in measuring economic size. While GDP provides a measure of the absolute size of national economies, however, it does not take into account population size. For a more revealing comparison, we use per capita GDP, which gives us a better idea of the relative economic development of different states.

Finally, we must not forget the importance of gauging political systems by looking at their relative performances in terms of providing their citizens with basic needs. There are different ways of understanding 'basic needs', but at a minimum they would include adequate nutrition, education, and health care, and in this regard the most often-used comparative measure of social conditions is the Human Development Index maintained by the UN Development Programme. Using a combination of life expectancy, adult literacy, educational enrolment, and per capita GDP, it rates human development for most of the states in the world as either very high, high, medium, or low. On the 2017 index, most democracies were in the top 30, while the poorest states ranked at the bottom of the table, with Niger in last place at 187 (see Map 1.1).

Table 1.4 Comparing economic size

Country	GDP (billion US $)	Per capita GDP (US $)
United States	19,390	59,531
European Union	17,278	33,715
China	12,238	8,827
Japan	4,872	38,428
Germany	3,677	44,470
UK	2,622	39,720
India	2,597	1,940
France	2,582	38,477
Brazil	2,055	9,821
Canada	1,653	45,032
Russia	1,577	10,743
Australia	1,323	53,800
Mexico	1,150	8,902
Turkey	851	10,540
Sweden	538	53,442
Iran	439	5,415
Nigeria	375	1,969
South Africa	349	6,160
Egypt	235	2,412
New Zealand	205	42,940
Burundi	3	320
WORLD	80,684	10,714

Source: World Bank (2018).
Note: Data are for 2017. Data for Venezuela not available.

DISCUSSION QUESTIONS

- What is government?
- What is politics? Where does it begin and end?
- Who has power, who does not, and how do we know?
- Does it necessarily follow that to be a democracy is to be legitimate, and to be legitimate is to be a democracy?
- Are the ideological distinctions in modern political systems as important and as clear as they once were?
- What are the strengths and weaknesses of the Democracy Index and Freedom in the World as means of classifying political systems?

KEY CONCEPTS

- Authority
- Comparative politics
- Concept
- Governance
- Government
- Gross domestic product
- Ideology
- Institution

- Legitimacy
- Political science
- Political system
- Politics
- Power
- Social science
- Three Worlds system
- Typology

FURTHER READING

Boix, Carles, and Susan C. Stokes (eds) (2007) *The Oxford Handbook of Comparative Politics* (Oxford University Press). At more than 1,000 pages in length, this is a rich survey of the many different dimensions of comparative politics.

Dogan, Mattei, and Dominique Pelassy (1990) *How to Compare Nations: Strategies in Comparative Politics*, 2nd edn (Chatham House). Although published many years ago, the arguments made by this short and readable book are still relevant.

Goodin, Robert E. (2009) *The Oxford Handbook of Political Science* (Oxford University Press). Another in the Oxford handbook series, offering a survey of the different facets of the study of political science.

Heywood, Andrew (2017) *Political Ideologies: An Introduction,* 6th edn (Red Globe Press). An informative and wide-ranging textbook that successfully introduces influential political creeds and doctrines.

Peter, Fabienne (2011) *Democratic Legitimacy* (Routledge). An exploration of the components of legitimacy in democracies, and the ways in which the concept has been understood and interpreted.

Woodward, Kath (2014) *Social Sciences: The Big Issues*, 3rd edn (Routledge). A useful general survey of the social sciences and the kinds of issues they include.

EORETICAL APPROACHES

2

CONTENTS

PREVIEW

In the opening chapter, we looked at comparative government and politics in broad terms, and it is probably already clear that it is a field of study that is both deep and complex. This is true enough at the level of the individual state, and the complexities grow when we add multiple political systems to the equation.

Theory comes to the rescue by pulling together a cluster of otherwise unstructured observations and facts into a framework that we can use to guide ourselves as we seek to answer political questions such as why some countries are democratic and others are not, or why democracy seems to be backsliding in some countries. Theory is a simplifying device or a conceptual filter that can help us sift through a body of facts, decide which are primary and which are secondary, enable us to organize and interpret the information, and develop complete arguments and explanations about the objects of our study.

This chapter offers some insights into the theoretical approaches used by comparative political scientists. There are so many that it is impossible in a brief chapter to be comprehensive; instead, we focus here on five of the most important: the institutional, rational, structural, cultural, and interpretive approaches. The chapter begins with a brief explanation of what theory is as well as a review of the changing face of comparative politics, then goes through each of the five key approaches in turn, explaining their origins, principles, and goals, and offering some illustrative examples.

KEY ARGUMENTS

◆ Theoretical approaches are ways of studying politics, and help in identifying the right questions to ask and how to go about answering them.

◆ The institutional perspective has done most to shape the development of politics as a discipline and remains an important tradition in comparative politics.

◆ The rational choice approach seeks to explain political outcomes by looking at the motives of the individuals involved.

◆ The structural approach focuses on networks, and looks at the past to help understand the present. In this way, it helps bridge politics and history.

◆ The cultural approach focuses on the ways in which cultural norms and practices support or undermine political preferences and forms.

◆ The interpretive approach, viewing politics as the ideas people construct about it in the course of their interaction, offers a contrast to more mainstream approaches.

THEORETICAL APPROACHES: AN OVERVIEW

Theory is a key part of the exercise of achieving understanding in any field of knowledge, opening our minds to different ways of seeing. For comparative politics, it means developing and employing principles and concepts that can be used to explain everything from the formation of states to the character of institutions, the process of democratization, the methods of dictators, and the dynamics of political instability, political participation, and public policy.

Theory
An abstract or generalized approach to explaining or understanding a phenomenon or a set of phenomena, supported by a significant body of hard evidence.

Several challenges face the political theorist. First, the field of comparative politics is so broad that it includes numerous theoretical approaches, ranging from the general to the specific. For some, there are so many choices that the diversity can sometimes seem too much, prompting charges that comparative politics lacks direction. Others see the variety as a strength, offering comparativists a multitude of approaches that can be shaped to meet different needs.

Second, political theory has been criticized for focusing too much on ideas emerging from the Western tradition, a consequence of the relatively large numbers of political scientists working in Western states. As comparison takes a more global approach – pressed by the influence of globalization – there have been calls for it to be more inclusive. This trend will further expand the already substantial range of theoretical approaches, but it will remain hard to develop universal theories so long as many parts of the world remain relatively under-studied.

Third, the value of political theory is often compromised by the way in which it is the victim of fad, fashion, and individual preference. For every theoretical approach that is proposed or applied, there often seems to be a long line of critics waiting to shoot it down and propose alternatives. It can sometimes seem as though the debate about the pros and cons of competing theoretical approaches is more vibrant than that about their practical, real-world applications.

Finally, the place of theory in the social sciences more generally is based on shaky foundations. The natural sciences have a strong record of developing theories that are well supported by the evidence, are broadly accepted, and can be used to develop laws, guide experiments, and make predictions. The social sciences suffer greater uncertainties (if only because they focus more on trying to understand human behaviour), with the result that they generate theories that are subject to stronger doubts, with a weaker record in generating laws and predicting outcomes.

In this chapter, we focus on five major theoretical approaches to the comparative study of politics. By 'approaches' we mean ways of understanding, or 'sets of attitudes, understandings and practices that define a certain way of doing political science' (Lowndes *et al.*, 2017). They are alternatives that influence how we go about political research, that structure the questions we ask, that offer guidance on where we might seek an answer, and that help us define what counts as a good answer. The chapter reviews the five approaches in an order that reflects the historical evolution of politics as an academic discipline, but by no means suggests that the list is complete. For the sake of clarity, we avoid the many subdivisions, crossovers, and reinventions within each perspective.

THE CHANGING FACE OF COMPARATIVE POLITICS

Although comparison lies at the heart of all research, the sub-field of comparative politics is relatively young, as is its theoretical base. As a systematic endeavour, it can be dated back to the formal origins of political science in the late nineteenth century, but it long lagged behind the study of domestic politics, and still lacks either a well-developed identity, or a single (or even dominant) theoretical approach. This makes it little different from political science more generally; political theory, argue Dryzek *et al.* (2006) 'is an unapologetically mongrel sub-discipline, with no dominant methodology or approach'.

Comparativists can draw from many different approaches, prompting Verba (1991) to describe the diversity of approaches as bordering on the anarchic. (There is no final and authoritative list of the options, but a representative selection of the theories most often used in political science is included in Table 2.1.) At the same time, he argued that there was strength in diversity because it 'left the field open to new and often unorthodox ideas and to a variety of approaches', a view supported by Przeworski (1995), who saw the variety as giving comparativists a wide array of options, allowing them to be 'opportunists' who can use whatever approach best works. Finnemore and Sikkink (2001) note that scholars of comparative politics, unlike their colleagues in international relations

> do not feel as compelled to maintain a consistent theoretical identity or to ensure that their work furthers a particular 'ism' in the paradigm trench wars, and it is not at all unusual for a comparative scholar to work on different problems using different theoretical approaches.

We saw in Chapter 1 how Aristotle is credited with the first attempt to classify political systems, but his work was mainly descriptive and did not establish principles that had much staying power. And while both comparative

The melting of the polar ice caps is one of the more dramatic effects of climate change, a phenomenon whose definition and solution is a classic collective action problem.
Source: iStock/Bernhard Staehli.

Paradoxically, the value of the rational choice approach lies not merely in the accuracy of its predictions, but also in explaining the reasoning behind what might, at first, appear to be irrational behaviour. If people behave in a surprising way, we have a puzzle in need of a solution. In 2016, for example, many British voters supported Brexit and many American voters supported Donald Trump, even though numerous political experts warned that they would often be acting against their best interests. The two events led to an avalanche of political analysis that tied the two results to shared concerns about immigration, globalization, loss of national sovereignty, distaste for political elites, and nostalgia for the (largely imagined) 'good old days'. Even if the choices of Brexit and Trump surprised many of the pundits, subsequent research found that both choices were a form of protest against the current situation.

Yet the rational choice approach, as any other, takes too much for granted. It fails to explain the origins of the goals that individuals hold; it is here, in understanding the shaping of preferences, that society re-enters the equation (as in the cases of the Brexit and Trump decisions, for example). Our aspirations, our fears, our status, and even our goals emerge from our interactions with others, rather than being formed beforehand.

Also, the rational choice approach is based on a universal model of human behaviour that leaves it with limited relevance in understanding variation across countries. Just as individual goals are taken for granted, so too are the different national settings which determine the choices available to individuals and within which they pursue their strategies. What may seem rational for one person, or community, or society, or country, may not seem rational for another. For voters in democracies, for example, it may seem irrational for Russian voters to keep on returning Vladimir Putin to office (helped, of course, by electoral irregularities – see Chapter 15). However, many Russian voters (particularly younger ones) define his administration – in spite of its authoritarianism – as being in their best interests, for reasons neatly encapsulated in a report in the *Washington Post* (Troianovski, 2018):

> Rather than dwell on Putin's crackdown on his opponents, young Russians draw a sense of personal liberty from those freedoms they do enjoy – a mostly open Internet, an open job market and open borders. Many of them reject

state TV as propaganda but nevertheless repeat its central tenet – that Russia needs Putin to stand up to U.S. aggression. And perhaps most important, these Russians seem shaped by a collective history they never knew – by fear of a return of the crisis-stricken 1990s or the stifling Soviet era.

In short, an action that might seem irrational for European or American voters familiar with the central tenets of liberal democracy is rational for Russian voters worried about the uncertainties of their country's past.

THE STRUCTURAL APPROACH

In contrast to theoretical approaches based on institutions or individuals, **structuralism** focuses on relationships: structuralists argue that we must go beyond the rationality of individual actors and, in the words of Lichbach and Zuckerman (1997), examine the 'networks, linkages, interdependencies, and interactions among the parts of some system'. A structure is defined by the relationships between its parts, with the parts themselves – including their internal organization and the individuals within them – being of little interest. For example, the relationship between labour and capital within a country is more important to structuralists than the internal organization or the leadership of trade unions and business organizations. The assumption is that capital and labour will follow their own real interests, regardless of who happens to lead the organizations formally representing their concerns.

> **Structuralism**
> An approach to the study of politics and government that emphasizes the relationships among groups and networks within larger systems.

The central tenet of structuralism is that 'groups matter', as in the examples of powerful groups in society, such as the bureaucracy, political parties, social classes, churches, and the military. These groups possess and pursue their own interests, creating a set of relationships which forms the structure underpinning or destabilizing the institutional politics of parties and government. Each group within the structure works to sustain its political influence in a society which is always developing in response to economic change, ideological innovations, international politics, and the effects of group conflict itself. It is this framework which undergirds, and ultimately determines, actual politics, because human actions are shaped by this bigger structural environment.

A good example of structuralism at work is found in the way that candidates running for public office in democracies will routinely campaign on a platform promising change, the injection of new ideas into government, and the avoidance of 'politics as usual'. Donald Trump's oft-repeated promise to 'drain the swamp' in Washington DC is just one particularly colourful example. Once in office, though, they find that change is more difficult to achieve than they thought, because they are only one small part of a complex structure involving a variety of organizations, ideologies, and interests. As the American politician Mario Cuomo said, 'You campaign in poetry. You govern in prose.' Meanwhile, voters continue to be seduced by promises of change, and continue voting for the 'candidates of change' instead of realizing that the barriers to change are often inherent in the structure of a political system, of which they are themselves a part. Structural constraints are central to governance, even though they rarely appear in campaigns.

Another example is offered by the persistence of poverty in many wealthy countries. Institutionalists might blame the problem on a failure of institutions to work efficiently or to coordinate with one another, but a structuralist would argue that poverty arises out of the contrasting interests and power positions of property owners and the working class. For the structuralist, the important factor is the framework of inequality, not the failure of institutions to be designed in such a way as to address the way in which particular families are confined to the bottom of the hierarchy of opportunity. 'At the core of structuralism', argues Mahoney (2003), 'is the concern with objective relationships between groups and societies. Structuralism holds that configurations of social relations shape, constrain and empower actors in predictable ways.'

Perhaps not surprisingly, the structural approach is strongly historical, often looking at how relationships change over time, seeking to understand how competition between powerful groups over time leads to specific outcomes such as a revolution, democracy, or a multi-party system. The authors of such studies argue that politics is about struggle rather than equilibrium, and they favour comparative history, giving us another contrast with the sometimes static descriptions of the institutionalists.

One of the leading figures in the field – who not only exemplifies the structural approach but helped to define it – was the American sociologist Barrington Moore. His 1966 book *Social Origins of Dictatorship and Democracy: Lord and Peasant in the Making of the Modern World* did more than any other to shape this format of historical analysis of structural forces. In trying to understand why liberal democracy developed earlier and more easily in France, Britain, and the United States than in Germany and Japan, he suggested that the strategy of the rising commercial class was the key.

In countries such as Britain, where the bourgeoisie avoided entanglement with the landowners in their battles with the peasants, the democratic transition was relatively peaceful. But where landlords engaged the commercial classes in a joint campaign against the peasantry, as in Germany, the result was an authoritarian regime which delayed the onset of democracy. Although later research qualified many of Moore's judgements, his work showed the value of studying structural relationships between groups and classes as they evolve over long periods (Mahoney, 2003). He asked important comparative questions and answered them with an account of how and when class relationships develop and evolve.

The structural approach asks big questions and, by selecting answers from the past, it interrogates history without limiting itself to chronology. Many authors working in this tradition make large claims about the positions adopted by particular classes and groups; specifically, interests are often treated as if they were actors, leading to ambitious generalizations which need verification through detailed research. Even so, the structural approach, in the form of comparative history, has made a distinctive contribution to comparative politics.

THE CULTURAL APPROACH

The relationship between culture and politics has long been a point of interest for political thinkers and analysts, with questions asked about how cultural norms and practices support or undermine different political preferences and forms. The challenge, though, has always been (and remains) just how to define **culture**, a term that is typically used in an anthropological or sociological context to describe a community of people with a shared history and common values, beliefs and customs. As we will see in Chapter 12, political culture describes the political personality of a society, reflected in the political norms and values that the community as a whole considers to be desirable and normal. More broadly, culture describes a set of assumptions associated with an institution or a society: a model of how it works, of what is considered normal or abnormal, and of the goals that are worth pursuing. Ross (2009) makes a distinction between culture as 'a system of meaning that people use to manage their daily worlds' and culture as 'the basis of social and political identity that affects how people line up and how they act on a wide range of matters'.

The earliest use of cultural theory focused on an assessment of how cultural practices either sustained or undermined different political forms. More recently, and particularly in Europe, there has been a vigorous debate about **multiculturalism** and its impact on states whose populations have become increasingly diverse in the wake of immigration since World War II. With this diversity has come new political and social tension, leading to a backlash that has fed in to the rise of nationalist movements and support for political parties that oppose immigration, notably in France, Britain, and Germany.

The troubled European record can be compared and contrasted with that of Canada, which has made a concerted political effort dating back decades to define, recognize, and build on its multicultural identity. The 1988 Canadian Multiculturalism Act acknowledges that 'multiculturalism reflects the cultural and racial diversity of Canadian society and acknowledges the freedom of all members of Canadian society to preserve, enhance and share their cultural heritage'. In the United States, meanwhile, which makes much of its immigrant history, racial differences are discussed more forthrightly than cultural differences, and there has been a backlash in some quarters against immigrants that parallels the European experience.

Culture is also a factor in contrasting global perspectives on politics and government; see Focus 2.2. We saw earlier the concerns raised about the close association between political theory (on the one hand) and Western ideas (on the other), which has been partly a consequence of the much bigger body of scholarship and analysis produced by Western political scientists. This is reflected in the research for this book, which is based in part on drawing examples from the 18 states listed in the Preface. Among those cases (chosen for their political and geographical variety), it has been easiest to find research sources on politics and government in the United States, the European Union, Britain, Germany, France, Russia, and China. Decades after the era of decolonization, however, it remains more difficult to find sources on what we once knew as the Third World, represented in this book by cases such as Mexico, Brazil, India, South Africa, and Nigeria.

Cultural approach
An approach to the study of politics and government based on understanding the influence of culture and cultural norms.

Culture
The values, beliefs, habits, attitudes, and/or norms to which a society subscribes and responds, often unconsciously and even in the face of individual differences.

Multiculturalism
A belief in a society made up of multiple cultures and ethnicities, and in the recognition of minority groups within the wider culture.

Focus 2.2
Culture and politics: Edward Said and *Orientalism*

The troubled efforts of comparative politics to bridge cultural differences are illustrated by the long-term results of the publication in 1978 of a book titled *Orientalism*. Written by the Palestinian-American scholar Edward Said (1935–2003), it argued that the forces of political and economic domination had long produced negative Western images and ideas regarding the East (or the Orient). The resulting orientalism, argued Said, embodied 'dogmas' regarding studies of the Arabs and Islam. These included a characterization of the West as 'rational, developed, humane, [and] superior', and of the Orient as 'aberrant, undeveloped, [and] inferior', and a view that the Orient was 'at bottom something either to be feared … or to be controlled'.

Orientalism
The habit by many in the West of defining the Orient (the East) in terms of stereotypical and often patronizing views about its peoples, cultures, and political systems.

Said's book was widely quoted and cited, opening up new possibilities in the debate about Western perceptions of the East, and also in comparative political study. It was also deeply controversial, however, creating something of a schism in studies of the Middle East and Islam, and Landes (2017) suggests that not much has actually changed in the wake of Said's thesis:

[When] one surveys the past two decades alone, Said's academic progeny have been spectacularly off the mark in their analyses of and prescriptions for action in the Middle East; and nowhere has this been more apparent than in the misreading of the disastrous Israeli-Palestinian Oslo 'peace process' and the 'Arab spring', with its rapid deterioration into a welter of tribal and sectarian wars.

The problem, Landes continued, was that in their excitement about the prospects for peace and democracy in the Middle East, scholars and journalists had failed to understand a critical feature of Arab and Muslim culture: the tension between honour and shame by which 'the acquisition, maintenance, and restoration of public honour trumps all other concerns', including the right of people to voice public criticism of those in power. 'In a radical misreading of the popular and social-media empowered protests that drove some Arab dictators from their perches,' Landes asserts, 'scholars interpreted the uprisings in light of European democratic revolutions.' In short, cultural misunderstandings continue to interfere with the way Western scholars interpreted political events in the Middle East.

THE INTERPRETIVE APPROACH

So far, we have looked at theories where the focus is on institutions, individuals, groups, and societies. With the interpretive approach, the focus is on ideas, summarized by Bevir and Rhodes (2004) when they argue that in order 'to understand actions, practices and institutions, we need to grasp the relevant meanings, beliefs and preferences of the people involved'. In other words, as Parsons (2018) puts it, people do some things and avoid others because of the presence of social constructs – ideas, beliefs, norms, assumptions, codes, identities, meanings, narratives, and values – that filter the way they see the world (hence the approach is also sometimes known as constructivism). The starting point is that we cannot take the actor's goals and definition of the situation for granted, as the rational actor approach does; instead, we must look to these kinds of constructs.

Interpretive approach
An approach to the study of politics and government based on the argument that politics is formed by the ideas we have about it.

In its strongest version, the interpretive approach argues that politics consists of the ideas participants hold about it. There is no political reality separate from our mental constructions, and no reality which can be examined to reveal the impact of ideas upon it. Rather, politics is formed by ideas themselves. In short, 'ideas matter' and there is nothing but ideas.

In a more restrained version, the argument is not that ideas comprise our political world but, rather, that they are an independent influence upon it, shaping how we define our interests, our goals, our allies, and our enemies. We act as we do because of how we view the world; if our perspective differed, so would our actions. Where rational choice focuses on how people go about achieving their individual objectives, the interpretivist examines the framing of objectives themselves and regards such interpretations as a property of the group, rather than the individual (hence interpretivists take a social rather than a psychological approach).

Because ideas are socially constructed, many interpretivists imagine that we can restructure our view of the world and, so, the world itself. For example, there is no intrinsic reason why individuals and states must act (as rational choice theorists imagine) in pursuit of their own narrow self-interests. To make such an assumption is to project concepts onto a world that we falsely imagine to be independent of our thoughts. Finnemore (1996) suggests that interests 'are not just "out there" waiting to be discovered; they are constructed through social interaction'. Also, ideas come before material factors because the value placed on material things is itself an idea (although Marxists and others would disagree).

For these reasons, interpretivists – like structuralists – often focus on historical narratives, examining how understandings of earlier events influence later ones. Take the study of revolutions as an example. Where behaviouralists see a set of cases (French, Russian, Iranian, and so on) and seek common causes of events treated as independent, interpretivists see a single sequence and ask how later examples (such as the Iranian revolution) were influenced by the ideas then held about earlier revolutions (such as the French). Alternatively, take the study of elections. The meaning of an election is not given by the results themselves but by the narrative that the political class later establishes about it: for example, 'the results showed that voters will not tolerate high unemployment' (see Chapter 17 for more about this).

Consider what this means for our understanding of states. They are often presented as entities existing independently of our thoughts, and by acting in a world of states – where we apply for passports, support national sports teams, or just use the word *citizen* – we routinely reinforce the concept of the state. But the state is not a physical entity such as a building or a mountain; it is an idea built over a long period by political thinkers, as well as by practical politicians. Borders between blocs of land were placed there not by nature but by people. There are no states when the world is viewed from outer space, as astronauts frequently tell us. It is this point that Steinberger (2004) has in mind when he says that his idea of the state is that the state is an idea. True, the consequences of states, such as taxes and wars, are real enough, but these are the effects of the world we have made, and can remake. Just as the idea of the state is socially reinforced or, as is often said, 'socially constructed', it can also be socially contested ('Why should I need a visa each time I visit this country?'), leading to gradual changes in the ideas themselves.

The interpretive/constructivist approach was used in two studies by Wedeen into Yemen (2008) and Syria (2015). In the first, she argued that the government continued to endure in spite of its inability to control violence or provide goods and services for its people. This happened because instead of attachments to institutions, Yemenis had formed strong attachments to one another, and regularly gathered to engage in wide-ranging discussions about even the most divisive political issues. In the second (the research for which was undertaken well before the outbreak of the Syrian civil war), she argued that although President Hafez al-Assad was omnipresent during his term in office (1971–2000), few people believed the claims of the official rhetoric of his administration. However, its inundation of public and political life with the symbols of his rule had a subtle effect on encouraging obedience, isolating Syrians from one another, and establishing guidelines for public speech and behaviour.

There is a clear and useful lesson in the interpretive approach for students of politics, and of comparative politics especially. When we confront a political system for the first time, our initial task is to engage in political anthropology: to make sense of the activities that comprise the system. What are the moves? What do they mean? What is the context that provides this meaning? And what identities and values underpin political action? Behaviour which has one meaning in our home country may possess a different significance, and constitute a different action, elsewhere. For example, offering a bribe may be accepted as normal in one place, but be regarded as a serious offence in another. Casting a vote may be an act of choice in a democracy, but of subservience in a dictatorship. Criticizing the president may be routine in one country, but sedition in another. Because the consequences of these acts vary, so does their meaning.

So far, so good. Yet, in studying politics we want to identify patterns that abstract from detail; we seek general statements about presidential, electoral, or party systems which go beyond the facts of a particular case. We want to examine relationships between such categories so as to discover overall associations. We want to know, for example, whether a plurality electoral system always leads to a two-party system – see Chapter 15. Through such investigations we can try to acquire knowledge which goes beyond the understandings held by the participants in a particular case.

We must recognize, also, that events have unintended consequences: the Holocaust was certainly a product of Hitler's ideas, but its effects ran far beyond his own intentions. With its emphasis on meaning, an interpretive approach misses the commonplace observation that much social and political analysis studies the unintended consequences of human activity. In short, unpacking the meaning of political action is best regarded as the start, but not the end, of political analysis. It provides a practical piece of advice: we must grasp the meaning of political behaviour, thus enabling us to compare like with like.

Compared with the other approaches reviewed in this chapter, the interpretive approach remains more aspiration than achievement. Some studies conducted within the programme focus on interesting but far-away cases when meanings really were different: when states did not rule the world; when lending money was considered a sin; or when the political game consisted of acquiring dependent followers, rather than independent wealth. Yet, such studies do little to confirm the easy assumption that the world we have made can be easily dissolved. As the institutionalists with whom we began this chapter are quick to remind us, most social constructs are social constraints, for institutions are powerfully persistent. Our ability to imagine other worlds should not bias how we go about understanding the world as it is.

DISCUSSION QUESTIONS

◆ Why is there so much disagreement among political scientists (or comparativists) about the best theoretical approach, and why are grand theories so elusive?
◆ Which of the different theoretical approaches outlined in this chapter do you find the most compelling or convincing, and which the least?
◆ How far can we understand politics and government by focusing on institutions?
◆ Which matter more to an understanding of government and politics: people, cultures, or ideas?
◆ What does 'rational' mean, and do people behave rationally?
◆ What influences have been most important in shaping how you view the political world?

KEY CONCEPTS

◆ Behaviouralism
◆ Collective action problem
◆ Cultural approach
◆ Culture
◆ Empirical
◆ Grand theory
◆ Institutionalism
◆ Institutionalization

◆ Interpretive approach
◆ Multiculturalism
◆ New institutionalism
◆ Normative
◆ Orientalism
◆ Rational choice
◆ Structuralism
◆ Theory

FURTHER READING

Dallmayr, Fred (ed.) (2010) *Comparative Political Theory: An Introduction* (Red Globe Press). An edited collection that tries to take the discussion of political theory away from its Western base, and focuses instead on Islamic, Indian, and East Asian ideas.

Dryzek, John S., Bonnie Honig, and Anne Phillips (eds) (2006) *The Oxford Handbook of Political Theory* (Oxford University Press). A detailed collection of essays on the many different options in the field of political theory.

Eriksson, Lina (2011) *Rational Choice Theory: Potential and Limits* (Red Globe Press). A broad-ranging review of the meaning, strengths, and weaknesses of rational choice theory.

Lichbach, Mark Irving, and Alan S. Zuckerman (eds) (2009) *Comparative Politics: Rationality, Culture and Structure,* 2nd edn (Cambridge University Press). Detailed essays on the rational, cultural and structural approaches to comparative politics.

Lowndes, Vivien, David Marsh, and Gerry Stoker (eds) (2018) *Theory and Methods in Political Science,* 4th edn (Red Globe Press). Includes chapters on most of the theoretical approaches introduced in this chapter.

Peters, B. Guy (2019) *Institutional Theory in Political Science*, 4th edn (Edward Elgar). A survey of the different facets of institutional theory, and its potential as a paradigm for political science.

COMPARATIVE METHODS

Source: iStock/ramihalir

CONTENTS

PREVIEW

So far we have looked at the conceptual and theoretical aspects of comparative politics. These provide us with critical context and guidance, helping provide direction to the practice of comparison: the kinds of questions that need to be asked, the methods that can be used to carry out research, the options for designing a comparative research project, and the pitfalls to be avoided. This chapter is partly a survey of methods and partly a practical *How To* guide to the comparative process, giving more insight into the dynamics of that process. The goal is not to cover the details of specific techniques such as interviewing or statistical analysis so much as to provide an outline of strategies that will help students working on comparative projects of their own.

The chapter begins with a discussion about the number and the use of cases chosen in comparison; these range from one to many, the research methods used being different for single-case studies, those involving a small numbers of cases (small-N studies), and those involving a large numbers of cases (large-N studies). The chapter then reviews the features of qualitative, quantitative, and historical research methods, arguing that the latter can be useful in offsetting some of the limitations inherent in the case study method. It ends with a discussion of some of the challenges faced by comparison, including the troubling problem of having too few cases and too many variables.

KEY ARGUMENTS

◆ There are many options for conducting comparative political research, each of which has advantages and disadvantages.

◆ Comparative researchers must make choices that include the unit of analysis, the level of analysis, and the variables to be studied.

◆ Research methods include the case study, the qualitative method (a small selection of cases), the quantitative method (large numbers of cases), and the historical method.

◆ Comparative research has different approaches and results according to whether it is empirical or normative, or quantitative or qualitative.

◆ In making comparisons between two or more factors, it is worth considering the relative strengths of the most similar and most different system designs.

◆ Comparative research can benefit from taking the historical approach: comparing current cases with past examples, or developments over time across countries.

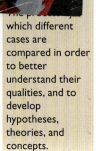

which different cases are compared in order to better understand their qualities, and to develop hypotheses, theories, and concepts.

Methodology
The systematic analysis of the methods used in a given field of enquiry. Also used to describe the body of methods used, or the means used to reach a particular set of conclusions.

Unit of analysis
The object of study in comparative politics.

Level of analysis
The level of study in comparative politics, ranging from the macro (political system) level to the micro (individual) level.

Case study method
A research method involving detailed study of a particular object and the context within which it exists.

Comparison is not only one of the oldest tools of political science (found, for example, in the work of Aristotle), but also one of the most important. Some have even argued that the scientific study of politics is unavoidably comparative (Almond, 1966, and Lasswell 1968), and that 'comparison is the methodological core of the scientific study of politics' (Powell *et al.*, 2014). In short, the **comparative method** lies at the heart of political research. Having said that, we saw in Chapter 2 that there are different theoretical approaches to comparison, and now – in looking at **methodology** – we will see that there are also different research methods, and differing opinions about the best way of realizing the potential of comparison (Munck and Snyder, 2007).

Once we have thought about the best theoretical approach to take, we then need to decide our **unit of analysis**, which could be the state, a political office, an institution, a process, a principle, a movement, a theme, or an area of policy. We then need to think about the **level of analysis**, which could be anything from the relations among and between states down through groups or social classes to politics at the level of the individual. We are then faced with several additional choices: the case or cases we wish to study, the combination of such cases, the variable that interests us, and the question of whether to use quantitative, qualitative, or historical research methods. Even if we opt for the most popular approach – the case study method – we are faced with several subsidiary questions regarding the number of cases we use, and whether or not the cases we use are representative.

Once we have made these choices, we have no shortage of methods from which to choose, depending on a combination of the research question we want to ask, the time and resources we have available, the method with which we are most comfortable, and our research preferences; that is, how we believe that understanding is best acquired (see Landman and Carvalho, 2017). In this chapter we will focus on four key methods: case studies, the qualitative method, the quantitative method, and the historical method, summarized in Figure 3.1. (These are broad groupings that contain many more specific methods, and treating them separately is not meant to suggest that they are distinct from one another, and in fact they often overlap and can be used in different combinations.)

THE CASE STUDY METHOD

The **case study method** is one of the most widely used strategies in research, lying at the heart of political science and being widely used also throughout the social and natural sciences, and the humanities. The method, says Gerring (2007), involves 'the intensive study of a single case for the purpose of understanding a larger class of cases (a population)'. The focus of that study might be an event, a policy, or a political institution or process. Although it might at first seem odd to suggest that we can compare using a single case, a case is necessarily comparative because it needs to be an example of a larger population, against which it can then be juxtaposed. (For example, Iran as a case of an Islamic republic, or Sweden as an example of a monarchy.) Single cases have the advantage of depth, and other researchers can use two or more single-country studies to explore broader similarities and differences, and single cases can be also compared with an ideal type or typology. The greatest advantage of a single case is that it offers an in-depth, real-world understanding of a phenomenon, a clearly defined example that helps to illustrate a wider principle.

Yin (2018) points out that case studies must be understood in terms of both their scope and their features. In terms of scope, they look in depth at a phenomenon within its actual context; case studies are different from experiments, for example, because the latter separate the phenomena to be studied from their context. In terms of features, case studies help address the problem of too many variables and not enough cases (discussed later in this chapter), and are broad-ranging in that they rely on multiple sources of evidence.

One key to a successful case study is to be clear what the case represents, and how a case differs from a study. By its nature, a case is an example of a more general category, such that to examine a case is to undertake an investigation with significance beyond its own boundaries. An account of the Japanese general election of 2017 which does not venture

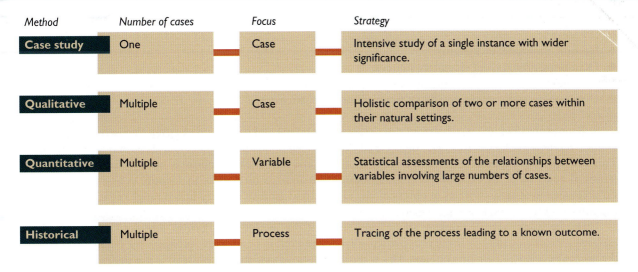

Method	Number of cases	Focus	Strategy
Case study	One	Case	Intensive study of a single instance with wider significance.
Qualitative	Multiple	Case	Holistic comparison of two or more cases within their natural settings.
Quantitative	Multiple	Variable	Statistical assessments of the relationships between variables involving large numbers of cases.
Historical	Multiple	Process	Tracing of the process leading to a known outcome.

Figure 3.1 Political science research methods

beyond the topic itself is a study, not a case study. However, an analysis which delves into the significance of the election being the first in Japan since 1953 in which an incumbent prime minister (Shinzō Abe) had a third consecutive victory makes it a case study, offering a detailed illustration of themes of wider interest. It raises many interesting questions about the evolution of political parties, about changes in the place of political factionalism, and about the dynamics of states with dominant political parties. The outcome of the election also had international ramification in that it gave Abe the support he needed to address constitutional limits on Japanese defence policy.

Prime minister Shinzō Abe stands to take a bow before the Diet after being re-elected to office for a second time, an event offering a case study with many potentially interesting insights into the changing nature of Japanese politics.
Source: Getty Images/Kyodo News.

By their nature, case studies use a wide range of techniques, including the following:

◆ Reading the academic literature.
◆ Examining primary and secondary sources.
◆ Interviews with participants and other observers in the unit.
◆ Direct observation, either as a 'fly on the wall' or as a participant.

As King *et al.* (1994) put it, scholars of cases engage in 'soaking and poking, marinating themselves in minutiae', aiming to provide what Geertz (1973) once called 'thick description', meaning that it is both rounded and detailed. This multi-method approach contrasts with a more specific and explicit approach using a single lens, such as statistical analysis, or an experiment. Unlike statistical analysis, which seeks to identify relationships between variables measured across a series of observations, case analysis aims to identify how a range of factors interact in the context of the example being studied.

There are many ways of thinking about cases, some of the modifying adjectives include *illustrative*, *descriptive*, *exploratory*, *cumulative*, and *critical*, but four particular types stand out in comparative politics – see Figure 3.2. Of these, the *representative case* is the most common. This is the workhorse of case studies, as useful as it is undramatic, and often focused on the home country of a researcher. For example, researchers may be interested in the formation of coalition governments in general, but they opt to study in detail how governments form in their homeland, hoping that the resulting research can contribute to broader understandings. A collection of representative case studies can go on to provide the raw material for comparative generalization by other scholars taking a wider approach.

By contrast, a *prototypical case* is chosen not because it is representative but because it is expected to become so. The point here is that studying a pioneer can help us understand a phenomenon which might become more widely significant. One example is the use of social media in elections in the United States, for which the Obama campaign in 2008 was a trendsetter. His campaign may not have been the first to do this, but it was clearly one of the most thorough and effective, setting new standards and exploiting new methods that were quickly adopted elsewhere. Campaigning via social media has quickly become the norm in many democracies, even moving into darker territory with allegations of Russian manipulation of elections in several countries. The use of social media to campaign was predictable, as was the earlier use of mass circulation newspapers, radio, and television, but one of the dangers of a prototypical case is that it is based on a bet on the future, and may come to nothing if it is not adopted more widely. (At which point, presumably, the focus of research can switch to an analysis of why it never took off.)

Where the study of prototypical cases looks to the future, *exemplary cases* look to the past in the sense that they are the archetypes that are considered to have generated the category of which they are taken as representative. For example, the parliamentary system was born in Britain, and thus a study of the features of the British Parliament is likely to provide insights into the manner in which legislatures and executives work in all those countries using this system. In similar fashion, the French presidency does far more than illustrate the semi-presidential system of government: it is the model upon which other semi-presidential systems – such as those in Russia, Ukraine, and several former French

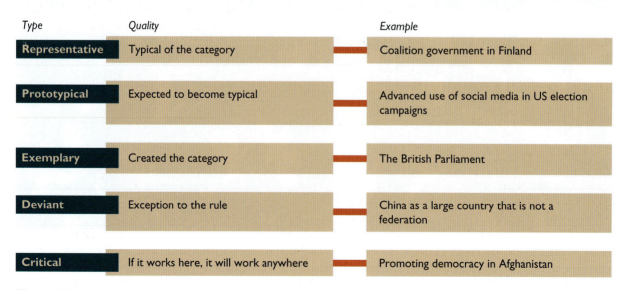

Type	Quality		Example
Representative	Typical of the category		Coalition government in Finland
Prototypical	Expected to become typical		Advanced use of social media in US election campaigns
Exemplary	Created the category		The British Parliament
Deviant	Exception to the rule		China as a large country that is not a federation
Critical	If it works here, it will work anywhere		Promoting democracy in Afghanistan

Figure 3.2 Five types of case study

colonies in Africa – were based. While an exemplar is often defined as a case to be emulated, in research design the term refers more neutrally to an influential example which illustrates the essential features of a phenomenon. An exemplary case is often, but need not be, prototypical.

The purpose of studying a *deviant case* is to seek out the exceptional and the atypical, rather than the usual: the few countries which remain communist, for example, or poor countries that have managed to be democratic, or those where the military still plays an important political role. Deviant cases are often used to tidy up our understanding of exceptions and anomalies. Why does India contradict the thesis that democracy presupposes prosperity? Why did tiny Switzerland adopt a federal administrative system when most federations are found in large countries? (Conversely, why is China – the largest country in the world by population – not a federation?) Why has voter turnout stayed high in Sweden and Denmark (more than 80 per cent in recent elections) while it has been more modest in neighbouring Estonia and Finland? Deviant cases always attract interest and, by providing a contrast with the norm, enhance our understanding of representative examples. Since the exceptional tends to the exotic, however, the danger is over-study: comparative politics should be more than a collection of curios.

Finally, a *critical case* (also known as a 'crucial case') enables a proposition to be tested in the circumstances least favourable to its validity. The logic is simple: if it is true here, then it is true everywhere. For instance, if we were to find that most Germans opposed further European integration, we could anticipate that the same would hold true in other EU countries. In this way, critical case studies can be highly efficient, providing exceptional returns on the research investment; by studying just one country, we can generalize to others. However, the pay-off comes with risk: a critical case design builds a potential for generalization into a single investigation but involves a bet that the relevant proposition will, in fact, be confirmed in the conditions least favourable to its validity.

Case studies are the building blocks from which we construct our understanding of the political world. In a similar way to judges in common law systems, political scientists (and politicians more so) usually proceed by comparing cases, rather than by making deductions from first principles. As a result, much comparative political analysis takes the form of drawing analogies between cases. For example, what are the similarities and differences between the causes of the Russian, Chinese, and Iranian revolutions? Why does the plurality electoral system produce a two-party system in the United States but a multi-party system in India? Why have several Eastern European countries (notably Hungary and Poland), after setting out on the road to democracy, started slipping back towards authoritarianism? As we will see in the next section, a comparison of cases can create space for a broader understanding.

THE QUALITATIVE METHOD

Implementing a comparative design involves making either qualitative or quantitative comparisons, or a blend of the two. The **qualitative method** is what we usually associate with the comparative method, and although it can involve comparing many cases (otherwise known as large-N, for the number of cases), it most often concentrates on the intensive examination of two cases (a paired or binary comparison), three cases (a triangular comparison), or a few cases. Cases are usually chosen so as to introduce variation into the dependent variable, thus overcoming an inherent limit of the single case study.

> **Qualitative method**
> A research method based on studying a few cases within their natural setting, with an emphasis on values, opinions, behaviour, and context.

The qualitative approach has the following features:

◆ A limited number of cases are studied in depth.
◆ It tends to be descriptive rather than predictive.
◆ An effort is made to understand the interaction of multiple variables.
◆ Meaning is allowed to emerge from the objects of study.
◆ Observation is the main means of data collection.
◆ Phenomena are studied within their natural setting.

An example of the qualitative approach is offered by recent research into nationalism, which (as we will see in Chapter 4) has been on the rise in multiple countries in different parts of the world. Much of it has come as a reaction to immigration, globalization, and multiculturalism, but the spark varies from place to place (lending itself to studies involving a few cases), and because nationalism can be highly emotional, it is hard to fit into the large-N statistical approaches that come with quantitative analysis.

In a book published in 1995, the author Michael Billig developed the idea of 'banal nationalism' to describe the 'banal' channels through which people in established nations experienced nationalism; these included routine symbols and habits, such as flags, anthems, sporting events, and use of terms that imply togetherness, such as '*the* president' or *us*

Focus 3.1
Hypotheses and variables

Hypothesis
A proposed explanation for a phenomenon that can be supported (confirmed) or refuted (falsified) through observation or experimentation.

Variable
A changeable feature, factor, quantity, or element.

Dependent variable
The factor or element we wish to explain.

Independent variable
The factor or element believed to influence the dependent variable. There are often many such variables.

At the heart of research in almost every field of study is the formulation and testing of a **hypothesis**. Although distinct from a theory, which – as we saw in Chapter 2 – is an explanatory framework, hypotheses might flow from theories, and can in turn be tested in order to support or refute theories. Examples of hypotheses include the following:

◆ The wealthier a country, the more likely it is to sustain a stable democracy.
◆ The violent end to a dictatorial regime is more likely to bring chaos than democracy.
◆ Colonialism is the root cause of the problems of the world's poorest states.

In much comparative research, the focus of interest lies with **variables**, the object usually being to explore the extent to which they co-vary with one another, such that knowing a country's score on one variable (such as literacy) allows us to predict its score on another (such as electoral turnout). In such analyses, one variable is **dependent**, in the sense that it is the one we want to better understand, while the others are **independent**, in the sense that we believe that they may explain or impact the dependent variable. For example:

◆ Higher participation in politics may be driven by factors such as greater wealth and higher education.
◆ The incidence of military coups may be tied to poverty, social division, and the past incidence of coups.
◆ An assertive foreign policy may be driven by a high sense of mission, the power of the defence industry, fear of the foreign, or (as in the case of Putin's Russia) a desire to reassert lost influence.

or *we*. (These are known as deixis, or 'pointing' words that cannot be understood without understanding the context in which they are used.)

In a book published in 2017, editors Michael Skey and Marco Antonsich brought together a group of nearly 20 scholars who used Billig's book as the basis for case studies on nationalism from different parts of the world, including Azerbaijan, France, Germany, Japan, New Zealand, Serbia, and Russia. They used a variety of techniques to undertake their research, including interviews, focus groups, survey data, ethnography (the study of people and cultures) and the analysis of Twitter campaigns. Skey and Antonsich comment on the manner in which national commemorative events build con-

Most similar system
A research design based on using cases that are as similar as possible, in effect controlling for the similarities and isolating the causes of differences.

nections 'between bodies, symbols and places that may generate feelings of awe, respect, sadness or joy', and that they are 'crucial in making the nation seem resonant and meaningful for substantial numbers'. They also argue that any understanding of the nation must pay attention to matters that are 'emotional or felt', otherwise there is a danger of failing to understand how 'passions, feelings and emotions drive people's involvement in political campaigns and public celebrations tied to the nation'. Clearly, then, studies of nationalism invite the use of qualitative approaches based on values, opinions, behaviour, and context.

The selection of cases is important to qualitative research, and there are two core strategies involved (see Anckar, 2008). The most common – known as the **most similar system** (MSS) design – involves selecting those cases which are as similar as possible except in regard to the object of study (the dependent variable). The underlying logic, argues Lipset (1990) is that 'the more similar the units being compared, the more possible it should be to isolate the factors responsible for differences between them'. If the units being studied are similar in, say, their history, culture, and government institutions, it should be possible to rule out such common factors as explanations for the particular difference being studied.

An example of the MSS method at work might be a study of attitudes towards membership of the European Union among its six founding states, or a selection of Western European members, or a selection of Eastern Europeans members. Attitudes towards integration differ among countries within each group, even though they have much else in common, so the goal would be to tease out the differences that accounted for the variation in levels of support for the EU within an otherwise similar group.

The **most different system** (MDS) design follows the opposite track. Here, the goal is to test a relationship between two factors by discovering whether it can be observed in a range of countries with contrasting political systems, histories, or cultures, for example. If so, our confidence that the relationship is real, and not due to the dependence of both factors on an unmeasured third variable, will increase (Landman and Carvalho, 2017). A well-known example of this approach is the historical analysis by Theda Skocpol (1979) of revolutions in France, Russia, and China. These three cases had quite different political, economic, and social systems, so she set out to ask what they had in common that would produce a similar political outcome. She concluded that regimes which were internationally weak and domestically ineffective became vulnerable to insurrection when well-organized agitators succeeded in exploiting peasant frustration with an old order to which the landed aristocracy offered only limited support.

> **Most different system**
> A research design based on using cases that are as different as possible, in effect controlling for the differences and isolating the causes of similarities.

THE QUANTITATIVE METHOD

Where the qualitative method takes a wide-angle approach to understanding political phenomena, often using small-N cases in their natural setting, the **quantitative method** usually takes a narrower approach based on larger-N cases, more variables, and statistical analysis; see summary in Table 3.1. It usually tries to quantify data and to generalize the results to a larger population, generates information through experiments and survey research, and demands a familiarity with the technical language of statistics. It calls for different skills than the qualitative approach, and is more likely to suffer from the variable quality and availability of data from multiple cases, but the results often provide more breadth.

The most basic form of quantitative research is counting numbers. For example: how many federations are there; how many states are democratic; or how many of the countries that were classified by the Democracy Index as full democracies in 2010 are flawed democracies today? Just as straightforward case studies can contribute more to comparative politics than elaborate attempts at theory testing, so descriptive counts can sometimes provide more useful results than sophisticated statistical analyses. Once we go beyond the basics, though, we enter the more analytical world of dependent and independent variables.

To illustrate the statistical approach, consider the example in Figure 3.3, which is a scatter plot showing the relationship between the number of members in a national legislature (the dependent variable) and a country's population (the independent variable). The simple question being asked is whether population size impacts the size of the legislature, and the graph reveals a modest positive **correlation**: the larger the population, the larger the assembly. The findings are summarized in the graph by calculating a **regression line**: the line giving the best fit to the data, and which is determined by a formula linking the two variables.

In this case, the equation reveals that, on average, the size of a legislature increases by a factor of one for each increment of a million in a country's population. Given such an equation, which also gives a base estimate for assembly size given a notional population of zero, we can use the population of any particular country to predict its assembly size. (If there had been a negative correlation, the regression line would have sloped down rather than up: in that unlikely case, a larger population would be associated with a smaller legislature.)

One important virtue of a regression line is that it allows us to identify **outliers**. The larger the difference between the predicted and the actual assembly size, the greater the need for additional explanation, thus providing a link to deviant case analysis. In our example in Figure 3.3, Nigeria has a legislature that is smaller per head of population than most: it has 360 members in a country with nearly 180 million people, or one representative for 494,000 people. This undersize is a reflection in part of its federal structure; federations tend to have smaller national legislatures

> **Quantitative method**
> A research method using more cases, more variables, and attempting to explain political phenomena using statistical analysis.
>
> **Correlation**
> A relationship between two or more variables or attributes.
>
> **Regression line**
> The line of best fit in a scatter plot, summarizing the relationship between two variables.
>
> **Outliers**
> The observations furthest away from the value predicted by the regression line.

Table 3.1 Comparing qualitative and quantitative approaches

	Qualitative	Quantitative
Goal	To understand underlying reasons and motivations in the setting of a phenomenon.	To quantify data and generalize results from a sample to the population of interest.
Method	Exploratory or 'bottom-up'; hypotheses and theory generated from data.	Confirmatory or 'top-down'; hypotheses and theory tested with data.
View of human thought and behaviour	Contextual, personal, and unpredictable.	Regular and predictable.
Focus	Wide-angle lens.	Narrow-angle lens.
Context	Natural setting.	Controlled conditions.
Sample size	Smaller.	Larger.
Core principles	Interpretive, exploratory.	Scientific, conclusive.
Types of information	Open-ended, narrative, non-numerical, words, images, themes.	Statistical, numerical.
Information collection	Interviews, focus groups, case studies, observation.	Experiments, audits, survey research, rating scales.
Results	Particularistic, respondent-framed.	Generalizable, researcher-framed.
Advantages	Best where ideas cannot be reduced to numbers.	Allows for large-scale studies.
Disadvantages	Can be difficult to analyse, generating conflicting conclusions.	Ideas and political phenomena cannot always be expressed in numbers.

Adapted from Johnson and Christensen (2017), Chapter 2.
Note: These contrasts should be regarded as tendencies rather than absolutes. There is much overlap between the two methods.

because their people are also represented in state/provincial legislatures. Conversely, Cuba's National Assembly of People's Power is large per head of population; it has 612 members in a country with just over 11 million people, or one representative for 18,000 people, giving Cubans a higher level of representation than almost any other country in the world. This could be because communist states created large legislatures as a way of reducing any threat they might pose to the party's power, giving us a plausible hypothesis for further investigation.

The value of quantitative comparison is that it can provide precise summaries of large amounts of data using standard techniques whose application can be checked by other researchers. But, as always, interpretation is the difficult

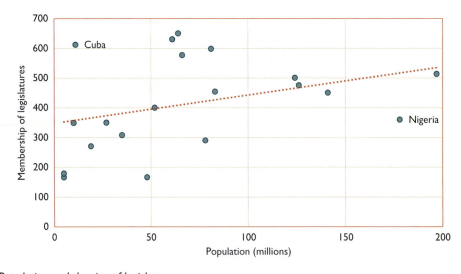

Figure 3.3 Population and the size of legislatures
Sources: Membership of legislatures from Inter-Parliamentary Union (2018); population size from World Bank (2018). Membership of legislatures refers to lower chamber only.

part, posing two main dangers. First, a strong correlation between two variables may arise simply because both depend on a third, unmeasured factor. In such cases, there is no relationship of cause and effect. For example, a correlation between proportional representation (PR) and multi-party systems might arise because both factors emerge in divided societies, not because PR itself increases the number of parties. This problem of a spurious correlation can be addressed by including all relevant variables in an analysis, but we may not know how many are relevant, and may not have data on all those we think might be relevant.

The second problem in interpreting statistical results is that, even if a relationship is genuine, the direction of causation remains to be established. Suppose we find that liberal democracies have higher rates of economic growth than authoritarian regimes; does the correlation arise because democracy encourages economic growth, or because economic growth encourages democracy? A case can be made either way, or both. A statistical correlation by itself will not provide the answer, and a correlation in itself does not show the direction of causation.

For Brady and Collier (2010), there are several potential dangers posed by quantitative approaches. 'Constructing a statistical model requires assumptions,' they warn, 'which often are not only untested, but largely untestable.' Those assumptions come into play when decisions are made about the parameters to include in a study, and the degree to which chance affects the results. They also warn that 'regression analysis depends on the model, and if the model is wrong, so is the analysis'. In short, the results of quantitative research vary with the quality and the quantity of the data used and the design of the models used. As often as not, scholars in political science will end up arguing about the construction of those models rather than about the results they produce.

THE HISTORICAL METHOD

Most studies in politics – and in comparative politics, especially – focus on the present and leave history to the historians. But this division of labour is both arbitrary and artificial, because today's present is tomorrow's past, and it is often hard to truly understand a political system without looking at its historical roots. Political science can, and perhaps should, make more use of the past as a treasure trove of additional cases, whether of rare events such as

The Cuban National Assembly in session. Given its unusually large number of representatives per voter, it stands as an outlier in studies of the size and membership of legislatures.
Source: Getty Images/Adalberto Roque.

genocide and revolution or of particular episodes that exemplify, challenge, or refine existing theories. The **historical method** has much to add to both qualitative and quantitative approaches to research, helping to examine the robustness of findings across distinct time periods.

The European Union offers a good example. One of the hardest challenges in EU studies is to provide an answer to the question 'What is the European Union?' There is nothing quite like it anywhere else in the world, and it is both more than a standard international organization while also being less than a United States of Europe. One possible answer to the question is that it is a confederation (a union of independent states – see Chapter 11 for more on this), but there are no true confederations in existence today with which it could be compared. This means that we have to go back in history and look at examples such as the Old Swiss Confederacy (prior to 1798) and the German confederation (1815–66) in order to better assess the question of the degree to which today's EU can be regarded as confederal.

We can connect political science with history by using **process tracing** to identify and describe the historical sequence linking a cause to an effect. For example, what were the steps leading from Hitler's anti-Semitism to the Holocaust? Through what mechanisms does defeat in war lead to a change of regime? Taking a more particular case: why does Iran have such a troubled relationship with the West? At first glance, it can appear that Iranians are over-concerned with criticizing the West, and the instinctive reaction of Western political leaders is to reward Iran's petulance with criticism, mistrust, and an unwillingness to engage. Although Iran was never a colony, its perspective is still coloured by the long history of Western interference in its politics and economics, and narratives on both sides have been altered, recycled, and manipulated to fit different agendas (Whiskin, 2018). It is only through an historical analysis of this kind that the present can be understood in terms of the past.

Pierson (2004) brings together some concepts for thinking about politics in the context of time, helping tease out our often-submerged thoughts about political change. First among these is **path dependence**, an idea borrowed from physics by economists trying to explain how changes in technology impacted the evolution of business practices, and which has since spread throughout the social sciences. It might be used, for example, to argue that the return of authoritarianism in Putin's Russia can be traced back to decisions made or steps taken during the reform era following the collapse of the USSR in 1991.

Path dependence implies an emphasis on history generally and branching points specifically. By contrast, path *in*dependence means that the same destination will be reached, regardless of the route; all roads lead to Rome. It implies an emphasis on underlying structures and resources rather than historical sequences. For example, the outcome of a war is path dependent if a particular battle proves decisive, and path independent if the stronger side is sure to win eventually, whatever the result of a specific confrontation.

Path dependence can be initiated by **critical junctures**, or key moments that clear a new path that continues to be followed long after the juncture itself has passed; see Focus 3.2 for an example. During the critical phase (often a crisis of some kind), all options are on the table and history is written. Revolutions are one example, constitutional conventions another. Once the new order has consolidated, however, politics settles down and the choices realistically available to decision-makers shrink. The revolutionary generation gives way to pragmatic operators of the new regime. As ideas are displaced by institutions, so the constitution as choice is supplanted by the constitution as constraint.

By dividing history into critical and normal eras, we arrive at a plausible perspective on the old debate about whether people make their own history. The answer is perhaps that they do, but only occasionally. In other words, critical junctures are rare choice points in which human agency really can be decisive for the long term.

Ideas, in particular, rise to prominence during critical junctures. In normal times, much of the political discussion defends established procedures and interests. But the existing stock of ideas sometimes becomes incapable of responding to a shift in circumstances, creating pressures for established procedures to be revised or completely rethought. A country may experience economic decline; a party may lose voter support; a trade union may experience a collapse in membership. Suddenly, ideas that had previously received little consideration find themselves at the centre of the table. When disintegration threatens, new thoughts are urgently needed.

Sequencing, the order in which events unfold, can help to account for path dependence. For example, communist regimes which introduced economic reform before political liberalization

Historical method
A research method based on studying cases from the past, often with a focus on their development through time.

Process tracing
The study of the sequence of events linking a cause to an effect.

Path dependence
The idea that the outcome of a political process depends on earlier decisions that lead down a particular path.

Critical juncture
A turning point which establishes interests, structures, or institutions persisting through time.

Sequencing
The idea that the order of events, not merely their occurrence, affects the outcome.

Focus 3.2
The Greek financial crisis: why it happened

The financial crisis that emerged in Greece in 2009 is an example both of path dependence at work, and of critical junctures at which decisions were taken leading to new paths.

The immediate beginnings of the crisis date to 2002, when Greece became one of 12 European Union states to adopt the new EU single currency, the euro. Even then, there were doubts about its readiness to take this step, because it had not met all the criteria needed to join the euro, including limits on its budget deficit. It was allowed to join regardless. One of the effects of membership of the euro was that poorer states such as Greece, Portugal, and Spain had access to lower interest rates on their loans; as a result, Greece went on a spending spree fuelled by cheaper borrowing, built a budget deficit that – at nearly 13 per cent – was far above the 3 per cent limit set for eurozone membership, manipulated its official statistics to exaggerate its levels of economic growth, and accumulated a national debt that was ultimately bigger than its national economy.

Greece might have struggled on indefinitely in this weakened condition but for the onset in 2007 of a financial crisis in the United States that quickly spread to Europe. European states felt the effects of the crisis, but those in a weaker condition suffered the most. In 2009, the Greek government finally admitted the size of its budget deficit, sparking a broader crisis within the eurozone. Greece was offered a financial bailout, but only on condition that it cut public spending and increased its tax revenues. The terms of the deal sparked riots in the streets of Athens and encouraged little improvement in investor confidence.

The European Union revised its policies on the management of the euro, making sure that a closer watch would be kept in future on the size of national budget deficits, but the crisis in Greece rumbled on. Questions were asked not only about how long it could remain within the eurozone, but also about the future of the euro and of Greece's membership of the European Union itself.

The entire history of the crisis is path dependent in that each effort to resolve the issue failed, leading only to further plans for reform. And what about the critical juncture: the decisive moment when Greece finally addressed its core economic problems and the euro zone carved out a more secure future for itself, with or without Greece? That moment has yet to arrive and may or may not ever do so. Talking up their story, journalists identify too many historical turning points; political scientists are right to be more cautious.

(such as China) were more likely to survive than those beginning the reform process with political change (such as the USSR). In European countries where trade unions developed before socialism became a full-blooded ideology (such as Britain), the labour movement took on a moderate reformist character. But where Marxist thought was already established, as in France, communist unions developed a more radical political agenda. So, whether trade unions emerged before or after the onset of Marxism helps to explain whether particular European countries developed a reformist or radical labour movement. The outcome was not predetermined but, rather, depended on the sequence of events.

One form of 'sequence' is a conjuncture in which separate events occur at the same time, enlarging their political impact. The collision of World War I with the emergence of working-class socialism, or of the Vietnam War with the student movement, generated political effects which were greater than would have been the case had these events unfolded separately. These confluences are typically made by history, and are another contributor to path dependence.

Slow-moving causes, finally, are processes that unfold over a long period. Examples include modernization and technological advance, the spread of education, globalization, and the growth of the mass media. Such processes often need to reach a threshold or a tipping point beyond which a variable begins to exert a visible, dramatic effect. For example, there has been a resurgence of right-wing anti-immigrant political parties in Europe that dates back at least to the early 1990s, reflecting long-term concerns about immigration, law and order, unemployment and, more recently, the 'Islamization' of Europe. At least in some countries, such as Austria and France, a threshold seems to have been passed; the Freedom Party of Austria, whose first leader was a former member of the Austrian Nazi Party and of the paramilitary SS, has even been part of Austrian coalition governments, in 2000–5 and again in 2017. When thresholds are involved, long-term but otherwise slow-moving causes need to be understood historically. Contemporary explosions have long fuses and political scientists need to search into the past to uncover them.

Slow-moving cause
An influence which changes slowly but, over a long period, dramatically.

THE CHALLENGES OF COMPARISON

As we saw in Chapter 1, comparison broadens our understanding of the political world, leads to improved classifications, and gives potential for explanation and even prediction. And as we have just seen, there are different approaches to using cases and variables in comparative study. Despite the variety of advantages and options, the very breadth of comparison brings its own challenges, of which four in particular stand out (summarized in Table 3.2).

Too few cases, too many variables

This is a problem for those who think of comparative politics as a version of the experimenter's laboratory, in which researchers patiently seek to isolate the impact of a single variable. As outlined by Lijphart (1971), it arises when a researcher wants to control for many variables at the same time and quickly runs out of cases. In other words, the number of variables exceeds the number of cases. Even with nearly 200 sovereign states, we do not have enough cases to allow political comparisons to be as precise as laboratory experiments. To make the same point from another angle, we will never be able to test all possible explanations of a political difference between states.

Why, for example, have green political parties done so much better in some countries and so much worse in others? The differences have often been clear even in neighbouring countries with almost identical economic structures and bodies of environmental law, as in the case of members of the European Union. However, green parties have done much better in Austria, Belgium, and Germany than in Britain, France, or Italy for example. The Greens have also done well in Latvia; Prime Minister Indulis Emsis in 2004 became the first Green head of government in the world, and President Raimonds Vējonis in 2015 became the first Green head of state in the world. There are many possible explanations for these contrasts between countries, including post-material values (see Chapter 12), levels of education, national cultural traditions, electoral systems, the extent of pollution, the political skill with which green parties have pursued their agendas, and the diffusion of environmental ideas across national boundaries. With so many potential explanations, and only a limited set of country cases, decisive conclusions are difficult.

There are several potential solutions to the problem. We could increase the number of cases in a study by turning to history and comparing cases over an extended period of time. We could also use most similar system designs to achieve a more focused study of a few cases, or a most different system design to reduce the number of variables. Finally, we could resort to asking hypothetical 'What if … ?' questions by using **counterfactuals**. Would green parties have developed in Europe even without the expansion of mass higher education? What would our world be like if Britain had won the US War of Independence, if Hitler had died in a car crash in 1932, or if the attacks of 9/11 had never happened? Tetlock and Belkin (1996) have developed useful guidelines for judging the plausibility of counterfactuals, but the outcome of such thought experiments can – by definition – never be tested against reality.

Selection bias

A second handicap to comparison is **selection bias**, which can happen whenever the units of analysis (such as states, cities, interest groups, or electoral systems) are chosen intentionally rather than randomly. In these circumstances, the danger is that these units are unrepresentative of the wider population and, in consequence, results may not be **generalizable** to the broader

Counterfactual
A thought experiment speculating on possible outcomes if a particular factor had been absent from a process, or an absent factor had been present.

Selection bias
Arises when selected cases and variables are unrepresentative of the wider class from which they are drawn.

Generalizable
Able to be accurately applied or extended to situations or circumstances other than those originally studied.

Table 3.2 The challenges of comparison

Too few cases, too many variables	The problem of having more explanatory factors for a given outcome than there are cases available to study.
Selection bias	The cases selected for study are often an unrepresentative sample, limiting the significance of the findings. The selection may be influenced in particular by survivorship, value, or confirmation bias.
Understanding meaning	The 'same' phenomenon can mean different things in different countries, creating difficulties in comparing like with like.
Globalization	States cannot be regarded as entirely independent of each other, thus reducing the effective number of cases available for testing theories.

category from which the cases are drawn. For example, studies of English-speaking democracies are unrepresentative of all democracies, and studies of political parties in sub-Saharan Africa are untypical of those in Europe or Latin America. Given the rarity of random sampling in qualitative comparisons, the point is not so much to eliminate such bias as to be aware of its presence.

This danger often emerges as an unintended result of haphazard selection. For example, we might choose to study those countries which speak our language, or which we feel are safe to visit. As a result, large and powerful states might be studied more intensively than small and less powerful ones, even though large states are untypical. By contrast, countries in which it is difficult to conduct research receive less attention. For example, Goode (2010) suggests that authoritarian regimes such as Russia are under-studied because of the political sensitivity of conducting research in such domains. The result of such selection biases is that published work is unrepresentative of all states.

One virtue of large-N statistical designs is that they reduce the risk of selection bias. If a study was to cover every existing state, selection bias should disappear altogether, but the problem may just resurface in another form, through an unrepresentative selection of variables, rather than countries. For example, much statistical research in comparative politics relies on data collected by governments, think-tanks, and international bodies whose priorities are often economic rather than political (this book, for example, draws on data gathered by the World Bank). The result is that financial and economic variables receive more attention, and politics runs the risk of being treated as a branch of economics.

A particularly troubling form of selection bias comes from examining only positive cases, thus eliminating all variation in the phenomenon we seek to explain. King et al. (1994) explain the problem as follows:

> The literature is full of work that makes the mistake of failing to let the dependent variable vary; for example, research that tries to explain the outbreak of wars with studies only of wars, the onset of revolutions with studies only of revolutions, or patterns of voter turnout with interviews only of non-voters.

When only positive cases are studied, several potential conclusions about the causes and consequences of a phenomenon are ruled out. Contrast is needed to give variation, so that we can then consider what factors distinguish times of war from times of peace, periods of revolution from periods of stability, and abstainers from voters.

Even without variation in the dependent variable, we can still identify common characteristics of the cases. For example, we may find that revolutions are always preceded by war, or that all non-voters are cynical about politics. However, we have no contrast to explore and explain. We do not know how often the conditions associated with revolution have existed without triggering a revolution, or whether the political cynicism we find among abstainers is equally prevalent among those who turn out on Election Day (Geddes, 2003). Put differently, war may be a necessary condition of revolution (no revolution in the absence of war) without being a sufficient condition (whenever there is a war, revolution follows).

Three particular forms of selection bias raise their own unique problems. First, **survivorship bias** arises when non-survivors of a temporal process are excluded, leading to biased results. Studying the few surviving communist states or military governments as representative of the entire class of such regimes (past and present) is a mistake because the few that have survived may be very different from those that have disappeared. Similarly, if we want to study federations, we should appreciate that some have failed and should ask not only whether current federations are successful, but also what proportion of all federations, past and present, have survived and prospered. And just because every example from history of a confederation has failed or morphed into a federation, does that mean that future examples are also doomed to fail? In designing our research, we need to look through both ends of the telescope – at starters as well as finishers, at casualties as well as survivors.

Second, **value bias** arises when researchers allow themselves to be guided by values or ideology. As we read reports, journal articles, and books (even this one), we have to allow that the authors will have political preferences. In the case of sponsored research we have to consider who paid for the research, whether conditions were imposed on the researchers by the sponsors, or whether there is an underlying political agenda at work. Value bias is a particular problem in comparative studies, because other than the country or countries in which researchers have spent most or all of their lives, they will know little directly about the objects of their study, and they face the danger of seeing other countries through the lenses of their own experiences, values, and learning. Without even trying, they will be biased by politics, culture, race, gender, religion, age, economic situation, and a host of other factors.

Finally, **confirmation bias** arises when researchers have a view in mind before they undertake their research, and pay attention only to the facts and analyses that support that view, ignoring

Survivorship bias
A form of selection bias that crops up when we study only surviving examples of political types, overlooking past examples.

Value bias
Allowing assessments, the choice of facts, and conclusions to be impacted by the values of the researcher.

Confirmation bias
The tendency to seek out or interpret information that confirms pre-existing beliefs and attitudes, and to ignore information that does not.

or downplaying any contrary evidence. Those who sponsor research are likely to seek out and support researchers who seek out data that support their interests. In regard to climate change, for example, both advocates and deniers sometimes seize on any study which supports their beliefs, while ignoring or rejecting findings which run against their entrenched positions. Whether it is conscious or unconscious, confirmation bias has the effect of producing skewed results and conclusions.

Understanding meaning

Because the meaning of a political action depends on the conventions of the state concerned, comparing like with like is not always as straightforward as it seems. The cultural approach discussed in the last chapter, and again in Chapter 12, plays an important role here. Before we begin any cross-national comparison we should ensure that we understand the relevant cultural codes of the states we are studying. Failure here results in cultural imperialism, in which the meaning of an action in our home state is incorrectly projected onto other societies.

Take, for example, the question of styles of political representation, which vary across states. Where Nigerian politicians might seek to impress their supporters by acts of flamboyant extravagance, Swedish politicians are more likely to set out to affirm their very ordinariness. The same goal of impressing constituents is achieved by culturally specific means, such that what works in Lagos would be disastrous in Stockholm, and what succeeds in Stockholm would be met with apathy in Abuja.

Similarly, when members of a legislature vote against their party's line, the consequences can range by state from complete indifference to expulsion from the party. What appears to be the same act carries varying significance, and thus meaning depends on context. Meaning and context also come into play in comparing the incidence of violence in national legislatures. Why is it, for example, that brawls have occasionally broken out among legislators in Italy, Mexico, South Korea, Taiwan, Ukraine, and Venezuela, but that they are rare – if unknown in recent history – in most other parts of the world. What, if anything, do the countries in this list have in common?

A scuffle breaks out among members of the Taiwanese legislature. What kind of meaning should comparativists attach to the number of such scuffles in some legislatures and their absence in others?
Source: Getty Images/Sam Yeh.

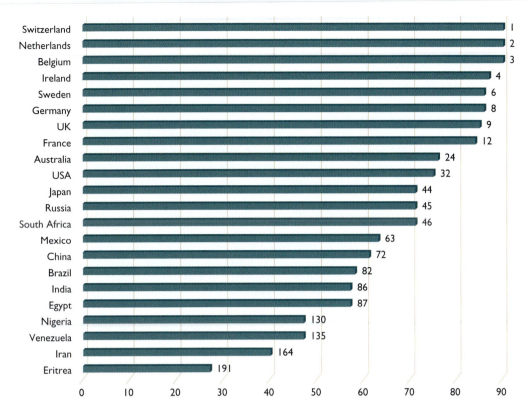

Figure 3.4 The KOF Globalization Index
Source: Swiss Economic Institute (2018).
Note: Numbers indicate scores out of 100, with 100 representing the most globalized and 0 indicating the least globalized. Numbers are rounded out to nearest whole figure. Figures at the end of bars indicate ranking out of 191.

Globalization

The final handicap to comparison (if we take the state as the unit of analysis) comes from **globalization** (Teune, 2010). Although 193 'independent' states belong to the United Nations in reality these states are interdependent, or even dependent. Countries learn from, copy, compete, and trade with, influence and even invade each other in a constant process of interaction. The result can be homogenization, where politics and government in different countries becomes increasingly similar (though specialization, where each country focuses on its distinctive strengths in the global order, is another possible outcome). (See also the discussion about policy diffusion and convergence in Chapter 19.)

The KOF Globalization Index maintained by the Swiss Economic Institute offers some insight into this phenomenon by ranking the countries of the world in terms of the extent to which they are globally connected in economic, political, and social terms. Among other things, Figure 3.4 reveals that it tends to be the smaller democracies with advanced economies – such as Switzerland and the Netherlands – that have achieved the highest levels of global connectivity. Large economies naturally rely more on their domestic market so in spite of their large economies and expansive trade networks, the United States and Japan remain less globalized, while large emerging powers such as China and India rank even lower. The poorest African states, perhaps unsurprisingly, sit at the lower reaches of the ranking.

Looking at these numbers, it might be reasonable to conclude that the most globalized states will have the fewest political differences, but opinion is divided on the implications of globalization. Does it mean the end of the state, are global and national processes interacting and adapting to one another, is globalization much older than we think, and does it even exist? (See debate in Holton, 2011.) It does exist, argues the sociologist George Ritzer (2018), who writes of the McDonaldization of society, suggesting that culture has come to be dominated by the goals of efficiency, calculability, predictability, and control; related arguments could be made about politics and political expectations. How

Globalization
The process by which the links between people, corporations, and governments in different states become integrated through trade, investment, and technology.

then, do we explain the political backlash as nationalists in countries such as Britain, France, the United States, India, and the Philippines work to reassert the sovereignty of states in the face of globalization?

The major transitions of world history – industrialization, colonialism, decolonization, democratization, and globalization – unfolded on a world stage. In that sense we inhabit one global system, rather than a world of independent states. Green (2002) puts the point well when he says the world is arranged 'as if national polities are in fact cells of a larger entity with a life all its own'. The implication is that we should study this larger organism, rather than comparing its component parts as if they were unconnected.

Specific institutional forms also reflect diffusion. The presidential systems of Latin America were imported from the United States; prime ministers and parliaments grew out of the specific circumstances of British political history; and the ombudsman (see Chapter 10) was a device copied from Sweden. The development of international organizations, from the United Nations to the European Union, also creates another layer of governance to which all member states must react.

These links do not invalidate comparative analysis; indeed, they allow studies comparing the impact of an international factor on different states, thus bridging the study of international and comparative politics. But interdependence creates technical difficulties for statistical analysis. Treating states as independent entities artificially inflates the effective sample size in statistical research, resulting in exaggerated confidence in the significance of the results obtained (Tilly, 1997). To put the point more intuitively, treating states as separate can lead to false inferences if in reality they are all subject to a common external influence, such as globalization.

DISCUSSION QUESTIONS

◆ What does it take for the study of politics to be scientific, and where is it most likely to fail?
◆ In what way (or ways) could your country serve as a representative or deviant case study?
◆ What are the advantages and disadvantages of quantitative and qualitative approaches to comparative political research?
◆ How does the study of politics differ from the study of history?
◆ How can comparative political research best be protected from value bias?
◆ What challenges does globalization pose for comparative politics?

KEY CONCEPTS

◆ Case study method
◆ Comparative method
◆ Confirmation bias
◆ Correlation
◆ Counterfactual
◆ Critical juncture
◆ Dependent variable
◆ Generalizable
◆ Globalization
◆ Historical method
◆ Hypothesis
◆ Independent variable
◆ Level of analysis
◆ Methodology
◆ Most different system

◆ Most similar system
◆ Outliers
◆ Path dependence
◆ Process tracing
◆ Qualitative method
◆ Quantitative method
◆ Regression line
◆ Selection bias
◆ Sequencing
◆ Slow-moving cause
◆ Survivorship bias
◆ Unit of analysis
◆ Value bias
◆ Variable

FURTHER READING

Box-Steffensmeier, Janet M., Henry E. Brady, and David Collier (2008) *The Oxford Handbook of Political Methodology* (Oxford University Press). An edited collection of chapters on the many different approaches to political research.

Gray, David E. (2018) *Doing Research in the Real World*, 4th edn (Sage). A general guide to undertaking research, offering detail on many of the topics covered in this chapter.

Halperin, Sandra, and Oliver Heath (2017) *Political Research: Methods and Practical Skills*, 2nd edn (Oxford University Press). An introduction to the methods, goals, and approaches used in political research.

Landman, Todd, and Edzia Carvalho (2017) *Issues and Methods in Comparative Politics*, 4th edn (Routledge). A concise survey of comparative methods and approaches, including chapters on particular themes in comparative politics.

Lange, Matthew (2013) *Comparative-Historical Methods* (Sage). A survey of the strategies and benefits to comparison of the historical method.

Yin, Robert K. (2018) *Case Study Research and Applications: Design and Methods,* 6th edn (Sage). A standard source on conducting case studies, using examples from a range of disciplines.

THE STATE

4

PREVIEW

The most popular unit of analysis in comparative politics is the state. It is far from the only such option, because comparison can be made at any level from the local to the multinational, and can involve any political institution, process, problem, or phenomenon. Even so, the use of states in comparison means that we need to understand what they are, how they work, how they evolved, the varieties in which they are found, and the current dynamic of the state system.

This chapter begins with a review of the features of states, with a particular focus on sovereignty. It then briefly examines the history of states, focusing on how and where they emerged, and at how political relationships changed both vertically (among rulers and the ruled) and horizontally (among different political communities). It then looks at the diversity that exists among states, before discussing the related concepts of *nation* and *nationalism*, ending with an analysis of today's debates over the condition and the future prospects of the state.

The state is a younger concept than most people think, and fewer than 50 were in existence at the beginning of the twentieth century. But even as the number has grown to its current total of about 190, so the questions about the long-term future of states have grown. Some argue that states are as strong as ever, others argue that they are undergoing fundamental change in the face of globalization, while yet others argue that they are in decline.

KEY ARGUMENTS

◆ The state lies at the heart of government and politics, which is why it is so important to understand its features and evolution.

◆ All states have five defining qualities: government, population, legitimacy, territory, and sovereignty.

◆ The modern state was born in Europe, and its form was exported to the rest of the world by imperial powers such as Britain, France, and Spain.

◆ States differ from one another in terms of their population, the reach of their political authority, and their income.

◆ A nation is quite different from a state, even if the terms are sometimes used interchangeably, and nations and states often overlap.

◆ The condition of the modern state is debatable. Some argue that states remain strong, some that they are declining, and some that they are simply evolving.

THE STATE: AN OVERVIEW

Although we take for granted the division of the world into states, we should assume neither that the **state** always was the dominant principle of political organization, nor that it always will be. There was a world before states and, as advocates of globalization like to point out, there may be a world after them, too.

Before the modern state, government and politics was mainly associated with kingdoms, empires, and cities. These were often governed in a personal and highly decentralized fashion, lacking many of the structured and formal features of states, most notably the sovereign authority to rule the population of a specific territory. And while those earlier formations had many political and economic links among them, they functioned within limited horizons, being influenced only by their near neighbours, and rarely being exposed to ideas about government from further afield.

> **State**
> The legal and political authority of a territory containing a population and marked by borders.

The modern idea of the state emerged in Europe between the sixteenth and eighteenth centuries, the use of the word *state* as a political term coming into common use towards the end of this period. (It stems from the Latin *status*, meaning 'condition' or 'manner of standing'. It is also quite different, as we will see, from the idea of a nation, with which it is often confused.) The number of states grew slowly: there were only 19 in existence in 1800 (most of them in Europe and Asia), and barely 30 more had been established by 1900 (mostly in Europe and the Americas).

At a global level, the most active period of state formation began after World War II as decolonization saw the end of European empires: nearly 70 mainly African and Asian states achieved independence in the 1960s and 1970s, more new states emerged with the break-up of the Soviet Union in 1991, and the balance of global power changed with the rise of emerging powers such as China, India, and Brazil in the 1990s. Along the way, debates about sovereignty, authority, and self-determination broadened and deepened, and political systems – even if they had many core features in common – took on a greater variety.

The world today has about 190 states (Focus 4.1 explains why we need to use the preposition *about* when discussing the number of states), and they have a quite different and more complex relationship with one another than they did even two generations ago. Their interactions influence domestic political and economic calculations, questions are frequently raised about their true independence, and in the wake of globalization we have seen an intensified debate under way about their future: are states becoming weaker, are they as strong as they ever were, or are they simply changing in the wake of new demands and pressures?

Whatever the answer, the state remains the basis for understanding government and politics all over the world. There are sub-national units of government, to be sure (as we will see in Chapter 11), and signs of governance at the global level, but almost everyone is a citizen of one state or another, and when we think of government we also think of states. The institutions and processes that will be covered in the rest of this book are mainly associated with states, and even if we study what happens below the level of the state, we will still find ourselves referring back to the governments of states; they drive and determine what can be done not just within their borders, but also in the relations between and among states, both regionally and globally.

WHAT IS A STATE?

Few concepts are more central to understanding government and politics than the state, and yet few concepts are also so contested. It is nearly impossible to meaningfully study government and politics without at least a working understanding of what the state looks like, because it is the world's dominant form of political organization, and states collectively form the building blocks of the international system. We experience the state when we pay taxes, are subject to state law, must carry a state passport in order to travel across borders, and take part in choosing governments. The further we move away from these practical signs of the state, though, the harder it is to pin down.

The usual benchmark for understanding the state is the classic definition offered by the German sociologist Max Weber, who described it as 'a human community that (successfully) claims the monopoly of the legitimate use of physical force within a given territory' (quoted in Gerth and Mills, 1948). There is more to the state than physical force, though, and it needs to be understood more particularly in its modern context, where it is best defined as a legal and political entity with five main features: a government, population, legitimacy, territory, and sovereignty (see Figure 4.1).

If all was neat and tidy, then every square metre of land in the world would be part of one state or another. But there are numerous parcels of territory around the world that lack one or more of these qualities, and cannot be considered states: examples include Hong Kong, Palestine, Puerto Rico, Taiwan, and Western Sahara. Furthermore, there are still

DEMOCRATIC RULE

5

PREVIEW

Democracy is both one of the easiest and one of the most difficult of concepts to understand. It is easy because democracies are abundant and familiar, and most of the readers of this book will probably live in one, while others will live in countries that aspire to become democracies. Democracy is also one of the most closely studied of all political concepts, the ease of that study made stronger by the openness of democracies and the availability of information regarding how they work. But our understanding of democracy is made more difficult by the extent to which the concept is misunderstood and misused, by the numerous and highly nuanced interpretations of what democracy means in practice, and by the many claims that are made for democracy that do not stand up to closer examination.

This chapter begins with a review of the key features of democracy, beginning with the Athenian idea of direct democracy (an important historical concept which has regained significance with the recent rise of e-democracy and social media), before assessing and comparing the features of representative and liberal democracy. It then looks at the links between democracy and modernization, and reviews the emergence of democracy in the three waves described by Samuel Huntington. The chapter ends with an assessment of the present state and future prospects for democracy. After several decades in which the number of democracies grew and the number of authoritarian countries shrank, there has been a reversal in trends.

KEY ARGUMENTS

◆ About half the people in the world today live under democratic rule, although there is still no universally agreed definition of democracy.

◆ Athenian direct democracy offers a standard of self-rule against which today's representative (indirect) democracies are often judged.

◆ Representative democracy limits the people to electing a government, while liberal democracy goes a stage further by placing limits on government and protecting the rights of citizens.

◆ There is a close association between democracy, modernization, and economic growth.

◆ The spread of democracy occurred in three distinct waves, but questions are now being asked about its prospect of continuing expansion.

◆ Democracy is threatened by a combination of internal shortcomings and the pressures from more confident authoritarian systems such as China and Russia.

DEMOCRATIC RULE: AN OVERVIEW

About half the people in the world today live under democratic rule (see Focus 5.1). At first glance, this may seem impressive, particularly since the number of democracies has more than doubled in the last generation, and democratic ideas have expanded beyond their Western core to embrace Southern Europe, Eastern Europe, Latin America, and more of Asia and Africa. But is the glass half full or half empty? Why have so many countries failed to achieve democracy? And why do many now argue that the spread of democracy may have come to a halt, and that it may actually be in retreat in several parts of the world?

Much depends on how we define **democracy**, which – in spite of being probably the most studied concept in the history of government and politics – is still not fully understood. At a minimum, it requires open and responsive government, free elections, freedom of speech, the protection of individual rights, respect for the rule of law, and government by 'the people' (see Table 5.1). But the precise meaning of these phenomena remains open to debate, and many democracies continue to be plagued by elitism, limits on representation, rule by a political class, barriers to equality, and the impingement of the rights of individuals and groups upon one another.

Democracy
A political system in which government is based on a fair and open mandate from all qualified citizens of a state.

It is hard to find a government that does not claim to be democratic, because to do otherwise would be to admit that it was restricting the rights of its citizens. But some states have stronger claims to being democratic than others; these are what the Democracy Index describes either as full or flawed democracies. Most of the former are found in Europe, while the latter include countries from many parts of the world. Until recently we could say with some confidence that many states were undergoing a process of **democratization**, where political institutions and processes are developing greater stability, where individual rights are built on firmer foundations, and where the voice of the people is heard more clearly. But there are signs in several parts of the world of a backsliding away from democracy, and growing confidence on the part of the world's most prominent authoritarian political systems, notably China and Russia. (See Chapter 6 for discussion of authoritarian rule.)

Democratization
The process by which states build the institutions and processes needed to become stable democracies.

The core principle of democracy is self-rule; the word itself comes from the Greek *demokratia*, meaning power (*kratos*) by the people (*demos*). From this perspective, democracy refers not to the election of rulers by the ruled but to the denial of any separation between the two. The model democracy is a form of self-government in which all qualified citizens participate in shaping collective decisions in an atmosphere of equality and deliberation, and in which state and society become one. But this is no more than an ideal, rarely found in practice except at the local level in decentralized systems of government.

Indeed, in trying to understand democracy, we should avoid the assumption that it is self-evidently the best system of rule. It certainly has many advantages over dictatorship, and it can bring stability to historically divided societies provided the groups involved agree to share power through elections. But it has many imperfections, as British political leader Winston Churchill once famously acknowledged when he argued that democracy was the worst form of government, except for all the others.

Table 5.1 Features of democratic rule

◆ Representative systems of government based on regular, fair, secret, and competitive elections.
◆ Well-defined, stable, and predictable political institutions and processes, based on a distribution of powers and a system of political checks and balances.
◆ A variety of institutionalized forms of political participation and representation, including multiple political parties with different platforms.
◆ Limits on the powers of government, and protection of individual rights and freedoms under the law, sustained by an independent judiciary.
◆ An active, effective, and protected opposition.
◆ A diverse and independent media establishment, subject to few political controls and free to share a wide variety of opinions.

DIRECT DEMOCRACY

Direct democracy
A system of government in which all members of the community take part in making the decisions that affect that community.

The purest form of democracy is the type of **direct democracy** that was exemplified in the government of Athens between 461 and 322 BCE. During this time, Greece consisted of several hundred small, independent city-communities known as *poleis* (singular: *polis*), each typically containing an urban core and a rural hinterland. The leader among these was Athens, where all male citizens could attend meetings of the Ekklesia (People's Assembly) at which they could address their peers; meetings were of citizens, not their representatives. In Aristotle's phrase, the assembly was 'supreme over all causes' (Aristotle, 1962 edn); it was the sovereign body, unconstrained by a formal constitution or even, in the early decades, by written laws. The Athenians believed that direct popular involvement and open deliberation were educational in character, encouraging informed and committed citizens who were sensitive both to the public good and to the range of interests and opinions found even in small communities.

Administrative functions were the responsibility of an executive council consisting of 500 citizens aged over 30, chosen by lot for a one-year period, with no repeat terms. Meanwhile, juries of several hundred people – again, selected randomly from a panel of volunteers – decided the lawsuits which citizens frequently brought against those considered to have acted against the interests of the *polis*. The courts functioned as an arena through which top figures (including generals) were brought to account. Above all, politics was an amateur activity, to be undertaken by all citizens not just in the interest of the community at large, but also to enhance their own development. To engage in democracy was to become informed about the *polis*, and an educated citizenry meant a stronger whole.

However, there were flaws in the system:

◆ Because citizenship was restricted to men whose parents were citizens, most adults – including women, slaves, and foreign residents – were excluded.
◆ Turnout was a problem, with most citizens being absent from most assembly meetings even after the introduction of an attendance payment.
◆ The system was time-consuming, expensive, and over-complex, especially for such a small society.
◆ The principle of self-government did not always lead to coherent policy, and the lack of a permanent bureaucracy eventually contributed to a period of ineffective governance, leading to the fall of the Athenian republic after defeat in war.

The Athenian democratic experiment proved that – in the right circumstances – direct democracy was an achievable goal, and yet it is hard to find in modern political systems. It exists most obviously in the form either of referendums and initiatives (see Chapter 15), or of decision-making at the community level, for example in a village or a school. To go any further, some would argue, would be to risk the dangers inherent in the lack of interest and knowledge that many people display in relation to politics, and this would undermine their ability to govern themselves effectively. But create a more participatory social environment, respond its supporters, and people will be up to – and up for – the task of self-government. Society will have schooled them in, and trained them for, democratic politics, given that 'individuals learn to participate by participating' (Pateman, 2012).

E-democracy
A form of democratic expression through which all those with an interest in a problem or an issue can express themselves via the internet or social media, thereby participating in the shaping of government decisions.

There has been some recent talk of the possibilities of electronic direct democracy, or **e-democracy** via the internet. This includes being able to vote online, launching or signing online petitions, and organizing demonstrations via social media. This is an option that might be a useful response to charges that representative government has become elitist, but the impact of internet in general on politics – and social media in particular – has been mixed. On the one hand, the internet provides for the instant availability of more political information, allows political leaders to communicate more often and more directly with voters (helping change the way that electoral campaigns are run), and can help people engage more directly in political discussions.

But there are several problems with e-democracy:

◆ The opinions expressed online are not methodically collected and assessed as they would be in a true direct democracy; the voices that are heard tend to be those of people who post most often, and there is often a bandwagon effect reflected – for example – in the phenomenon of trending hashtags on Twitter.

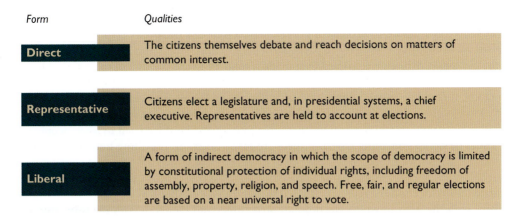

Form	Qualities
Direct	The citizens themselves debate and reach decisions on matters of common interest.
Representative	Citizens elect a legislature and, in presidential systems, a chief executive. Representatives are held to account at elections.
Liberal	A form of indirect democracy in which the scope of democracy is limited by constitutional protection of individual rights, including freedom of assembly, property, religion, and speech. Free, fair, and regular elections are based on a near universal right to vote.

Figure 5.1 Forms of democracy

◆ Many of those who express themselves via social media are either partisan or deliberately provocative, as reflected in the often inflammatory postings of anonymous internet 'trolls'. The result is to skew the direction taken by debates, and we can never be sure exactly who is behind the opinions posted.

◆ The use of social media has led to heightened concerns about privacy, perhaps feeding in to the kind of mistrust of government that has led to reduced support for conventional forms of participation (see Chapter 13).

◆ E-democracy relies upon having access to the internet, which is a problem in poor countries, and even, sometimes, in poorer regions of wealthy countries.

There are also particular problems with the internet as a medium of political communication, discussed in more detail in Chapter 14.

REPRESENTATIVE DEMOCRACY

In its modern state form, the democratic principle has transmuted from self-government to elected government, resulting in the phenomenon of **representative democracy**, an indirect form of government. To the ancient Greeks, the idea of representation would have seemed preposterous: how can the people be said to govern themselves if a separate class of rulers exists? As late as the eighteenth century, the French philosopher Jean-Jacques Rousseau (1762) warned that 'the moment a people gives itself representatives, it is no longer free. It ceases to exist.'

Yet, as large states emerged, so too did the need for a new way in which the people could shape collective decisions. One of the first authors to graft representation on to democracy was Thomas Paine, a British-born political activist who experienced both the French and the American revolutions. In his *Rights of Man* (1791/2), Paine wrote:

> The original simple democracy … is incapable of extension, not from its principle, but from the inconvenience of its form. Simple democracy was society governing itself without the aid of secondary means. By ingrafting representation upon democracy, we arrive at a system of government capable of embracing and confederating all the various interests and every extent of territory and population.

Representative democracy
A system of government in which members of a community elect people to represent their interests and to make decisions affecting the community.

In ancient Athens, the upper limit for a republic was reckoned to be the number of people who could gather together to hear a speaker. However, modern representative government allows enormous populations (such as 1.3 billion Indians and 320 million Americans) to exert some popular control over their rulers. But there have been many critics of representative democracy, prime among them the Austrian-born political economist Joseph Schumpeter (1883–1950), who doubted the ability of ordinary voters to make informed political choices:

> The typical citizen drops down to a lower level of mental performance as soon as he enters the political field. He argues and analyzes in a way that he would recognize as infantile within the sphere of his real interests. He becomes a primitive again. (Schumpeter, 1943)

As for elections, Schumpeter saw them not as a means by which voters could elect representatives to carry out their will, but simply as a device to produce a government. From this perspective, the voter becomes a political accessory, restricted to choosing among broad packages of policies and leaders prepared by the parties. The deciding of issues by the electorate, Schumpeter argued, was made secondary to the election of the people who are to do the deciding.

Representation, it could be argued, offers a valuable division of labour, allowing those who want to participate to do so, and everyone else to limit their participation to monitoring government and voting at elections (Schudson, 1998). After all, how serious would our commitment to a free society be if we tried to force people to participate who would rather be doing something else? But there are many questions regarding how representation works in practice:

◆ The standard means for choosing representatives is through elections, but – as we will see in Chapter 15 – there are problems with the ways in which elections are structured, and therefore with the ways voices are counted and citizens are represented (see Figure 5.2).

◆ Political parties and candidates are never given the same amount of attention by the media, and money and special interests often skew the attention paid to competing sets of policy choices.

◆ Questions are raised about varying and often declining rates of voter turnout; rates vary by age, gender, education, race, income, and other factors.

◆ Elections can be manipulated in many ways, including complex or inconvenient registration procedures, the intimidation of voters, the poor organization of polling stations, and the miscounting of ballots. New challenges have been created by charges that Russia has interfered in US and European elections by manipulating social media and hacking computerized electoral systems.

◆ There are questions – as we will see in Chapter 8 – about the manner in which elected officials actually represent the needs and opinions of voters. Specifically, how should they guard against being influenced excessively by interest groups, big business, social movements, or the voices of those with the means to make themselves heard most loudly?

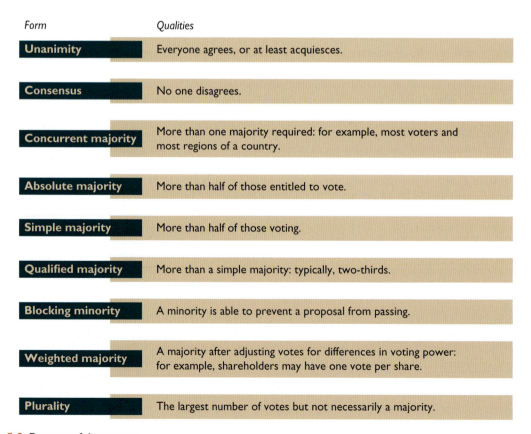

Form	Qualities
Unanimity	Everyone agrees, or at least acquiesces.
Consensus	No one disagrees.
Concurrent majority	More than one majority required: for example, most voters and most regions of a country.
Absolute majority	More than half of those entitled to vote.
Simple majority	More than half of those voting.
Qualified majority	More than a simple majority: typically, two-thirds.
Blocking minority	A minority is able to prevent a proposal from passing.
Weighted majority	A majority after adjusting votes for differences in voting power: for example, shareholders may have one vote per share.
Plurality	The largest number of votes but not necessarily a majority.

Figure 5.2 Degrees of democracy

Focus 5.1
How many democracies are there?

We saw in Chapter 4 that there are questions about the number of states in the world. There are related questions about the number of those states that can be considered to be democracies. It is generally agreed that their number has more than doubled since the 1980s, thanks mainly to two developments. First, the end of the Cold War freed several Eastern European states from the centralized political and economic control of the Soviet Union. Second, an expansion of the membership of the European Union (EU) helped build on and strengthen the democratic and capitalist credentials of those Eastern European states that are now EU members, or would like to be members.

Even so, there is no agreement on just how many democracies that gives us, out of the world's approximately 190 independent states. The Democracy Index in 2017 listed 19 full democracies and 57 flawed democracies, for a total of 76, while Freedom in the World in 2017 classified 87 countries as Free. Another source for a possible answer is the Center for Systemic Peace, a US-based research body that undertakes research on political behaviour. Its Polity IV project has gathered data on political systems dating back to 1800, the results suggesting that there has been much volatility since 1945 as more countries have become independent, and that the number of democracies has grown since the end of the Cold War (reaching 95 in 2016) while the number of autocracies has fallen in tandem: see Figure 5.3. How the retrenchment of democracy in several countries in recent years will affect these numbers remains to be seen.

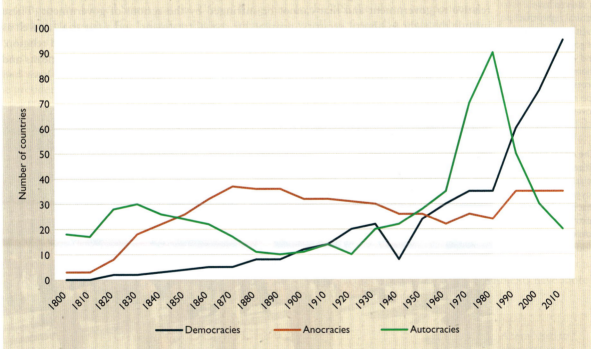

Figure 5.3 The changing number of democracies
Source: Simplified version of data from Center for Systemic Peace (2016).
Notes: Indicates only those countries with a population exceeding 500,000. An autocracy is a political system in which power is concentrated in the hands of one person. An anocracy is a system that combines features of democracy and autocracy.

The result of such doubts is to raise the question of just how much true representation we find in representative democracy. All animals are equal, wrote George Orwell in his novel *Animal Farm*, but some animals are more equal than others.

Focus 5.2
Full and flawed democracies

The Democracy Index makes a distinction between what it calls full democracies and flawed democracies. The former group (consisting of 19 countries in the 2017 index, containing less than 5 per cent of the world's population) is characterized by the efficient functioning of government with an effective system of checks and balances, respect for basic political freedoms and liberties, a political culture that is conducive to the flourishing of democracy, a variety of independent media, and an independent judiciary whose decisions are enforced. For their part, flawed democracies (of which there were 57 in the 2017 index, containing just under half of the world's population) enjoy most of these features but experience weaknesses such as problems in governance, an underdeveloped political culture, and low levels of political participation. Examples of the two types include the following:

Full democracies	Flawed democracies
Australia	Brazil
Canada	France
Germany	Ghana
Mauritius	Greece
Netherlands	India
New Zealand	Indonesia
Norway	Italy
Spain	Japan
Sweden	Mexico
United Kingdom	South Africa
Uruguay	United States

Two countries which notably fell from a ranking of full to flawed democracy in 2017 were the United States and Japan, the first because of a decline in public faith in political institutions and a growing partisan divide, and the latter because of weaknesses in political participation.

Modernization

The process of acquiring the attributes of a modern society, or one reflecting contemporary ideas, institutions, and norms.

The political sociologist Seymour Martin Lipset (1959) provided the classic statement of the impact of **modernization**, suggesting that 'the more well-to-do a [country], the greater the chances that it will sustain democracy'. Using data from the late 1950s, Lipset found strong correlations between affluence, industrialization, urbanization, and education, on the one hand, and democracy, on the other. Later, Diamond (1992) commented that the relationship between affluence and democracy remained 'one of the most powerful and stable … in the study of national development'. In an analysis of all democracies existing between 1789 and 2001, Svolik (2008) concluded that 'democracies with low levels of economic development … are less likely to consolidate'. Boix (2011) agrees, with the qualification that the effect of affluence on democracy declines once societies have achieved developed status.

Not everyone agrees that there is a link between modernization and democracy, however – see Przeworski and Limongi (1997) – and there continue to be exceptions to the argument, both apparent and real. The record of the oil-rich kingdoms of the Middle East suggests that affluence, and even mass affluence, is no guarantee of democracy. But these seeming counter-examples show only that modernity consists of more than income per head; authoritarian monarchs in the Middle East rule societies that may be wealthy, but are also highly traditional. A more important exception is India, a lower-middle-income country with a consolidated, if distinctive, democracy (see Spotlight India).

So, why does liberal democracy seem to be the natural way of governing modern societies? Lipset (1959) offered several possible answers:

◆ Wealth softens class differences, producing a more equal distribution of income and turning the working class away from 'leftist extremism', while the presence of a large middle class tempers class conflict between rich and poor.
◆ Economic security raises the quality of governance by reducing incentives for corruption.
◆ High-income countries have more interest groups to reinforce liberal democracy.
◆ Education and urbanization also make a difference. Education inculcates democratic and tolerant values, while towns have always been the wellspring of democracy.

Although Lipset's argument has been contested by some, particularly those who argue that global capitalism has been a major cause of political and economic underdevelopment, his conclusions have held up well with later research. Diamond and Marks (1992), for example, concluded that the level of economic development continued to be 'the single most powerful predictor of the likelihood of democracy'. Research by Boix (2003) led him to conclude that 'democracy prevails when either economic equality or capital mobility are high in a given country', while authoritarianism prevailed in countries where levels of equality were low. More recently, Luce (2017) has argued that liberal democracy's 'strongest glue' is economic growth:

> When groups fight over the fruits of growth, the rules of the political game are relatively easy to uphold. When those fruits disappear, or are monopolized by a fortunate few, things turn nasty.

As we will see in the following section, much of the story of democracy has been about its steady expansion. In recent years, though, there has been some backsliding, with growing inequality being among the leading causes.

HUNTINGTON'S WAVES OF DEMOCRACY

When and why did modern democracies emerge? As with the phases of decolonization discussed in Chapter 4, so today's democracies emerged – argues political scientist Samuel Huntington (1991) – in a series of distinct **waves of democratization** (see Figure 5.4). Just as each period of decolonization deposited a particular type of state on the political shore, so too did each democratic wave differ in the character of the resulting democracies.

Waves of democratization
A group of transitions from non-democratic to democratic political systems that occurs within a specified period of time and that significantly outnumbers transitions in the opposite direction during that period.

First wave

This took place between 1828 and 1926, when the earliest representative democracies emerged. During this first period, nearly 30 countries established at least minimally democratic national institutions, including Argentina, Australia, Britain, Canada, France, Germany, the Netherlands, New Zealand, the Scandinavian countries, and the United States. However, some backsliding occurred as fledgling democracies were overthrown by fascist, communist, or military dictatorships during what Huntington describes as the 'first reverse wave' from 1922 to 1942.

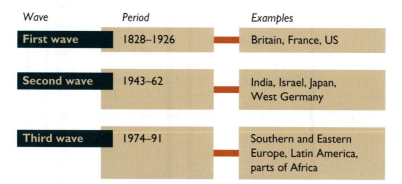

Wave	Period	Examples
First wave	1828–1926	Britain, France, US
Second wave	1943–62	India, Israel, Japan, West Germany
Third wave	1974–91	Southern and Eastern Europe, Latin America, parts of Africa

Figure 5.4 Huntington's waves of democratization
Source: Huntington (1991).
Note: The first wave partly reversed between 1922 and 1942 (e.g. in Germany and Italy) and the second wave between 1958 and 1975 (e.g. in much of Latin America and postcolonial Africa). Many such reversals were later themselves reversed.

SPOTLIGHT INDIA

Brief profile

Often described as the world's largest democracy, India is also one of the most culturally and demographically varied countries in the world, and has the second biggest population after that of China (with which it is rapidly catching up). After centuries of British imperial control (some direct, some indirect), India became independent in 1947. While it has many political parties, it spent many decades dominated by a single party (Congress), which has recently lost much ground to the Hindu nationalist Bharatiya Janata Party. India has a large military and is a nuclear power, but its economy long remained notably staid, with many analysts arguing that its enormous potential was being held back by excessive state intervention and endemic corruption; changes in policy have recently helped address these problems, but India still suffers from religious and cultural divisions that have produced communal strife, and has had difficulties addressing its widespread poverty.

Form of government	Federal parliamentary republic consisting of 29 states and seven union territories. State formed 1947, and most recent constitution adopted 1950.
Executive	Parliamentary. The prime minister selects and leads the Council of Ministers (cabinet). The president, indirectly elected for a renewable five-year term, is head of state, formally asks a party leader to form the government, and can take emergency powers.
Legislature	Bicameral Parliament: lower Lok Sabha (House of the People, 545 members) elected for renewable five-year terms, and upper Rajya Sabha (Council of States, 245 members) with most members elected for fixed and single six-year terms by state legislatures.
Judiciary	Independent Supreme Court consisting of 31 judges appointed by the president following consultation. Judges must retire at age 65.
Electoral system	Elections to the Lok Sabha are by single-member plurality. The Election Commission of India, established by the constitution, oversees national and state elections.
Parties	Multi-party, with a recent tradition of coalitions. The two major parties are the Bharatiya Janata Party and the once dominant Congress Party. Regional parties are also important.

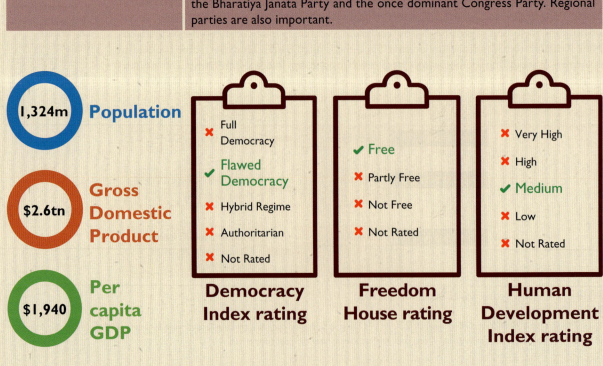

1,324m **Population**

$2.6tn **Gross Domestic Product**

$1,940 **Per capita GDP**

Democracy Index rating
- ✗ Full Democracy
- ✓ Flawed Democracy
- ✗ Hybrid Regime
- ✗ Authoritarian
- ✗ Not Rated

Freedom House rating
- ✓ Free
- ✗ Partly Free
- ✗ Not Free
- ✗ Not Rated

Human Development Index rating
- ✗ Very High
- ✗ High
- ✓ Medium
- ✗ Low
- ✗ Not Rated

A candidate gives an address during an election campaign in India. Although often described as the world's largest democracy, India's limitations mean that it is ranked as a flawed democracy.

Source: Getty Images/Hindustan Times.

Democracy in India

India is the great exception to the thesis that stable democracy is restricted to affluent states. In spite of enormous poverty and massive inequality, democracy is well entrenched in India, which is often described as the world's largest democracy. This story begs the question of how it has been able to consolidate democracy against the background of major economic and social challenges.

Part of the answer lies in India's experience under British control: Britain often used indirect rule in India, allowing local elites to occupy positions of authority, where they experienced a style of governance which accepted some dispersal of power and often allowed the expression of specific grievances. The transition to independence was also gradual and considered, led by the Indian National Congress (founded in 1885), which built an extensive, patronage-based network that helped it govern a disparate country after independence. Congress also gained experience of elections as participation widened even under colonial rule. Even before independence in 1947, about 40 million people were entitled to vote in elections, contests which functioned as training grounds for democracy.

Perhaps the critical factor in India's democratic success, however, was the pro-democratic values of the Congress elite. Put simply, democracy survived in India because that is what its leaders wanted. Practices associated with British democracy – such as parliamentary government, an independent judiciary, and the rule of law – were seen as worthy of emulation. In India, then, the consolidation of democracy was fundamentally an elite project.

The quality of India's democracy has since inevitably been constrained by economic, religious, ethnic, and class inequalities in Indian society: it is because of such limitations that India is ranked in the Democracy Index as a flawed democracy. On the positive side of the ledger, Corbridge *et al.* (2013) note the increasing self-confidence of India, at least among its urban middle classes: there is a growing sense, they argue, that India is taking its place 'at the heart of the Asian growth machine'. At the same time, though, there is concern about the resurgence of Hindu nationalism and about what it means not just for India but for South Asia.

Further reading

Corbridge, Stuart, John Harris, and Craig Jeffrey (2013) *India Today: Economy, Politics and Society* (Polity Press).
Datta, Rekha (2018) *Contemporary India* (Routledge).
Mitra, Subrata K. (2017) *Politics in India: Structure, Process and Policy*, 2nd edn (Routledge).

A distinctive feature of many first wave transitions was their slow and sequential character. Political competition, traditionally operating within a privileged elite, gradually broadened as the right to vote extended to the wider population. Unhurried transitions lowered the political temperature; in the first wave, democracy was as much outcome as intention. In Britain, for example, the expansion of the vote occurred only gradually (see Figure 5.5), with each step easing the fears of the propertied classes about the dangers of further reform. The biggest increases occurred with women's suffrage; women over the age of 30 were given the right to vote in 1918, and women over the age of 21 in 1928.

In the United States, the idea that citizens could only be represented fairly by those of their own sort gained ground against the founders' view that the republic should be led by a leisured, landed gentry. Within 50 years of independence, nearly all white men had the vote (Wood, 1993), but women were not given the vote on the same terms as men until 1919, and the franchise for black Americans was not fully realized until the Voting Rights Act of 1965. In that sense, America's democratic transition was also a prolonged affair.

Second wave

Huntington's second wave of democratization began during World War II and continued until the early 1960s. As with the first wave, some of the new democracies created at this time did not consolidate; for example, elected rulers in several Latin American states were quickly overthrown by military coups. But established democracies did emerge after 1945 from the ashes of defeated dictatorships, not just in Germany, but also in Austria, Japan, and Italy. These post-war democracies were introduced by the victorious allies, supported by local partners. The second-wave democracies established firm roots, helped by an economic recovery which was nourished by US aid. During this second wave, democracy also consolidated in the new state of Israel and newly independent India.

Political parties played a key role in the transition. First-generation democracies had emerged when parties were seen as a source of faction, rather than progress. By the time of the second wave, parties had emerged as the leading instrument of democracy in a mass electorate. As in many more recent constitutions, Germany's Basic Law (1949) went so far as to codify their role: 'political parties shall take part in forming the democratic will of the people'. In several cases, though, effective competition was reduced by the emergence of a single party which dominated government for a generation or more: Congress in India, the Christian Democrats in Italy, the Liberal Democrats in Japan, and Labour in Israel. Many second-wave democracies took a generation to mature into fully competitive party systems.

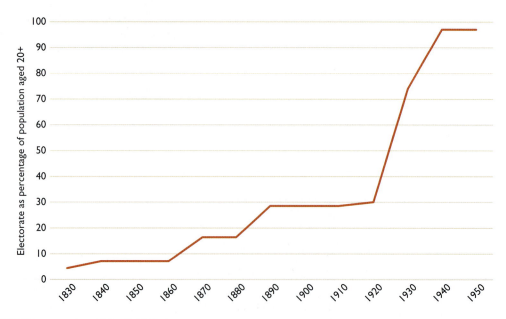

Figure 5.5 The expansion of the British electorate
Note: The last major change was made in 1969, when the voting age was reduced from 21 to 18.

Third wave

This was a product of the final quarter of the twentieth century, and included the following elements:

◆ The ending of right-wing dictatorships in Greece, Portugal, and Spain in the 1970s.
◆ The retreat of the military in much of Latin America in the 1980s.
◆ The collapse of communism in the Soviet Union and Eastern Europe at the end of the 1980s.

The third wave transformed the global political landscape, providing an inhospitable environment for those non-democratic political systems that survived. Even in sub-Saharan Africa, presidents subjected themselves to re-election (though rarely to defeat). With the end of the Cold War and the collapse of any realistic alternative to democracy, the European Union and the United States also became more encouraging of democratic transitions while still, of course, keeping a close eye on their own shorter-term interests.

DEMOCRATIZATION

Huntington was writing at a time of great change, and – as we will see later in this chapter – there was reason then to be optimistic about the future of democracy. Before looking at what has happened since the end of his third wave, though, it is worth looking in more detail at how democratization occurs, and at the conditions needed for countries to democratize. The stages of democratization outlined by O'Donnell *et al.* (1986) (see Figure 5.6) offer one perspective.

The first step in the process comes with the liberalization of an authoritarian **political regime**. Much as we would like to believe in the power of public opinion, transitions are rarely initiated by mass demonstrations against a united dictatorship. Rather, democracy is typically the outcome – intended or unintended – of recognition within part of the ruling group that change is inevitable, or even desirable. As O'Donnell *et al.* (1986) assert:

> There is no transition whose beginning is not the consequence – direct or indirect – of important divisions within the authoritarian regime itself, principally along the fluctuating cleavage between hardliners and softliners … In Brazil and Spain, for example, the decision to liberalize was made by high-echelon, dominant personnel in the incumbent regime in the face of weak and disorganized opposition.

Political regime
Although, strictly speaking, this has the same meaning as the term *political system*, it is typically used pejoratively to refer to authoritarian political systems.

In the more liberal environment that emerges, opportunities increase to express public opposition, inducing a dynamic of reform, moving the process to the second stage of a fraught and often lengthy transition to democracy. During this time, arrangements are made for the new system of government, with efforts to overcome threats to the transition from hardliners (who may consider a military coup) and radical reformers (who may seek a full-scale revolution, rather than just a change of regime). Constitutions must be written, institutions designed, and elections scheduled. Negotiations frequently take the form of round-table talks between rulers and opposition, often leading to an elite settlement.

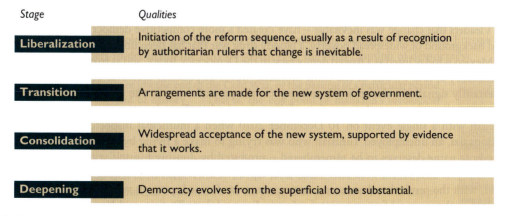

Stage	Qualities
Liberalization	Initiation of the reform sequence, usually as a result of recognition by authoritarian rulers that change is inevitable.
Transition	Arrangements are made for the new system of government.
Consolidation	Widespread acceptance of the new system, supported by evidence that it works.
Deepening	Democracy evolves from the superficial to the substantial.

Figure 5.6 Stages of democratization

DISCUSSION QUESTIONS

◆ Is democracy – in practice – truly government by the people, or have other voices come to be heard more loudly?
◆ Does the internet allow the recreation of Athenian-style direct democracy in today's states?
◆ What are the appropriate limits on government in a democracy?
◆ What conditions are needed in order for democracy to flourish?
◆ How can democracies respond to the international threats posed by authoritarian regimes?
◆ Should we be optimistic or pessimistic about the future of democracy?

KEY CONCEPTS

◆ Checks and balances
◆ Civil liberties
◆ Democracy
◆ Democratization
◆ Direct democracy
◆ E-democracy
◆ End of history
◆ Liberal democracy
◆ Liberalism

◆ Limited government
◆ Modern
◆ Modernization
◆ Political regime
◆ Populism
◆ Representative democracy
◆ Structural violence
◆ Waves of democratization

FURTHER READING

Altman, David (2012) *Direct Democracy Worldwide* (Cambridge University Press). A study of the meaning, effects, and use of direct democracy in different parts of the world.

Dahl, Robert A. (2015) *On Democracy*, 2nd edn (Yale University Press). An accessible primer on democracy by one of its most influential proponents.

Diamond, Larry, and Marc F. Plattner (eds) (2015) *Democracy in Decline?* (Johns Hopkins University Press). An edited collection looking at recent trends in democratic rule, asking if democracies are in decline.

Grugel, Jean, and Matthew Louis Bishop (2014) *Democratization: A Critical Introduction* (Red Globe Press). A textbook assessment of democratization in theory and in practice, including chapters dealing with five regions of the world.

Levitsky, Steven, and Daniel Ziblatt (2018) *How Democracies Die* (Crown). A critical assessment of the possible dangers faced by democracy, using examples from history to speculate on modern regime breakdown.

Morlino, Leonardo (2012) *Changes for Democracy: Actors, Structures, Processes* (Oxford University Press). An extensive review of the academic literature on democratization, including hybrid regimes.

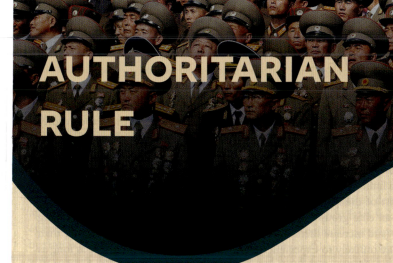

AUTHORITARIAN RULE

6

Source: Getty Images/Alexander Demianchuk

CONTENTS

PREVIEW

While democracy has spread to many parts of the world since 1945, and many people now live in democracies, about as many still live under authoritarian rule. This means centralized government, power for the elite, and limits on the rights and freedoms of citizens. These conditions are not only widespread today, but have been the norm for most of human history. The last century will be remembered at least as much for the dictatorships it spawned – including Hitler's Germany, Stalin's Russia, and Mao's China – as for the democratic transitions at its close. And in spite of the spread of democracy, the most prominent authoritarian states remain globally significant, whether judged by their economic reach (China), as incubators of terrorism (Afghanistan), by their natural resources (Russia), or by their actual or seemingly intended possession of nuclear weapons (Pakistan and Iran).

This chapter follows the lead of the Democracy Index by dividing non-democracies into hybrid and authoritarian systems. It begins with a survey of hybrid regimes that give some of the appearances of being democratic, but where institutions are manipulated to keep rulers in power. Examples include Iraq, Kenya, Nigeria, and Turkey. It goes on to look at authoritarian regimes, breaking them down into five different types: absolute monarchy, personal rule, ruling parties, military government, and theocracy. Many Middle Eastern and African states fall into one of these categories. The chapter ends with a review of the particular problem of corruption, which is so much a part of the political landscape in authoritarian systems.

KEY ARGUMENTS

- Authoritarianism is just as complex and nuanced as democracy, with the added problem that it operates within unspoken limits.
- The concept of hybrid regimes offers a transitional stage between democracy and authoritarianism.
- At the heart of authoritarianism is rule by an individual or a clique, whose belligerence is often a cover for vulnerability.
- Coercion and patronage lie at the heart of authoritarianism, the means used ranging from the subtle to the brutally obvious.
- Authoritarian systems take five main forms: absolute monarchies, personal rule, ruling parties, military government, and theocracy.
- Corruption exists wherever people are willing to abuse the offices they hold for private gain, but it plays a particularly telling role in authoritarian regimes.

SPOTLIGHT CHINA

Brief profile

China is the world's largest state by population, the second biggest by economic output, and has been undergoing a process of political and economic change which is changing the global order. It has one of the world's oldest cultures, but is normally reviewed only in terms of the changes it has seen since the institution of communist rule in 1949. Until 1976 it was under the idiosyncratic and hard-line control of Mao Zedong, since when several generations of leaders have overseen pro-market changes that have helped China become the world's fastest-growing economy. Political reform has not moved as quickly, however, and China remains under the watchful control of the Chinese Communist Party. Dissent and opposition are controlled and limited, corruption is a persistent problem, China's human rights record is poor, and in spite of the changes it has undergone, it ranks low on most comparative political and economic rankings.

Form of government	Unitary communist republic. State formed 1949, and most recent constitution adopted 1982.
Executive	The once mainly ceremonial role of president has been transformed recently into a powerful executive position, the previous limit of two five-year terms removed in 2018 and replaced with a lifetime tenure. The position of general secretary of the CCP is also powerful, while the State Council, headed by the premier, supervises the work of government ministries.
Legislature	Unicameral National People's Congress of nearly 3,000 members, chosen indirectly through local and provincial congresses, serving five-year terms. Meets only for brief periods, its work carried out when in recess by a 150-member Standing Committee.
Judiciary	No independent constitutional court. Rule through law has strengthened but the judicial system remains underdeveloped.
Electoral system	Elections have been introduced to many of China's villages and to some townships. However, elected officials still operate under the party's supervision. Indirect election is usual at higher levels.
Parties	Single party. The Chinese Communist Party (CCP) remains the dominant political force, its leadership being a parallel government within which most real power is focused.

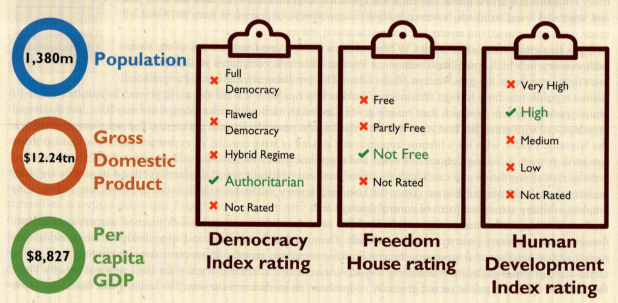

1,380m Population

$12.24tn Gross Domestic Product

$8,827 Per capita GDP

Democracy Index rating
- ✗ Full Democracy
- ✗ Flawed Democracy
- ✗ Hybrid Regime
- ✔ Authoritarian
- ✗ Not Rated

Freedom House rating
- ✗ Free
- ✗ Partly Free
- ✔ Not Free
- ✗ Not Rated

Human Development Index rating
- ✗ Very High
- ✔ High
- ✗ Medium
- ✗ Low
- ✗ Not Rated

Authoritarian rule in China

A portrait of Chairman Mao dominates Tiananmen Square in Beijing, offering a reminder of the dominant role in Chinese politics and government of the Chinese Communist Party.
Source: iStock/Nikada.

China is an authoritarian system within which the degree of central government control has waxed and waned according mainly to the preferences and political skills of its leaders. During the era of Mao Zedong it veered between totalitarianism and chaos, but his successors began a process that saw China moving towards new openness both in its politics and its economic policy. Much has recently changed thanks to the efforts of Xi Jinping, president since 2013.

Government continues to be dominated by the Chinese Communist Party (CCP), but Xi was able to convince the party in 2018 to convert the position of president into a job for life, and he has used a campaign against corruption to tighten his control. He has even been able to integrate 'Xi Jinping Thought on Socialism with Chinese Characteristics for a New Era' into the Chinese constitution. This philosophy has been summarized by Buckley (2018) as follows: a 'great rejuvenation' for China in the world (through its economic and military power), revitalized control of the CCP over every corner of society, and a central role for Xi in Chinese leadership.

The degree of political control witnessed in China can be ascribed mainly to the skills of the CCP in both maintaining its monopoly position while also becoming less intrusive and more supervisory. In local communities, informal networks of power-holders now determine 'who gets rich first' – a political market, rather than a free market. These alliances are composed not only of well-placed party members, but also of officials in the bureaucracy, local government, and the army. Local officials provide favoured businesses (including their own) with contracts, land, sympathetic regulations, information, supplies, transport, and other subsidies.

Minzner (2018) concludes that China's era of reform is ending. Its leaders have rejected fundamental changes to the one-party system, so that while the country creates an impression of political stability and remarkable economic growth, the reality is less positive: economic cleavages have widened, the entrenched interests of the CCP have deepened, and the collective governance of the past is trending towards one-man rule. Uncertainty hangs in the air, raising many troubling questions about the new directions being taken by the world's biggest country.

Further reading

Economy, Elizabeth C. (2018) *The Third Revolution: Xi Jinping and the New Chinese State* (Oxford University Press).

Heilman, Sebastian (ed.) (2016) *China's Political System* (Rowman & Littlefield).

Li, Cheng (2016) *Chinese Politics in the Xi Jinping Era: Reassessing Collective Leadership* (Brookings Institution).

establishment consists of competing factions of middle-aged to elderly men exploiting the revolutionary heritage in a successful effort to build and retain power and wealth. Neither a strong party nor a royal family exist to impose overall direction.

Unsurprisingly in a country where the median age was just 27 years in 2011, rule by this theocratic elite has intensified generational divisions. Well-educated young people, including many female graduates, chafe at the restrictions imposed by the religious establishment. This desire for freedom is not necessarily rooted in a secular outlook; rather, it reflects opposition to the cultural repression imposed by a religious leadership lacking a positive vision of the country's future (Gheissari, 2009).

THE POLITICAL IMPACT OF CORRUPTION

Corruption is far from unique to authoritarian systems, and can be found at every level of government and administration in every society where people are willing to abuse public office for private gain, even in full and flawed democracies. However, corruption plays a particularly telling role in hybrid and authoritarian regimes, being both a cause and effect of the kind of power that authoritarian leaders wield. In the famously cynical observation of the nineteenth-century British politician Lord Acton:

> **Corruption**
> The abuse of office for private gain.

> Power tends to corrupt, and absolute power tends to corrupt absolutely. Great men are almost always bad men, even when they exercise influence and not authority: still more when you super add the tendency or the certainty of corruption by authority. (Acton, quoted in Figgis and Laurence, 1907)

Corruption occurs when an official – who could be a member of a government, a judge, a bureaucrat, a customs official, or someone else in a position of authority – seeks or provides a benefit in exchange for an incentive, rather than on the basis of entitlement. The incentive may persuade officials to do what they should have done anyway, or to do it promptly, but it typically involves breaking the law. Most worryingly, corruption can undermine the quality of governance and the efficiency of an economy. It replaces efforts to promote the public good with efforts to promote the private good, diverts limited resources away from those who most need them, discourages foreign investment, corrodes public trust in government, and places the interests of those willing and able to break the law above the interests of the population as a whole.

Political corruption comes in many different forms, including the following:

◆ *Electoral fraud* involves manipulating the outcome of elections, whether by redrawing electoral districts, making it difficult for voters to cast their ballots, intimidating opposition candidates and their supporters, or artificially expanding the electoral roll by double-counting voters or adding fake or dead voters.

◆ The giving of a *bribe* to a government official or a police officer.

◆ *Influence peddling*, where someone sells their influence in government to benefit a third party, as when officials use their office to ensure that a particular company is awarded a public contract.

◆ *Patronage* was discussed earlier, and in many forms is legitimate, but becomes corrupt when it involves leaders selecting less qualified over more qualified candidates for office in return for their political support.

◆ *Nepotism* or *cronyism*, the former involving favouring relatives, while the latter involves favouring personal friends, for example in being selected as candidates in elections, in being appointed to important government office, or in being awarded government contracts.

◆ *Embezzlement* involves the theft of public funds, as in the case of the nearly $175 million spent on property, luxury cars, and artwork bought by Teodorin Obiang, son of President Teodoro Obiang of Equatorial Guinea, an oil-rich state in west Africa. The younger Obiang was found guilty of embezzlement in absentia by a French court in October 2017.

◆ *Kickbacks* occur when government officials use their position to offer a contract for public work to a company in return for a share of the payment made to the company.

Measuring and quantifying corruption is not easy, mainly because it is – by definition – an illegal and covert activity. In terms of making comparisons, the best guide we have comes in the form of the reports published by Transparency International, an organization headquartered in Berlin that works to limit corruption and promote

Focus 6.2
Totalitarianism

There is a sixth and final form of authoritarian rule (**totalitarianism**, in which rigid support is demanded for a supreme leader), but it was rare even in the twentieth century, and there is only one example left today: North Korea. In spite of its rarity, totalitarianism cannot be ignored as a political type, and it is worth reviewing if only as the benchmark for the most extreme form of political control we have seen in the modern era. Its features include a dominating leader portrayed as working in the benevolent interests of the people, and a single guiding ideology based on a pessimistic view of human nature and claims of the need to strive towards building an ideal society (see Goodwin, 2014).

The archetypal totalitarian regime was that dominated by Joseph Stalin in the Soviet Union between the late 1920s, when he came to power, and his death in 1953 (see McCauley, 2013). Under his iron fist, the USSR moved away from Marxist ideals towards an absolutist and unyielding dictatorship that demanded unquestioning support for the state, the party, and its leaders. Stalin used systematic and calculated oppression to enforce his reforms, in the process of which perhaps as many as 20 million people died from famine, execution, or war, and many millions more were purged, or exiled to concentration camps. Stalinism also meant the elimination of human rights, the encouragement of a cult of personality, and the use of secret police to identify and remove rivals. It also meant the establishment of a command economy (see Chapter 20) in which all economic decisions were made by state planners, as a result of which the Soviet bureaucracy became both massive and massively inefficient.

Today, North Korea has many of the same qualities (see French, 2014), prime among which is rule by a leader (Kim Jong-Un since 2011) who sits at the apex of a system controlled by a ruling dynasty; his grandfather Kim Il-Sung was Supreme Leader from 1948 until 1994, and his father Kim Jong-Il held the position from 1994 until 2011. The current Kim is the uncontested holder of numerous key positions, including chair of the ruling Workers' Party, chair of the Central Military Commission, and Supreme Commander of the military, in which he holds the rank of Marshal.

Kim maintains a cult of personality, his administration routinely abusing the human rights of North Korean citizens and maintaining a network of prison camps for the most incorrigible opponents of the regime. There is an elected Supreme People's Assembly, but it meets only twice annually for a few days at a time, and while elections are held every five years, only one candidate is fielded for each district. But even Kim's power is far from unlimited; he depends on patronage by China and the continued support of his own military. Meanwhile, an inflexible economic system has led not just to stagnation but also to mass starvation.

> **Totalitarianism**
> The most absolute form of authoritarian rule, based either on a guiding ideology or the goal of major social change, with total control exercised by a leader, state, or party over all aspects of public and private life.

transparency. It publishes an annual Corruption Perceptions Index (CPI) which uses a variety of governmental and non-governmental sources to rank perceptions of corruption around the world. The key word here is *perception*; the index reflects how countries are regarded by those who know them, rather than providing a direct and objective measure of corruption itself. The index is based on a compilation of information from banks, foundations, and interest groups. The overlap with forms of political rule is close, the least corrupt countries corresponding with full democracies, and the most corrupt overlapping with authoritarian regimes (see Map 6.1).

That even the most advanced democracies experience corruption is reflected in the cases of Denmark and New Zealand, which usually sit at the top of the Transparency International rankings (although this does not mean that they are the least corrupt countries so much as those where corruption is less evident). Recent CPI reports note that Denmark lacks transparency in political and campaign financing, has outdated laws on freedom of information, and provides insufficient protection to whistle-blowers, while New Zealand is criticized for its failure to ratify the United Nations Convention Against Corruption.

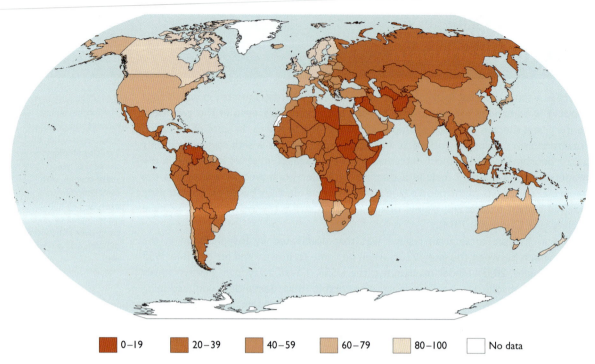

Map 6.1 The Corruption Perceptions Index
Source: Transparency International (2018).
Note: Ranked on a scale between 100 (Very Clean) and 0 (Highly Corrupt).

These are minor concerns when compared with the situation in North Korea and Somalia, which routinely rank at the bottom of the Corruption Perceptions Index. In the case of North Korea, information is gleaned mainly from defectors, whose reports suggest that a culture of corruption has infiltrated the entire society. Bribery, notes Lankov (2013), has become a matter of basic survival, given the country's food shortages, lack of basic resources, and harsh penalties for any actions that might be defined as threatening the governing regime. Somalia experiences comparable problems, with the addition of even more high-level corruption involving patronage and the misappropriation of public funds.

DISCUSSION QUESTIONS

◆ What are the key differences between hybrid and authoritarian regimes?
◆ How does patronage differ in its democratic and authoritarian forms?
◆ Even if personal rule is unique to authoritarian regimes, could it also be a useful tool for helping us understand and describe government in democracies?
◆ What is the line between ruling parties in authoritarian regimes and dominant parties in democracies?
◆ Why are military governments so much more unusual today than they once were?
◆ Why are so many authoritarian regimes corrupt?

KEY CONCEPTS

◆ Absolute monarchy
◆ Authoritarian regimes
◆ Coercion
◆ Corruption
◆ *Coup d'état*
◆ Cult of personality
◆ Despotism

◆ Hybrid regimes
◆ Islamic Republic
◆ Patronage
◆ Personal rule
◆ Theocracy
◆ Totalitarianism

FURTHER READING

Brooker, Paul (2014) *Non-Democratic Regimes*, 3rd edn (Red Globe Press). An assessment of the different types of non-democratic regime, how they emerge, the means they use, and how they survive.

Ezrow, Natasha, and Erica Frantz (2011) *Dictators and Dictatorships: Understanding Authoritarian Regimes and Their Leaders* (Continuum). A comparative survey of the different forms taken by dictatorships, focusing on the importance of leader-elite relations.

Heywood, Paul M. (ed.) (2015) *Routledge Handbook of Political Corruption* (Routledge). A review of the meaning and causes of corruption, with chapters offering cases from different parts of the world.

Levitsky, Steven, and Lucan A. Way (2010) *Competitive Authoritarianism: Hybrid Regimes After the Cold War* (Cambridge University Press). A detailed account of the rise and diverging fate of competitive authoritarian regimes since 1990.

Marquez, Xavier (2016) *Non-Democratic Politics: Authoritarianism, Dictatorship and Democratization* (Red Globe Press). A comprehensive analysis of the main types of authoritarian regime and the means by which authoritarian governments wield and retain power.

Svolik, Milan W. (2012) *The Politics of Authoritarian Rule* (Cambridge University Press). Another comparative survey of the causes, methods, and strategies of dictatorship, explaining why its takes different forms in different situations.

CONSTITUTIONS AND COURTS

7

PREVIEW

So far we have looked mainly at broad concepts and ideas in comparative politics, including theoretical approaches and research methods. We now focus on political institutions, opening in this chapter with a review of constitutions and the courts that lie at their foundation. Constitutions outline the rules of political systems, and tell us much about the structure and aspirations of government, as well as the rights of citizens. For their part, courts strive to make sure that the rules are respected and equally applied. Just as humans are imperfect, however, so are the political institutions they create and manage; there are significant gaps between constitutional ideals and practice.

This chapter begins with an assessment of constitutions: what they are, what they do, their character and durability, how their performance can be measured, and how they are changed. There is no fixed template for constitutions, they vary widely in terms of their length and efficacy, and the gap between aspiration and achievement differs from one constitution to another.

The chapter goes on to look at the role of courts and their relationship with constitutions, examining the differences between supreme courts and constitutional courts, and the incidence of judicial activism. It then focuses on judges: how they are recruited, the terms of their tenure, and how such differences impact judicial independence. It then briefly reviews the three major legal systems found in the world – common law, civil law, and religious law – before assessing the place of constitutions and courts in authoritarian regimes.

KEY ARGUMENTS

◆ Constitutions are critical to achieving an understanding of government, offering a power map through key political principles and rules.

◆ Understanding governments requires an appreciation not just of the content of constitutions, but also of their durability and how they are amended.

◆ Awareness of the structure and role of courts is also critical, as is the distinction between supreme courts and constitutional courts.

◆ Judges have become more willing to enter the political arena, making it more important to understand the rules on judicial recruitment.

◆ In comparing constitutions and courts, the distinction between common and civil law has long been important, and more attention needs to be paid to the political significance of religious law.

◆ In authoritarian regimes, constitutions and courts are weak, with governments either using them as a facade or entirely bypassing them.

CONSTITUTIONS AND COURTS: AN OVERVIEW

A **constitution** is a power map containing a set of rules and principles outlining the structure and powers of a system of government, describing its institutions and the manner in which they work and relate to one another, and typically describing both the limits on governmental power and the rights of citizens. A system of government without a constitution is not a system at all, but rather an unorganized collection of habits that can be changed at the whim of the leaders or the people. In the case of democracies, the authority provided by a constitution helps provide predictability and security. In the case of authoritarian regimes, the constitution is more often a fig leaf behind which elites hide, the terms of the constitution being interpreted to suit their needs, or ignored altogether. As well as providing the rules of government, constitutions also offer benchmarks against which the performance of government can be measured.

> **Constitution**
> A document or a set of documents that outlines the powers, institutions, and structure of government, as well as expressing the rights of citizens and the limits on government.

Recent decades have seen a growth of interest in the study of constitutions, for four main reasons:

◆ There has been an explosion of constitution-making, with 105 countries adopting new constitutions between 1990 and 2014 (Comparative Constitutions Project, 2018).
◆ Judges and courts in many democracies have become more willing to step into the political arena, in a process known as judicial or constitutional review. (See later in the chapter for more details.)
◆ The growing interest in human rights lends itself to judicial engagement.
◆ The expanding body of international law increasingly impacts domestic politics, with judges called on to arbitrate the conflicting claims of national and supranational law.

A key link between constitutions, law, and government is found in the idea of the **rule of law**. In the words of the nineteenth-century English jurist, A. V. Dicey (1885), this means that no one can be punished except for a breach of the law, that no one is above the law, that everyone is equally subject to the law, and that we substitute 'a government of laws' for a 'government of men'. Under the rule of law, political leaders cannot exercise arbitrary power and the powerful are (in theory, at least) subject to the same laws as everyone else (see Bingham, 2011).

> **Rule of law**
> The principle that societies are best governed using clear, stable, and just laws to which all residents are equally subject regardless of their status or background.

The implementation of the rule of law and due process (respect for an individual's legal rights) is perhaps the most important distinction between democracies and authoritarian regimes. In the case of the latter, the adoption and application of laws is more arbitrary, and based less on tried and tested principles than on the political goals and objectives of leaders and elites. No country provides completely equal application of the law, but democracies fare much better than authoritarian regimes, many of whose political weaknesses stem back to constitutional weaknesses.

THE CHARACTER OF CONSTITUTIONS

Most constitutions are structured similarly in the sense that they include four elements (see Figure 7.1). They often start out with a set of broad aspirations, declaring in vague but often inspiring terms the ideals of the state, most often including support for democracy and equality. The core of the document then goes into detail on the institutional structure of government: how the different offices are elected or appointed, and what they are allowed and not allowed to do. There will usually be a bill of rights or its equivalent, outlining the rights of citizens relative to government. Finally, there will be a description of the rules on amending the constitution.

> **Codified constitution**
> One that is set out in a single, self-contained document.

While most countries have constitutions that are **codified** and can be found in a single document, a few (such as Britain, Canada, Israel, New Zealand, and Saudi Arabia) have **uncodified** constitutions based on different sources. In the case of Britain, we must look for its constitution in a large body of statute and common law, European Union law, commentaries written by constitutional experts, and customs and traditions. This is because, unlike most countries, Brit-

> **Uncodified constitution**
> One that is spread among several documents.

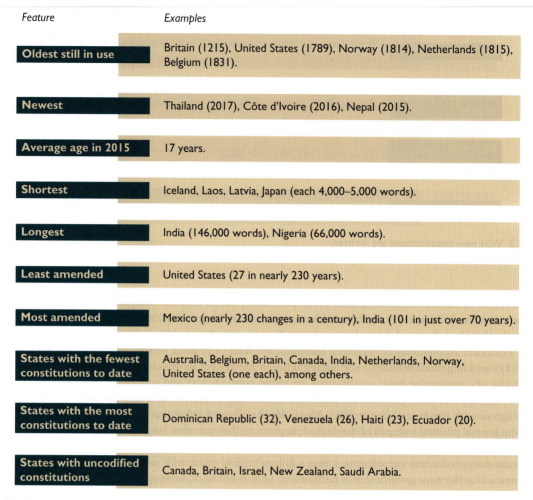

Feature	Examples
Oldest still in use	Britain (1215), United States (1789), Norway (1814), Netherlands (1815), Belgium (1831).
Newest	Thailand (2017), Côte d'Ivoire (2016), Nepal (2015).
Average age in 2015	17 years.
Shortest	Iceland, Laos, Latvia, Japan (each 4,000–5,000 words).
Longest	India (146,000 words), Nigeria (66,000 words).
Least amended	United States (27 in nearly 230 years).
Most amended	Mexico (nearly 230 changes in a century), India (101 in just over 70 years).
States with the fewest constitutions to date	Australia, Belgium, Britain, Canada, India, Netherlands, Norway, United States (one each), among others.
States with the most constitutions to date	Dominican Republic (32), Venezuela (26), Haiti (23), Ecuador (20).
States with uncodified constitutions	Canada, Britain, Israel, New Zealand, Saudi Arabia.

Figure 7.3 Ten facts about constitutions
Source: Based partly on information in Comparative Constitutions Project (2018).

Judiciary
A collective term for the judges within the system of courts that interpret and apply the law in keeping with the constitution.

Judicial review
The power of courts to nullify any laws or actions proposed or taken by government officials that contravene the constitution. Otherwise known as constitutional review.

yet India suffers massive poverty, widespread corruption, human rights abuses (particularly in regard to women), unequal access to education, and an extraordinarily slow-moving legal process.

Recent developments in the United States offer additional insights into the problem. The US constitution did not change after the terrorist attacks of 11 September 2001, but the detention of alleged terrorists in Guantanamo Bay and revelations about the use of torture and the increased monitoring by government agencies of phone and electronic communications raised troubling questions about the health of individual rights in the United States. It is often said that truth is the first casualty of war; in a similar vein, it is often the case with countries facing external threats that the rule of law takes second place to national security, and needs to be rebuilt subsequently through the courts.

THE ROLE OF COURTS

Constitutions are neither self-made nor self-implementing, and they need the support of institutions that can enforce their provisions by striking down unconstitutional laws and practices. This role has fallen to the **judiciary**: with their power of **judicial review**, judges occupy a unique position both in and above politics. Few constitutions initially had this provision (not even the US constitution, which is often seen as a template for judicial review; the US Supreme Court gave itself this power with a decision in 1803), but the vast

Focus 7.1
Amending constitutions

Times, needs, and expectations change, and constitutions should change with them, up to a point. So while there should always be allowances for amendment, the procedures involved have critical implications: too many amendments can result in instability, while too few can result in stagnation. Here we meet the matter of **entrenchment**, a term referring to procedures which set a higher level and wider spread of support for amendments than is the case for ordinary legislative bills.

In the case of a **flexible constitution**, changes can be made relatively easily, while changing a **rigid constitution** is more difficult, usually demanding super- or concurrent majorities (see Figure 7.4). Rigidity offers the benefit of a stable political framework, and benefits rulers by limiting the damage should political opponents win power, because they would face the same barriers to change. On the other hand, non-entrenchment (which is rare) offers the advantage of ready adaptability. In New Zealand, this flexibility allowed changes to the electoral system and government administration in the 1980s and 1990s, while in the United Kingdom it allowed the devolution of significant powers to Scotland and Wales in 1999 without much constitutional fuss.

The most extreme form of entrenchment is a clause that cannot be amended at all. For example, the French and Turkish constitutions guarantee the republican character of their regimes. These statements were designed to enforce a break with the old regime, but they also provide ammunition to those who see constitutions as the dictatorship of the dead over the living. In new conditions, past solutions sometimes have a way of turning into current problems.

A key element of the amendment procedure concerns the role of the legislature. On the one hand, some constitutions can be amended simply through special majorities within the legislature, thereby reducing the relative status of the constitution. This approach is found in European states with a strong commitment to parliamentary supremacy, such as Germany: amendments there (where permitted) require only a two-thirds majority in both houses. On the other hand, where modifications cannot be approved by the legislature alone, the constitution stands supreme over the legislature. In Australia, for example, amendments must be endorsed not only by the national parliament, but also by a referendum achieving a concurrent majority in most states and in the country as a whole. A total of 44 amendments have been proposed, of which only eight won enough support to go through, the most recent in 1977.

Changes can also be initiated by other means than a formal amendment. The most important of these devices are judicial review (the rulings of constitutional courts), and the passage of new laws that modify some aspect of the rules of government. And even when constitutions are codified, simple customs and traditions should not be forgotten; there is often much about the structure of government that is not written down, but has simply become a tradition. Political parties play a critical role in government all over the world, for example, but there may not always be much said about them in constitutions.

Entrenchment
The question of the legal procedures for amending a constitution.

Flexible constitution
One that can be amended more easily, often in the same way that ordinary legislation is passed.

Rigid constitution
One that is entrenched, requiring more demanding amendment procedures.

majority now include some provision for review. As a result, courts have come to play an increasingly important role in government and politics. Ginsburg (2008) describes this development as 'a global institutional norm' that has spread to nearly every democracy as well as several authoritarian regimes, and is increasingly seen in transnational contexts as well. Hirschl (2008) has gone so far as to refer to the rise of juristocracy, or government by judges.

The function of judicial review can be allocated in one of two ways. The first and more traditional method – used in the United States and much of Latin America – is for the highest or supreme court in the ordinary judicial system to

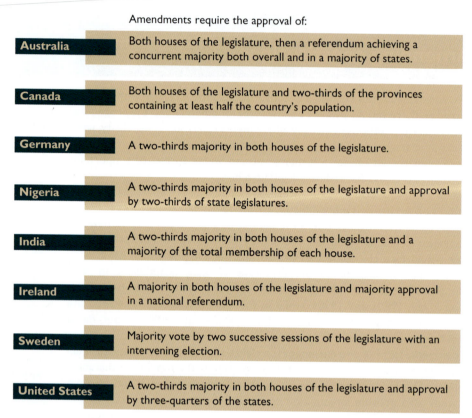

Amendments require the approval of:

Australia	Both houses of the legislature, then a referendum achieving a concurrent majority both overall and in a majority of states.
Canada	Both houses of the legislature and two-thirds of the provinces containing at least half the country's population.
Germany	A two-thirds majority in both houses of the legislature.
Nigeria	A two-thirds majority in both houses of the legislature and approval by two-thirds of state legislatures.
India	A two-thirds majority in both houses of the legislature and a majority of the total membership of each house.
Ireland	A majority in both houses of the legislature and majority approval in a national referendum.
Sweden	Majority vote by two successive sessions of the legislature with an intervening election.
United States	A two-thirds majority in both houses of the legislature and approval by three-quarters of the states.

Figure 7.4 Comparing constitutional amendments
Notes:
Germany: The federal, social, and democratic character of the German state, and the rights of individuals within it, cannot be amended.
India: Selected amendments, such as those changing the representation of states in parliament, must also be approved by at least half the states.
United States: An alternative method, based on a special convention called by the states and by Congress, has not been used.

take on the task of constitutional protection. A supreme court rules on constitutional matters, just as it has the final say on other questions of common and statute law. A second and more recent method – favoured in Europe – is to create a special constitutional court, standing apart from the ordinary judicial system.

Supreme courts

Concrete review
Judgments made on the constitutional validity of law in the context of a specific case. Sometimes known as the American model.

Abstract review
Advice (not usually binding) given by a court on the constitutionality of a law or public policy. Sometimes known as the European model.

As the name implies, a supreme court is the highest court within a jurisdiction, whose decisions are not subject to review by any other court. Supreme courts are usually the final court of appeal, listening – if they choose – to cases appealed from a lower level. They also mainly use **concrete review**, meaning that they ask whether, given the facts of the particular case, the decision reached at lower level was compatible with the constitution. By contrast, constitutional courts mainly practise **abstract review**, judging the intrinsic constitutional validity of a law without limiting themselves to the particular case. In addition, constitutional courts can issue advisory judgments on a bill at the request of the government or legislature, often without the stimulus of a specific case. These latter judgments are often short and are usually unsigned, lacking the legal argument used by supreme courts. So concrete review provides decisions on cases with constitutional implications while abstract review is a more general assessment of the constitutional validity of a law or bill.

Confusingly, the name of a given court does not always follow its function. Hence the supreme courts of Australia and Hong Kong go under the title of High Court, those of France and Belgium under the title *Cour de Cassation* (Court of Appeal), and that of the European Union is the European Court of Justice, while a number of European countries – including Spain – have supreme courts whose decisions (some or all) can be appealed to constitutional courts.

Table 7.1 Comparing supreme courts and constitutional courts

	Supreme court	Constitutional court
Form of review	Primarily concrete	Primarily abstract
Relationship to other courts	Highest court of appeal	A separate body dealing with constitutional issues only
Recruitment	Legal expertise plus political approval	Political criteria more important
Normal tenure	Until retirement age	Typically one non-renewable term (6–9 years)
Examples	Australia, Brazil, Canada, China, India, Japan, Mexico, Nigeria, Sweden, United States	Austria, Egypt, France, Germany, most of Eastern Europe, Russia, South Africa

The United States is the prototypical case of a supreme court with concrete review. Although the US Supreme Court possesses **original jurisdiction** over cases to which a US state or a representative of another country is a party, its main role is **appellate**. That is, constitutional issues can be raised at any point in the ordinary judicial system and the Supreme Court selects only those cases that it believes raise significant constitutional questions; the vast majority of petitions for the Court to review a case are turned down.

Constitutional courts

This approach was born with the Austrian constitution of 1920, and became established in continental Europe after World War II. The success of Germany's Federal Constitutional Court encouraged non-European countries to follow suit, such that nearly half the world's states had such a court by 2005 (Horowitz, 2006). Where a supreme court is a judicial body making the final ruling on all appeals (not all of which involve the constitution), a constitutional court is more akin to an additional legislative chamber. In this system, ordinary courts are not empowered to engage in judicial review, with appeals to the supreme court; instead, the review function is exclusive to a separate constitutional authority (see Vanberg, 2015).

Germany has become the exemplar of the constitutional court approach. Its Federal Constitutional Court (FCC) has the following powers: judicial review, adjudication of disputes between state and federal political institutions, protection of individual rights, and protection of the constitutional and democratic order against groups and individuals seeking to overthrow it (Langenbacher and Conradt, 2017). The 'eternity clause' in Germany's constitution (the Basic Law) holds that the FCC's judgments in key areas of democracy, federalism, and human rights are the final word.

The FCC's public reputation has been enhanced by the provision of constitutional complaint, which allows citizens to petition the Court directly once other judicial remedies are exhausted. Kommers (2006) describes the Court as 'the guardian of German democracy', pointing to its decisions on voting rights, public funding of election campaigns, the electoral system, and the rights of smaller political parties. It has also kept a careful eye on whether European Union laws and policies detract from the autonomy of the country's legislature, and has been active on policy topics as varied as abortion, immigration, religion in schools, and university reform.

THE ROLE OF THE JUDICIARY

Judicial intervention in public affairs has grown throughout the liberal democratic world since 1945, marking a transition from **judicial restraint** to **judicial activism**. Studies from as far afield as Bangladesh, India, South Africa, Canada, and the United States have reflected on the implications of judges becoming more willing to enter political arenas that would have once been left to elected politicians and national parliaments (see Coutinho *et al.*, 2015).

For example, the US Supreme Court decided the outcome of the 2000 presidential election by voting along party lines that George W. Bush had won the election in the state of Florida, and thus the presidential election. One outraged commentator described the vote as 'the single most corrupt decision in Supreme Court history' and 'a violation of the judicial oath' because the majority decided on the basis of 'the personal identity and political affiliation of the litigants' (Dershowitz, 2001). Later, during Barack Obama's final term in office in 2016, Republicans in

Original jurisdiction
The power of a court to review cases that originate with the court itself.

Appellate
The power of a court to review decisions reached by lower courts.

Judicial restraint
The view that judges should apply the letter of the law, leaving politics to elected bodies.

Judicial activism
The willingness of judges to venture beyond narrow legal reasoning so as to influence public policy.

SPOTLIGHT SOUTH AFRICA

Brief profile

South Africa languished for many decades under a system of institutionalized racial separation known as apartheid. This ensured privileges and opportunities for white South Africans at the expense of black, mixed-race, and Asian South Africans. In the face of growing resistance, and ostracism from much of the outside world, an agreement was reached that paved the way for the first democratic elections in 1994. Much was originally expected from a country with a wealth of natural resources, but corruption is a major problem, unemployment remains stubbornly high, many still live in poverty, and South Africa faces major public security challenges: it has one of the highest per capita homicide and violent assault rates in the world. Despite being the second largest economy in Africa (after Nigeria), it has only partly realized its potential as a major regional power.

Form of government	Unitary parliamentary republic. State formed 1910, and most recent constitution adopted 1997.
Executive	Presidential. A president heads both the state and the government, ruling with a cabinet. The National Assembly elects the president after each general election. Presidents limited to two five-year terms.
Legislature	Bicameral Parliament: lower National Assembly (400 members) elected for renewable five-year terms, and upper National Council of Provinces with 90 members, ten appointed from each of the nine provinces.
Judiciary	The legal system mixes common and civil law. The Constitutional Court decides constitutional matters and can strike down legislation. It has 11 members appointed by the president for terms of 12 years.
Electoral system	The National Assembly is elected by proportional representation using closed party lists; half are elected from a national list and half from provincial lists.
Parties	Dominant party. The African National Congress (ANC) has dominated since the first full democratic and multi-racial election in 1994. The more liberal Democratic Alliance, now the leading party in the Western Cape, forms the official opposition.

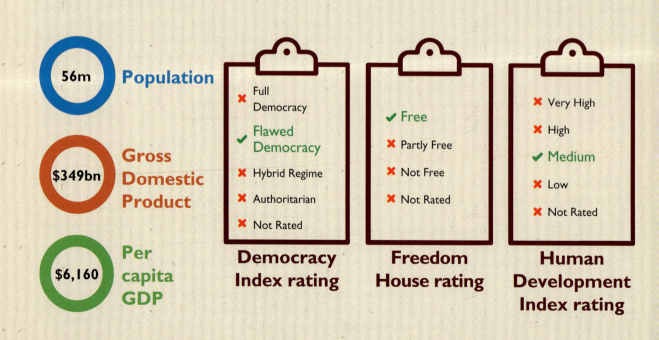

56m Population

$349bn Gross Domestic Product

$6,160 Per capita GDP

Democracy Index rating
- ✘ Full Democracy
- ✔ Flawed Democracy
- ✘ Hybrid Regime
- ✘ Authoritarian
- ✘ Not Rated

Freedom House rating
- ✔ Free
- ✘ Partly Free
- ✘ Not Free
- ✘ Not Rated

Human Development Index rating
- ✘ Very High
- ✘ High
- ✔ Medium
- ✘ Low
- ✘ Not Rated

The constitution of South Africa

South Africa's transformation from a state based on apartheid (institutionalized racial segregation) to a more constitutional order based on democracy was one of the most remarkable political transitions of the late twentieth century. In 1996, after two years of hard bargaining between the African National Congress (ANC) and the white National Party (NP), agreement was reached on a new 109-page constitution to take effect in February 1997. For a contextual analysis, see Klug (2010).

In a phrase reminiscent of the US constitution, South Africa's constitution declares that 'the Executive power of the Republic vests in the President'. Unlike the United States, though, presidents are elected by the National Assembly after each general election. They can be removed through a vote of no confidence in the legislature (although this event would trigger a general

Images of Cyril Ramaphosa, South Africa's president, on sale at the annual conference of the African National Congress, a party that has dominated the country since the end of apartheid in 1994.
Source: Getty Images/Bloomberg.

election), and by impeachment. The president governs in conjunction with a large cabinet.

Each of the country's nine provinces elects its own legislature and forms its own executive headed by a premier. But far more than in the United States, authority and funds flow from the top down. In any case, the ANC provides the glue linking not only executive and legislature, but also national, provincial, and municipal levels

of government. So far, at least, the ruling party has dominated the governing institutions whereas, in the United States, the institutions have dominated the parties.

South Africa's rainbow nation faces some difficulties in reconciling constitutional liberal democracy with the political dominance of the ANC. Some have argued that the constitution should be replaced with a document that is more reflective of the needs and realities of African society, replacing the compromises that were made at the end of the apartheid era. Others argue that it is a landmark attempt to create a society based on social, economic, and political rights for all citizens, and that its true implementation has yet to be achieved (Dixon and Roux, 2018). But the effects of the constitution, more than most, should be judged by what preceded it. By that test the achievements of the new South Africa are remarkable indeed.

Further reading

Butler, Anthony (2017) *Contemporary South Africa*, 3rd edn (Red Globe Press).
Deegan, Heather (2011) *Politics South Africa*, 2nd edn (Pearson).
Klug, Heinz (2010) *The Constitution of South Africa: A Contextual Analysis* (Hart).

the US Senate refused to consider his nominee for a vacancy in the Supreme Court, instead delaying the process in the hope that a Republican would win the presidency and would nominate a more conservative judge (which is exactly what happened). In Israel, meanwhile, the Supreme Court has addressed such controversial issues as the West Bank barrier, the use of torture in investigations by the security service, and the assassination of suspected terrorists (Hirschl, 2008).

There are three key reasons for the drift from restraint to activism:

◆ The increasing reliance on regulation as a mode of governance encourages court intervention. A government decision to oppose same-sex marriage, for example, is open to judicial challenge in a way that a decision to go to war or raise taxes is not.

◆ International conventions give judges an extra lever to move outside the limits of national law. Documents such as the Universal Declaration of Human Rights and the European Convention on Human Rights provide a base on which judges can construct what would once have been viewed as excessively political statements. The emergence of international courts such as the International Criminal Court (founded in 2002) has also encouraged national courts to become more assertive.

◆ The continuing prestige of the judiciary has encouraged some transfer of authority to its domain. The judicial process in most democracies has retained at least some reputation for integrity and impartiality, whereas the standing of many other institutions – notably political parties – has declined.

Whatever the factors lying behind the expansion of judicial authority, the process seems to reinforce itself. Sensing the growing confidence of judges in addressing broader political issues, interest groups, rights-conscious citizens, and even political parties have become more willing to continue their struggles in the judicial arena. In few states has judicial activism gone further than the United States. The US is founded on a constitutional contract and legions of lawyers forever quibble over the terms. Armed with a written constitution, federalism, judicial independence, no system of separate administrative courts, a legal system based on judge-made case law, and high esteem for judges, the US has moved ever further into a culture of judicial activism. So far has this gone that discussions about which way the Court will vote on an issue boil down less to constitutional principles than to the relative number of conservatives and liberals on the nine-person bench.

Fewer conditions of judicial autonomy are met in Britain, where parliamentary sovereignty long reigned supreme. Lacking the authority to annul legislation, judicial review in the British context normally refers to the capacity of judges to review executive decisions against the template provided by administrative law. Even so, judicial activism grew in Britain as the European Court of Justice established a legal order applying to all member states of the European Union (and has even influenced those outside the EU). Judicial assertiveness was further encouraged by Britain's belated adoption of the European Convention on Human Rights in 1998, the decay of the royal prerogative which once allowed the state to stand above the law, and the establishment of a Supreme Court for England and Wales in 2009. This is the final court of appeal for all UK civil cases, and for criminal cases from England, Wales, and Northern Ireland.

Formal statements of rights have also encouraged judicial expansion in other English-speaking countries. In Canada, a Charter of Rights and Freedoms was appended to the constitution in 1982, giving judges a more prominent role in defending individual rights. Similarly, New Zealand introduced a bill of rights in 1990, protecting 'the life and security of the person' and also confirming traditional, but previously uncodified, democratic and civil rights.

SYSTEMS OF LAW

As well as understanding constitutions and courts, it is also important to understand systems of law. The two most important of these are common law and civil law, whose contrasting principles are essential to an appreciation of the differences in the political role of judiciaries everywhere outside the Middle East. The third is religious law, the most important example of which is the sharia law found in most Muslim countries, and coexisting with common or civil law in countries with large Muslim populations, such as Nigeria, or in countries with a colonial history, such as Egypt.

Common law

The key feature of **common law** systems is that the decisions made by judges on specific cases form a legal framework which remains distinct from the authority of the state. It is

Common law
Judicial rulings on matters not explicitly treated in legislation, based on precedents created by decisions in specific cases.

Focus 7.2
Judicial independence

If courts are to provide an objective assessment of the constitutionality of laws and the actions of government, then judges need to be independent. In spite of this, Melton and Ginsburg (2014) argue that not much effort was made until recently to insulate them from external interference. At the same time, we must make a distinction between de facto protection and *de jure* protection, because giving judges legal protection does not mean that they will always be completely isolated from the influence of political leaders, the media, or public opinion. At the heart of judicial independence is the question of how judges are recruited and removed: if recruitment was controlled by politicians, the judiciary would simply reinforce partisan authority, providing an integration (rather than a separation) of powers. But is there really any way of protecting judges from political influence?

As judicial independence has moved up the political agenda, so governments have developed multiple possible solutions to judicial selection, ranging from democratic election to co-option by judges already in post (see Figure 7.5). The former is democratic but political, while the latter offers the surest guarantee of independence but can lead to a self-perpetuating elite because it runs the danger that the existing judges will seek out new recruits with an outlook resembling their own. In between these extremes come more conventional methods: appointment by the legislature, by the executive, and by independent panels. Many countries combine these methods, with the government choosing from a pool of candidates prepared by a professional body. Alternatively, and more traditionally, some judges on the senior court can be selected by one method, while others lower down are chosen by a different method.

For most courts charged with judicial review, selection still involves a clear political dimension. For example, the stature of the US Supreme Court combines with the unusual rule of lifetime appointments to make sure that nominations are key decisions in which the judicial experience and legal ability of the nominee may matter less than ideology, partisanship, and a clean personal history. A political dimension is also apparent in selection to constitutional courts. Typically, members are selected by the legislature in a procedure that can involve party horse-trading. For example, 8 out of the 12 members of Spain's Constitutional Court are appointed by the party-dominated parliament.

found mainly in Britain and in countries that were once British colonies, such as Australia, Canada (except Quebec), India, Kenya, Nigeria, Pakistan, and the United States (except Louisiana). Originally based on custom and tradition, such decisions were first published as a way of standardizing legal judgments across the territory of a state. Because judges abided by the principle of *stare decisis* (stand on decided cases), their verdicts created precedents and established a predictable legal framework, contributing thereby to economic exchange and nation-building.

Where common law is judge-made law, **statute law** is passed by the legislature in specific areas but these statutes usually build on case law (the past decisions of courts) and are themselves refined through judicial interpretation. The political significance of common law systems is that judges are an independent source of authority. They form part of the governance, but not the government, of society. In this way, common law systems contribute to political pluralism.

Statute law
Laws enacted by a legislature.

Civil law

Civil law springs from written legal codes rather than cases, the goal being to provide a single framework for the conduct of public affairs, including business contracts. It is found throughout Latin America, in all of continental Europe, in China and Russia, and in most African countries that were once colonies of continental European powers. The original codes date back to Roman times, and have since evolved into distinct codes which are elaborated through laws passed by national legislatures.

In civil law, judges (rather than juries) identify the facts of the case, and often even direct the investigation. They then apply the relevant section of the code to the matter at hand. The political

Civil law
Judicial rulings founded on written legal codes which seek to provide a single overarching framework for the conduct of public affairs.

20 to 32, Chávez supporters were appointed to the 12 new seats, and the rules were modified so that the government could remove judges without the two-thirds majority of the National Assembly required by the constitution. By the time of Chávez's death in office in March 2013, a series of incremental changes had removed almost all judicial checks on the Venezuelan executive.

A second more subtle strategy is to bypass the judicial process. For example, many non-democratic regimes use Declarations of Emergency as a cover to make decisions which are exempt from judicial scrutiny. In effect, a law is passed saying there is no law. Once introduced, such 'temporary' emergencies can drag on for decades. Alternatively, rulers can make use of special courts that do the regime's bidding without much pretence of judicial independence; Egypt's State Security Courts were an example, hearing matters involving 'threats' to 'security' (a concept that was interpreted broadly) until they were closed down in 2008. Military rulers have frequently extended the scope of secret military courts to include civilian troublemakers. Ordinary courts can then continue to deal with non-political cases, offering a thin image of legal integrity to the world.

Lurking behind the claims of constitutions, it is abundantly clear to outside observers (and to many at home) that authoritarian regimes have a poor record on human rights. Comparative data in this area lacks the established record of the indices we have reviewed for democracy and corruption, but the Human Freedom Index offers some useful insights. Maintained by three think tanks from the United States, Canada, and Germany, it defines human freedom as 'the absence of coercive constraint' and uses nearly 80 indicators, including a mixture of economic freedoms and civil liberties such as freedom of movement, religion, association, and expression. On a scale of 0 to 10, with 10 representing the most freedom, it found that the average score for countries assessed in 2015 was 6.93, and that the lowest levels were in the Middle East, North Africa, Eastern Europe, South Asia, and sub-Saharan Africa. The countries with the lowest scores are shown in Figure 7.7.

As the figure suggests, Zimbabwe has a poor record on human freedom, having languished under the government of Robert Mugabe between independence in 1980 and his forced removal from office in 2017. Following a period of growing political conflict and economic decline, a new constitution was adopted in 2013, offering hope that life for Zimbabweans might become more secure. But the governing party ZANU-PF – which won nearly three-quarters of the seats in the Zimbabwean legislature in deeply flawed 2013 elections – dragged its feet in implementing the provisions of the constitution and in amending existing laws restricting freedom of expression and assembly. Under Mugabe, media and academic freedom remained limited, opponents of the regime were routinely harassed, property rights were ignored, the military was used to support the regime, and the courts were manipulated to suit the purposes of the governing regime. For example, they ruled the 2013 elections to be free and fair in spite of clear evidence to the contrary.

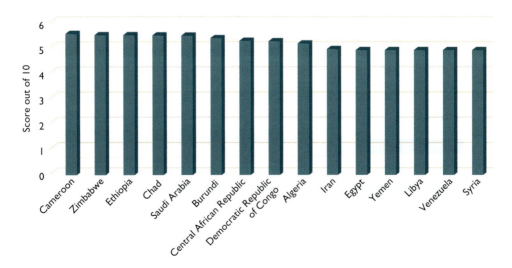

Figure 7.7 Human Freedom Index: the lowest-ranked countries
Source: Vásquez and Porčnik (2017).
Note: Based on data for 2015. For context, the average global score was 6.93, and Switzerland ranked highest with 8.89. Only 159 countries ranked. Those unranked include Afghanistan, Belarus, Cuba, Iraq, North Korea, and Somalia.

Another example of an authoritarian system with a poor human rights record is Iran. To be sure, the country exhibits all the trappings of a constitution supported by a court system. The constitutional document makes noble blueprint-style statements about an Islamic Republic 'endorsed by the people of Iran on the basis of their long-standing belief in the sovereignty of truth and Quranic justice', and about the 'exalted dignity and value of man' and the independence of the judiciary. But Iran has one of the weaker records on human rights in the world. Many activists languish in jail on political charges, Iran has a rate of execution that is probably second only to that of China (there are many capital offences in Iran, include apostasy (abandonment of Islam) and *moharebeh* ('enmity against God')), and women and minorities face discrimination of many kinds. In contrast to Western states, the constitution expresses Islamic more than liberal values and the court system is a channel of, rather than a limitation on, power.

In hybrid regimes, too, constitutions and the law are subsidiary to political authority. Leaders may be elected within a constitutional framework, but that environment has been shaped by previous leaders and the exercise of power is rarely constrained by an independent judiciary. Presidents occupy the highest ground, defining the national interest under the broad authority granted to them by the voters. In other words, presidential accountability is vertical (to the voters) rather than horizontal (to the judiciary). In contrast to a democracy, where the main parties have concluded that being ruled by law is preferable to being ruled by opponents, in a hybrid regime the commanding figure still sees the constitution, the law, and the courts as a source of political advantage. Legal processes operate more extensively than in pure authoritarian regimes but remain subject to political manipulation.

In states with a ruling party, courts are viewed not as a constraint upon political authority but as an aid to the party in its policy goals. China is currently on its fourth and most recent constitution (dating from 1982), and even though it begins by affirming the country's socialist status, and warning against 'sabotage of the socialist system', it is the least radical of the four. Offering an example of the billboard function of an authoritarian constitution, it seeks to establish a more predictable environment for economic development and to limit the communist party's historic emphasis on class conflict, national self-reliance, and revolutionary struggle. The leading role of the party is

The president of the Supreme People's Court of China and nearly 370 other judges take the oath of office at a ceremony in Beijing. In spite of an extensive court system, China remains an authoritarian regime.
Source: Getty Images/China News Service.

now mentioned only in the preamble, with the main text even declaring that 'all political parties must abide by the Constitution'.

In addition to moderating the content of its constitution, today's China also gives greater emphasis to law in general. There were few laws at all in the early decades of the People's Republic, reflecting a national tradition of unregulated power, and leaving the judiciary as, essentially, a branch of the police. However, laws did become more numerous, precise, and significant after the hiatus of the Cultural Revolution (1966–76). In 1979, the country passed its first criminal laws; later revisions abolished the vague crime of 'counter-revolution' and established the right of defendants to seek counsel. Law could prevail to the benefit of economic development. For law-abiding citizens, life became more predictable.

Despite such changes, Chinese politics remains authoritarian. 'Rule by law' still means exerting political control through law, rather than limiting the exercise of power. The courts are regarded as just one bureaucratic agency among others, legal judgments are not tested against the constitution, and many decisions are simply ignored. Rulings are unpublished and difficult cases are often left undecided. In comparison with liberal democracies, legal institutions remain less specialized, and legal personnel less sophisticated. Trial procedures, while improving, still offer only limited protection for the innocent. The death penalty remains in use, the police remain largely unaccountable, political opponents are still imprisoned without trial, and party officials continue to occupy a protected position above the law. Because the party still rules, power continues to trump the constitution and human rights, while Zhang (2012) notes that political and religious rights remain dormant.

It is always important, whether reviewing democracies or authoritarian systems, to distinguish the headline-making developments in government and politics from the underlying trends. Relatively few court decisions make the headlines, and when they do it is mainly because they have some notable effect tied to an issue that attracts public attention; the routine day-to-day work of the courts, and the constitutional principles upon which they are based, meanwhile goes on without much public attention.

This is an argument made by Hendley (2014) in regard to Russia, for example. She points to events that made international headlines – such as the conviction in 2012 of the punk rock group Pussy Riot after holding an anti-Putin event in a Moscow cathedral, or the repeated arrests of opposition politician Alexei Navalny – and notes that these and other cases have created an image of Russian law as 'an instrument used by the state to impose its will on dissenters'. She also argues, though, that they have obscured the role of law in the everyday life of Russians, who – in spite of misgivings about the weakness of judges relative to the executive – use the courts in ever-increasing numbers to resolve their disputes.

Russia during the Soviet era had a large body of law and elected judges. It also experienced several constitutions. But the legal structure was designed to underpin the role of the communist party, which meant that the Russian people had to undergo a crash course in the meaning of the rule of law following the adoption of Russia's post-communist constitution in 1993. This set out an array of individual rights (including that of owning property); proclaimed that 'the individual and his rights and freedoms are the supreme value'; and established a tripartite system of general, commercial, and constitutional courts. The introduction of the Constitutional Court, in particular, represented a major innovation in Russian legal thinking.

Under Boris Yeltsin (in office 1991–99), notes Hendley (2014), the Constitutional Court challenged some of the policies of president, if only indirectly. Under Vladimir Putin, though, the court has become more quiescent, and numerous problems continue to plague the legal system:

◆ The conviction rate in criminal cases remains suspiciously high.
◆ Expertise and pay within the legal system are low, sustaining a culture of corruption.
◆ Violence by the police is common.
◆ Politics overwhelms the law on sensitive cases.
◆ Legal judgments, especially against the state, can be difficult to enforce.
◆ The public still shows little faith in the legal system.

Russia may have made more progress towards achieving the rule of law than has China, but assuming that law in Russia will eventually acquire the status it possesses in liberal democracies still involves drawing a doubtful cheque against the future. Smith (2010) concedes that much progress has been made in establishing 'a workable and independent judiciary and legal system', with new laws enacted and legal reforms undertaken, but notes that 'the enforcement of laws has been uneven and at times politicised, which erodes public support and belief in the courts'. This is a problem that applies to many authoritarian systems.

DISCUSSION QUESTIONS

◆ Which is best: a constitution that is short and ambiguous, leaving room for interpretation, or one that is long and detailed, leaving less room for misunderstanding?
◆ What are the advantages and disadvantages of codified and uncodified constitutions?
◆ What are the advantages and disadvantages of supreme courts and constitutional courts?
◆ Judicial restraint or judicial activism – which is best for the constitutional well-being of a state?
◆ What is the best way of recruiting judges, and what are the most desirable limits on their terms in office, if any?
◆ Can religious and secular law coexist?

KEY CONCEPTS

◆ Abstract review
◆ Appellate
◆ Civil law
◆ Codified constitution
◆ Common law
◆ Concrete review
◆ Constitution
◆ Entrenchment
◆ Flexible constitution
◆ Judicial activism

◆ Judicial restraint
◆ Judicial review
◆ Judiciary
◆ Original jurisdiction
◆ Rigid constitution
◆ Rule of law
◆ Sharia law
◆ Statute law
◆ Uncodified constitution

FURTHER READING

Bobek, Michael (2013) *Comparative Reasoning in European Supreme Courts* (Oxford University Press). A study of how international trends influence judicial decisions in several European countries.

Ginsburg, Tom, and Alberto Simpser (eds) (2014) *Constitutions in Authoritarian Regimes* (Cambridge University Press). An edited collection on the design, content, and consequences of constitutions in authoritarian regimes.

Harding, Andrew, and Peter Leyland (ed.) (2009) *Constitutional Courts: A Comparative Study* (Wildy, Simmonds & Hill). A comparative study of constitutional courts, with cases from Europe, Russia, the Middle East, Latin America, and Asia.

Issacharoff, Samuel (2015) *Fragile Democracies: Contested Power in the Era of Constitutional Courts* (Cambridge University Press). Argues that strong constitutional courts are a powerful antidote to authoritarianism, because they help protect against external threats and the domestic consolidation of power.

Lee, H. P. (2011) *Judiciaries in Comparative Perspective* (Cambridge University Press). An edited collection of studies of judiciaries in Australia, Britain, Canada, New Zealand, South Africa, and the United States.

Rosenfeld, Michel, and András Sajó (eds) *The Oxford Handbook of Comparative Constitutional Law* (Oxford University Press). A comparative collection of studies of history, types, principles, processes, and structures of constitutions.

EXECUTIVES

8

CONTENTS

◆ Executives: an overview
◆ Heads of state and government
◆ Presidential executives
◆ Parliamentary executives
◆ Semi-presidential executives
◆ Executives in authoritarian states

PREVIEW

The focus of this chapter is the most visible tier in any system of government: the top level of leadership. Whether we are talking about presidents, prime ministers, chancellors, dictators, or despots, those who sit at the peak of the pyramid of governmental power typically excite the most public interest, whether opinions are positive or negative. To be sure, executives – in democracies, at least – consist not just of individual leaders but of large networks of people and institutions, including the ministers and secretaries who form the cabinet or the council of ministers. But a single figure usually becomes the best-known face of government, representing its successes and failures and acting as a focus of popular attention.

The chapter begins with a review of the roles of head of state and head of government, which are organized differently from one form of executive to another, with important and contrasting consequences. It then looks in turn at the three major forms of executive: presidential, parliamentary, and semi-presidential. It compares and contrasts their roles and powers, focusing in particular depth on the various sub-types of parliamentary executives and the experience they have had with legislative coalitions. The chapter then looks at executives in authoritarian systems, and at the particular qualities and effects of personal rule. Authoritarian leaders may enjoy more power than their democratic peers, but they also enjoy fewer formal protections on their person or their tenure in office. This inevitably affects the way they approach their positions.

KEY ARGUMENTS

◆ The political executive is responsible for setting priorities, mobilizing support, resolving crises, making decisions, and overseeing their implementation.

◆ Executives must carry out the functions of head of state and head of government, jobs that are combined in some political systems and divided in others.

◆ Although presidential executives come in many different forms, the usual arrangement is one in which power is shared between a presidency and other branches of government.

◆ In parliamentary executives, the government comes out of the legislature, and the power of the executive depends heavily on the balance of party support in the legislature.

◆ Semi-presidential executives combine elements of the presidential and parliamentary formats. They are less common, and less thoroughly studied.

◆ Executives in authoritarian states face fewer constraints than those in liberal democracies, as well as fewer guarantees regarding their tenure.

EXECUTIVES: AN OVERVIEW

The political **executive** is the core of government, consisting as it does of the political leaders who form the top level of the administration: presidents, prime ministers, ministers and cabinets. The executives that interest us here are national leaders, but the term executive also applies to leaders at lower levels, such as the governors of states or provinces, and the mayors of towns and cities. The institutional approach to comparison focuses on the role of the executive as a government's energizing force, setting priorities, mobilizing support, reacting to problems, resolving crises, making decisions, and overseeing their execution. Governing without a legislature or judiciary might be feasible, but ruling without an executive is arguably impossible. In authoritarian systems, the executive is often the only institution that wields true power, but – even so – other theoretical approaches such as structuralism may have more to offer to understanding how authoritarian executives work.

> **Executive**
> The political institution responsible for overseeing the execution of laws and policies, and most often associated with the idea of national leadership.

It is important to distinguish the political executive (which makes policy) from the bureaucracy (which puts policy into effect). Unlike appointed officials, the members of the political executive – in democracies, at least – are chosen by political means, most often by election, and can be removed by the same method. The executive is accountable for the activities of government; it is where the buck stops. The bureaucracy, meanwhile, consists mainly of career employees without direct accountability; secretaries and ministers at the top of the bureaucratic structure are typically political appointees, who serve at the pleasure of the government, but the vast majority of bureaucrats are unelected, as we will see in Chapter 10. At the same time, they are very much part of the work of the executive.

In democracies, understanding the executive begins with the study of institutional arrangements. Democracies have succeeded in the delicate and difficult task of subjecting executive power to constitutional constraint. The government is not only elected, but remains subject to rules which limit its power; it must also face regular re-election. In authoritarian regimes, by contrast, constitutional and electoral controls are either absent or ineffective. The scope of the executive is limited not so much by the constitution as by political realities, and the executive tends to be more fluid, patterned by informal relationships rather than formal rules.

Executives come in three main types: presidential (with two sub-categories: limited and unlimited), parliamentary, and semi-presidential. In all three types, power is diffused, and they can each be understood as contrasting methods for dividing and controlling executive authority. In presidential and semi-presidential regimes, the constitution sets up a system of checks and balances between distinct executive, legislative, and judicial institutions. In parliamentary systems, the government is constrained in different ways, its survival depending on retaining the confidence of the legislature. Typically, its freedom of action is limited by the need to sustain a coalition between parties that have agreed to share the task of governing.

Having said all this, though, there is no fixed and unchangeable template for any of these types. They change over time, and vary within and between different countries, according to the constitutional rules, the leadership style of office-holders, and the constantly changing balance between the executive and the legislature. Some states fit firmly within one of these types, while others have features that are a blend of types, even slowly moving from one to another as the powers of offices change.

> **Head of state**
> The figurehead leader of a state, who may be elected or appointed, or – in the case of monarchs – may inherit the position.

HEADS OF STATE AND GOVERNMENT

Before looking in turn at the different kinds of executive, it is important to distinguish between two distinct roles carried out by executives:

> **Head of government**
> The elected leader of a government, who comes to office because of the support of voters who identify with their party and platform.

◆ The **head of state** is a figurehead who acts as a representative of the state and all its citizens. The head of state is expected to rise above politics and to work in the general interests of all the citizens of a state, although the lines between the ceremonial leader and the politician are sometimes unclear, particularly in presidential systems, where one person is both head of state and head of government. Much of what the head of state does is symbolic: for example, hosting visiting leaders, engaging in foreign state visits, and providing leadership in times of war or national crisis.

◆ The **head of government** is the political leader of a government. In this capacity, the executive is either elected or is appointed by elected politicians, or – in authoritarian states – comes to power through other less transparent means. Heads of government usually make little effort to hide their partisan preferences, and they are more interested in retaining the

SPOTLIGHT BRAZIL

Brief profile

The recent rise of Brazil exemplifies the phenomenon of the emerging economy, placing it among the BRICs with Russia, India, and China. As the world's fifth biggest country by land and population, Brazil is also one of the world's largest democracies. It is the most important state in South America and has expanded its influence to the developing world more broadly. However, Brazil still faces many domestic problems. There is a wide gap between rich and poor, much of the arable land is owned by a few wealthy families, social conditions in its major cities are poor, the deforestation of the Amazon basin has global ecological implications, and corruption is rife at all levels of government. Recent economic developments have sent mixed signals, with oil discoveries pointing to energy self-sufficiency, but an economic downturn and a return to politics as usual casts clouds over Brazil's continued progress.

Form of government	Federal presidential republic consisting of 26 states and a federal capital district. State formed 1822, and most recent constitution adopted 1988.
Executive	Presidential. A president directly elected for no more than two consecutive four-year terms.
Legislature	Bicameral National Congress: lower Chamber of Deputies (513 members) elected for renewable four-year terms, and upper Senate (81 members) elected from the states (three members each) for renewable eight-year terms.
Judiciary	A dual system of state and federal courts, with justices of superior courts nominated for life by the president and confirmed by the Senate. Supreme Federal Court serves as constitutional court: 11 members, nominated by president and confirmed by Senate for life, but must retire at 70.
Electoral system	A two-round majority system is used for elections to the presidency and the Senate, while elections to the Chamber of Deputies use proportional representation.
Parties	Multi-party, with more than a dozen parties organized within Congress into four main coalitions and a cluster of non-attached parties.

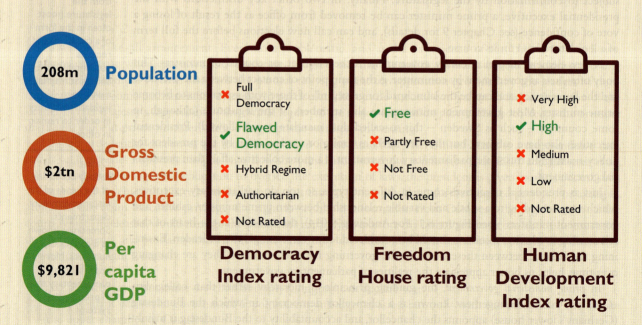

208m Population

$2tn Gross Domestic Product

$9,821 Per capita GDP

Democracy Index rating
- ✗ Full Democracy
- ✓ Flawed Democracy
- ✗ Hybrid Regime
- ✗ Authoritarian
- ✗ Not Rated

Freedom House rating
- ✓ Free
- ✗ Partly Free
- ✗ Not Free
- ✗ Not Rated

Human Development Index rating
- ✗ Very High
- ✓ High
- ✗ Medium
- ✗ Low
- ✗ Not Rated

Jair Bolsonaro campaigning ahead of his victory in the 2018 Brazilian presidential election.
Source: Getty Images/NurPhoto.

The political executive in Brazil

Brazil uses a presidential executive, but gives its leader more constitutional powers than its American equivalent; the president of Brazil can issue decrees in specified areas, declare bills to be urgent (forcing Congress to make a prompt decision), initiate bills in the National Congress, and propose a budget which goes into effect, month by month, if Congress does not itself pass a budget. But Brazilian presidents must work with two features of government that are absent in the United States, and that make it more difficult to bend Congress to their will.

First, thanks to the use of proportional representation, they are faced by a much more complex party landscape. The October 2018 legislative elections resulted in 30 parties winning seats in the Chamber of Deputies, with none winning more than 56 seats, 15 each winning less than ten seats, and the parties forming themselves into several different groupings.

Second, party discipline is exceptionally weak. Deputies often switch party in mid-term, and are more concerned with winning resources for their districts than with showing loyalty to their party. In response, Brazil's presidents are obliged to build informal coalitions by appointing ministers from a range of parties in an attempt to encourage their loyalty. The result, argue Melo and Pereira (2013), has been a form of multi-party presidentialism combining a constitutionally strong president and a robust system of checks and balances emerging from healthy political competition.

The coalitions formed in Brazilian politics are more informal, pragmatic, and unstable than the carefully crafted inter-party coalitions which characterize parliamentary government in Europe. In presidential systems, after all, the collapse of a coalition does not mean the fall of a government, reducing the incentive to sustain a coalition. So, although Latin American constitutions appear to give the chief executive a more important political role, appearances are deceptive. The Latin American experience confirms that presidents operating in a democratic setting confront inherent difficulties in securing their programme.

Further reading

Melo, Marcus André, and Carlos Pereira (2013) *Making Brazil Work: Checking the President in a Multiparty System* (Red Globe Press).

Reid, Michael (2014) *Brazil: The Troubled Rise of a Global Power* (Yale University Press).

Roett, Riordan (2016) *Brazil: What Everyone Needs to Know* (Oxford University Press).

Table 8.3 The parliamentary executive

◆ Prime minister (or chancellor, premier) is normally head of the governing party of coalition.
◆ Governments emerge from the legislature and the prime minister can be dismissed from office by losing a legislative majority or a vote of confidence.
◆ Executives can serve an unlimited number of terms in office.
◆ The executive is collegial, taking the form of a cabinet (or council of ministers) in which the prime minister is traditionally first among equals.
◆ Prime minister is head of government, working with a separate ceremonial head of state.
◆ Examples: most of Europe and Caribbean, Australia, Canada, India, Iraq, Japan, New Zealand, Pakistan.

through the chancellor's office (Langenbacher and Conradt, 2017). The chancellor answers to parliament, while ministers answer to the chancellor. The strong position of Germany's chief executive derives from the Basic Law (the German constitution) which says that the 'chancellor shall determine, and be responsible for, the general policy guidelines'. Elsewhere, there have been concerns that the office of prime minister has become 'presidentialized' in the sense that prime ministers have become more powerful and more prominent. This is thanks in part to greater media exposure (more prime ministers have communications offices designed to ensure greater public coverage of their policies), the growing international role of the chief executive, and the emerging need for policy coordination as governance becomes more complex (Poguntke and Webb, 2004).

For advocates of the parliamentary system, *cabinet government* has the advantage of encouraging more deliberation and collective leadership than occurs in a presidential system. The system works best in smaller countries; in many larger countries, the number and complexity of decisions means they cannot all be settled around the cabinet table. Finland provides a clear case of cabinet government at work: by law, the Finnish State Council (the cabinet) has extensive decision-making authority, prime ministers are mainly chairs of Council meetings, and it is at these meetings that decisions are reached and compromises made. Meanwhile, both the prime minister and individual ministers are constrained by Finland's complex multi-party coalitions.

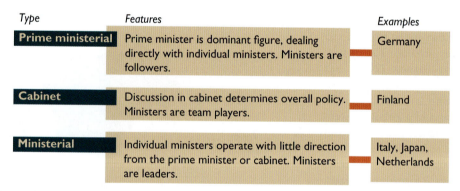

Type	Features	Examples
Prime ministerial	Prime minister is dominant figure, dealing directly with individual ministers. Ministers are followers.	Germany
Cabinet	Discussion in cabinet determines overall policy. Ministers are team players.	Finland
Ministerial	Individual ministers operate with little direction from the prime minister or cabinet. Ministers are leaders.	Italy, Japan, Netherlands

Figure 8.1 Types of parliamentary government
Note: None of these features is institutionalized or constitutionalized. Instead, each is a matter of politics and tradition.

In *ministerial government*, ministers operate without extensive direction from either prime minister or cabinet (except in coalitions, where they routinely find themselves constrained by the pressures of the coalition agreement (Moury, 2013)). This decentralized pattern can emerge either from respect for expertise, or from the realities of a coalition. Looking again at Germany, the chancellor sets the overall guidelines but the constitution goes on to say that 'each Federal Minister shall conduct the affairs of his department autonomously and on his own responsibility'. Ministers are appointed for their knowledge of the field and are expected to use their professional experience to shape their ministry's policy under the chancellor's guidance. So, Germany mixes two models, operating ministerial government within the framework of chancellor democracy.

In many coalition governments (see Focus 8.2), parties appoint their own leading figures to head particular ministries, again giving rise to ministerial government. In the Netherlands, for example, the prime minister does not appoint, dismiss, or reshuffle ministers. Cabinet members serve with, but not under, the government's formal leader. In these conditions, the prime minister's status is diminished, with ministers owing more loyalty to their party than

Focus 8.2
Executives and party numbers

One of the core distinguishing features of parliamentary systems, in contrast to presidential systems, is that the power of the executive depends upon the party balance in the legislature following elections. There are several different potential outcomes:

Majority government. In this case, one party wins a clear majority over all the others, and the leader of that party normally becomes the prime minister with a strong mandate to govern. Prime ministers must still work with a cabinet, whose support is essential, and governing effectively is also reliant on the prime minister exerting tight discipline over members of the party in the legislature. Assuming these two conditions, prime ministers are in a strong position.

Britain has traditionally been the classic example of parliamentary government based on a single ruling party with a secure majority. The plurality (or winner-take-all) method of election (see Chapter 15) usually delivers a working majority in the House of Commons to a single party, allowing the prime minister to appoint a cabinet made up of parliamentary colleagues from the same party. Because the governing party spans the cabinet and the legislature, domination of the parliamentary agenda is usually ensured.

Coalition government. In this case no one party wins a clear majority, obliging two or more parties – usually with adjacent positions on the ideological spectrum – to govern in tandem. The success of this arrangement depends on the extent to which the coalition partners reach a deal suitable to both, and the number of parties involved. Majority coalitions (where two parties control a majority of seats) are the most stable, coalitions involving more and occasionally smaller partners will have less stability, and minority coalitions in which the partner parties lack a majority are potentially the least stable.

> **Coalition government**
> An arrangement in which the government is formed through an agreement involving two or more parties which divide government posts between them.

In some cases, coalitions are promised or arranged before an election is held, helping voters to make a more informed judgement about the likely consequences of their voting choices. Most often, though, coalitions are worked out after an election, with the outgoing government remaining in place as a caretaker while negotiations are under way. Agreements can be reached in a matter of days, but the more complex negotiations take longer: it took a record 541 days (18 months) for a new Belgian government to be formed in 2010–11 because of deep divisions in the Chamber of Representatives, where 11 parties won seats.

Coalition governments are the norm in most of continental Europe, but their records vary. Denmark has not had a majority government since 1909, and has mainly managed well on minority coalitions since the 1980s. In Germany, grand coalitions involving the two major parties (the Christian Democrats and the Social Democrats) are not unusual. In Italy, meanwhile, it is a different story: see Chapter 9.

Minority government. In some cases, no party wins a majority after an election, and agreement among them is hard to reach, leaving one party to govern as a minority or two as a minority coalition. The latter happened, for example, in Sweden in 2014, when the Social Democrats and the Greens (having won 38 per cent of the vote in the general election, and 39 per cent of the seats in the Riksdag) formed one of the weakest minority coalitions ever seen in a country where coalition government is quite usual. It could only govern effectively so long as it had the informal support of other parties in the Riksdag.

to either the prime minister or the cabinet. The chief executive is less a chief or an executive than a skilled conciliator. In India's multi-party coalitions, too, open defiance of the prime minister is far from unknown (Mitra, 2017: Chapter 4).

Moreover, in Japan, ministers must often operate without strong guidance from the prime minister. The prime minister is more like the keeper of the helm than captain of the ship and few office-holders leave a lasting personal stamp on government (see Shinoda, 2011). Turnover has been rapid: while France had five presidents and Britain had

Table 8.5 Comparing executives

Characteristic	Presidential	Parliamentary	Semi-presidential
Method of election?	Direct, whole country	Indirect via legislature	President: direct, whole country. Prime minister: indirect
Separate head of state?	No	Yes	No
Does executive serve in legislature?	No	Yes	Prime minister only, not president
Separation of powers?	Yes	No	To some extent
Fixed terms in office?	Yes, except with unlimited presidencies	No	President only
Means for dismissal from office?	End of term, loss of presidential election, impeachment, resignation	Loss of legislative election, loss of vote of confidence, loss of party leadership, resignation	President: end of term, loss of presidential election, impeachment, resignation
Role of cabinet?	More marginal and individualistic	More central and collective	More marginal and individualistic
Can executive work with legislature controlled by another party?	Yes, but weakened, except with unlimited presidencies	Only in case of minority government	Yes, but weakened

EXECUTIVES IN AUTHORITARIAN STATES

Constitutional rules and political realities help define what a democratic executive can or cannot do. By contrast, understanding executives in authoritarian states is more about the latter; there are constitutions and rules, to be sure, but there is less constraint on their capacity to execute policy, and there are fewer formal protections on the office-holder. As Svolik (2012) points out, dictators lack the support of independent political authorities that would help them enforce agreements, as well as the rules that govern the work of formal government institutions. As a result, they might be inclined to use more extreme methods to win and wield power, but they also often face greater personal risks than their democratic counterparts. They can use the military to repress, for example, but once the military becomes essential to the survival of a regime, it acquires leverage that it can use against the regime (Svolik, 2012).

The most common form of executive in hybrid and authoritarian regimes is presidential, but this is a quite different kind of presidency than the limited form found in democracies. What we find instead is an **unlimited presidential executive**, although the adjective *unlimited* should not be taken too literally: there are always functional limits on the powers of anyone in government, and the powers of authoritarian leaders are often less a reflection of the terms of the constitution than of the capacity of office-holders to manipulate the political system to their own advantage.

Unlimited presidential executive
A presidential executive whose powers face few constitutional or political limits.

Dictatorship
A political system in which a leader or ruling elite uses a combination of repression and loyalty to remain in power.

The term *unlimited* instead means that presidents in such systems lack most of the constitutional and/or political limits of their democratic counterparts, including – in many cases – term limits, or the need to run in competitive elections; see Table 8.6. Even where term limits exist, a dominant political party might be able to make sure that opposition candidates are unable to win office, and sometimes dictators will change the rules so as to give themselves unlimited terms in office. They go through the motions of running for re-election, but are able to manipulate the process – repressing their opponents and encouraging loyalty among their supporters (Wintrobe, 2007) – in order to ensure themselves an unending string of victories. By this means, a dictator creates a **dictatorship** (see Ezrow and Frantz, 2011).

Presidential government in authoritarian settings provides a natural platform for leaders who seek to set themselves apart from – and above – all others. In such systems, the president operates without the same constitutional restraints faced by the chief executive of a liberal democracy.

Table 8.6 The unlimited presidential executive

- Most significant power focused in the office of the president, the office-holder often being more important than the office.
- Presidents usually face elections, but the outcome is assured by vote rigging, threats, and the marginalization of any opponents.
- Presidents face few political limits on their terms in office; absolute monarchs face none.
- All other government institutions are subservient to the executive, who typically uses patronage to keep them malleable.
- President serves as head of state and de facto head of government.
- Examples: China, Cuba, Egypt, Venezuela.

Instead, presidents use what they define as their direct mandate from the people to cast a shadow over competing institutions such as the courts and the legislature. While they do not usually go so far as to reduce these bodies to completely token status (they particularly need the courts and the bureaucracy to keep things running), they work to concentrate power on themselves and their supporters rather than to distribute it among institutions. It is this lack of institutionalization that is the central feature of the authoritarian executive, and what we find in its place is the tradition of personal rule discussed in Chapter 6. The institutional approach to understanding government in such systems has limitations; structuralism, with its interest in relationships among the parts of a political system, probably has more to offer.

In some instances, authoritarian leaders successfully groom family members to succeed them: examples include the al-Assads in Syria, the Kims in North Korea, Omar Bongo and his son Ali Bongo Ondimba in Gabon, and Laurent Kabila and his son Joseph in the Democratic Republic of Congo. In many absolute monarchies, succession is assured by heredity. Otherwise, the lack of a succession procedure can create a conflict among potential successors not only after the leader's exit, but also in the run-up to it. Authoritarian leaders keep their job for as long as they can ward off their rivals, which means that they must monitor threats and be prepared to neuter those who are becoming too strong. Politics, as a result, comes before policy.

The price of defeat, furthermore, is high; politics in authoritarian systems can be a matter of life and death. When the leaders of Western democracies leave office, they can often give well-paid lectures, write and sell their memoirs for large sums, be appointed to well-paid consultancies, or set up foundations to do good works. Ousted dictators risk a harsher fate, assuming they even live long enough to have a 'retirement'. The lucky ones might live in wealthy exile, while others languish in prison, and yet others are executed on the street. It is hardly surprising, then, that the governing style of authoritarian rulers inclines to the ruthless.

At the same time, personal rule is sometimes far from absolute, because many dictators find themselves constrained by other political actors, including the military, leaders of ethnic groups, landowners, the business class, the bureaucracy, multinational companies, and even factions in the leader's own court. To survive, leaders must distribute the perks of office so as to maintain a viable coalition of support, which is why personal rule is closely tied to corruption, and the gallery of the world's most corrupt leaders includes many who have held presidential office in authoritarian regimes; examples include Ferdinand Marcos of the Philippines (1972–86), Mobutu Sese Seko of Zaire (now Democratic Republic of the Congo) (1965–97), Suharto of Indonesia (1967–98), Zine Al-Abidine Ben Ali of Tunisia (1987–2011), and Teodoro Obiang Nguema Mbasogo of Equatorial Guinea (1979–present).

In the Middle East, the absolute monarchs discussed in Chapter 6 continue to rule oil-rich kingdoms in traditional patriarchal style, which emphasizes *ruling* over *governing*. In Saudi Arabia, for example, advancement within the ruling family depends less on merit than on proximity to the family's network of advisers, friends, and guards. Public and private are interwoven, each forming part of the ruler's sphere. Government posts are occupied on the basis of good behaviour, as demonstrated by unswerving loyalty to the ruler's personal interests. Change is in the wind, however, as an aged leadership cedes power to a new generation, the number of young people entering the job market is expanding, and expectations for political participation and transparency in governance are growing (Haykel *et al.*, 2015).

Systems of personal rule have survived for centuries in the Middle East, limiting the development of strong institutions. The Arab Spring revealed their weaknesses, however, as frustrated populations in several Arab states protested against the absence of opportunity in corrupt, conservative regimes headed by staid autocrats. But the challenges of switching from autocracy to democracy are not easy to meet, as reflected in the example of Egypt. There, President Hosni Mubarak was ousted from office in 2011 in the wake of demonstrations against his 30-year regime, and in 2012 the country's first-ever truly competitive elections resulted in the victory of Mohamed Morsi.

President Obiang Nguema of Equatorial Guinea (centre) during a visit to China. One of the most enduring leaders in the world, he claims to have never won an election with less than a 90 per cent share of the vote.
Source: Getty Images/Pool.

However, because Morsi came from the Islamist Muslim Brotherhood, nervousness grew abroad, particularly in the United States. When Morsi started showing signs of authoritarianism, he was removed in a July 2013 military coup led by military chief General Abdel Fattah el-Sisi. The general then reinvented himself as a civilian, turning in his military uniform for a two-piece suit, won elections held in May 2014, and quickly showed an unwillingness to tolerate opposition. After a brief and hopeful flirtation with democracy, Egypt was soon back to its old ways. This was not what most Egyptians wanted, and opposition to the el-Sisi regime began to grow. But Egypt's other political institutions were too weak to resist a return to personal rule, and el-Sisi was returned to office for a second term after March 2018 elections that were widely condemned as fraudulent.

Although it is easy to identify most autocrats, and most would probably lose office fairly quickly if they ran in truly open and competitive elections, a few have done a convincing job of persuading most of their citizens that they are the right person to confront their country's challenges. Few have been as successful in this regard as Vladimir Putin, who inherited the presidency of Russia in 1999, and whose regime has spent the years since, moving it away from democracy while retaining the support of the vast majority of Russians (see Ambrosio, 2016).

Formally, Russia is a semi-presidential system arranged along French lines, with a directly elected president coexisting with a prime minister who is nominated by the president and approved by the Duma (the lower chamber of the legislature). In some respects, the Russian president's position is only slightly stronger than that of a US president:

◆ Both are limited to two terms in office, but the Russian leader can stand again after a term out.
◆ Both are subject to impeachment, but the US requires only a majority of members in favour in the House of Representatives, while Russia requires a two-thirds majority in both parliamentary chambers plus confirmation by the courts.
◆ Theoretically, the Russian president could end up with a hostile opposition in the Duma, making him or her even weaker than the US president.

In reality, Russian presidents have a wide array of impressive powers: they are the head of state, the commander-in-chief, and the guarantor of the constitution. They can suspend the decisions of other state bodies, issue decrees, and remove ministers without the consent of the Duma. They are also charged – according to the constitution – with 'defining the basic directions of the domestic and foreign policy of the state', and with 'ensuring the coordinated functioning and collaboration of bodies of state power'. These powers affirm Russia's long tradition of executive power, a norm which both pre-dates and was reinforced by the communist era; strong government is regarded as a necessary source of effective leadership for a large and sometimes lawless country.

Putin has gone further by eliminating meaningful opposition and working within the constitution to maintain control. He had no choice but to step down as president upon the completion of his two terms in 2008, but he continued to hold on to power through the cynical means of becoming prime minister to the weak new president, Dmitry Medvedev, who was little more than a placeholder awaiting Putin's successful return in 2012. By then, the term of the president increased from four years to six, so Putin was able to further strengthen his grip before sailing to an easy and predictable victory in the 2018 presidential election. He ensured that he faced no serious competition, scooped up nearly 77 per cent of the vote, and now has another six-year term.

Not all executive systems fit neatly into the three categories of presidential, parliamentary, and semi-presidential, as we find in the cases of the five remaining communist regimes: China, Cuba, Laos, North Korea, and Vietnam. These are distinctive for the way in which executive, legislative, and judicial powers are intertwined with a one-party system, such that leadership goes beyond simply holding executive powers. China has – at least until recently – combined some of the formal features of a semi-presidential system with political dominance by the Chinese Communist Party (CCP). In understanding this system, two points are key:

◆ In spite of China's intricate governmental structure (which includes a cabinet, a legislature, and a network of supporting agencies), these bodies do little more than legitimize the decisions already taken by the party leadership (Saich, 2015: Chapter 4).
◆ Identifying who holds power is less a question of formal titles and offices than of understanding links across institutions, personal networks, and the standing of key figures in the system. For example, Deng Xiaoping was 'paramount leader' of China from 1978 until his death in 1997, yet the most senior posts he ever held were those of party vice chairman and chairman of the party's Military Commission. By 1993, the only position of any kind that he held was the presidency of China's bridge association.

As China emerged out of isolation in the 1990s, changes to the rules seemed to be headed towards producing an executive that looked in form more like some of its democratic counterparts. At the apex is the president, who is nominated by the leadership of the Chinese legislature, the National People's Congress (NPC), and then elected (or confirmed) by the NPC for a maximum of two five-year terms. The presidency was, at first, mainly a ceremonial head of state, but it had many conventional executive powers, such as the ability to appoint (with NPC approval) all members of the State Council (the functional equivalent of a cabinet). The office-holder was also conventionally head of the CCP and of the Central Military Commission, posts that provided enormous political power, and the president also had to work with a premier, the de facto head of government, and a senior member of the party nominated by the president and confirmed by the NPC.

Matters changed after 2013, when Xi Jinping became president and exerted more control over China, cracking down on dissent and corruption, supporting internet censorship, and advocating a more assertive foreign policy for China. In March 2018 he solidified his control by arranging for the CCP to abandon a clause in the constitution limiting the president to two five-year terms. The old days of the paramount leader are apparently back.

Military leaders are perhaps the ultimate form of the authoritarian executive, combining as they do control over civilian and military institutions. They are currently much more uncommon then they once were, but even if fully-fledged military leaders are unusual, there are still many civilian leaders who rely for office on keeping the military happy. If great power in democracies comes with great responsibilities, then power in dictatorships comes with great risks. If executives in democratic states must always worry about their standing in the opinion polls, their capacity to work with legislatures, and threats to their leadership from others seeking power, authoritarian leaders face threats that are both closer to home (from within the ruling elite) and more unpredictable and violent.

The story of Nigeria's leaders is illustrative. Since independence in 1960, it has had 15 leaders: six civilian presidents (although two of these six were former military leaders who came back to office as civilians) and nine military leaders. Of the 15, three were removed from office through military coups in which the leaders were killed, and four were removed from office but survived. All have had to keep a careful eye on critics within the military, who have always been ready to organize opposition and, if necessary, a coup to remove the incumbent.

DISCUSSION QUESTIONS

◆ What are the advantages and disadvantages of dividing the roles of head of state and head of government?
◆ How does the concept of winner-take-all help or hinder political systems with presidential executives?
◆ Which option is most efficient and/or most democratic in a parliamentary system: prime ministerial government or cabinet government?
◆ Have prime ministers become presidential and, if so, why?
◆ Do semi-presidential systems offer a useful compromise, offsetting the advantages and disadvantages of presidential and parliamentary executives?
◆ Are the potentially greater risks and uncertainties experienced by authoritarian leaders enough to discourage them from using extreme methods to govern?

KEY CONCEPTS

◆ Cabinet
◆ Coalition government
◆ Cohabitation
◆ Constitutional monarchy
◆ Dictatorship
◆ Executive
◆ Head of government

◆ Head of state
◆ Limited presidential executive
◆ Parliamentary executive
◆ Presidential executive
◆ Semi-presidential executive
◆ Separation of powers
◆ Unlimited presidential executive

FURTHER READING

Bennister, Mark (2012) *Prime Ministers in Power: Political Leadership in Britain and Australia* (Palgrave Macmillan). A study of the office of prime minister, comparing two of its leading examples.

Elgie, Robert (2011) *Semi-Presidentialism: Sub-Types and Democratic Performance* (Oxford University Press). Examines how different forms of semi-presidentialism affect the quality and durability of democracy.

Ezrow, Natasha M., and Erica Frantz (2011) *Dictatorships: Understanding Authoritarian Regimes and Their Leaders* (Continuum). An assessment of the types, causes, methods, and effects of authoritarian leadership.

Krasno, Jean, and Sean LaPides (eds) (2015) *Personality, Political Leadership, and Decision Making: A Global Perspective* (Praeger). A study of a selection of individual leaders – democratic and authoritarian – that provides helpful insight into the traits and actions of the people who lead countries.

Mezey, Michael L. (2013) *Presidentialism: Power in Comparative Perspective* (Lynne Rienner). A comparative survey of presidential executives, looking at their history, their relative powers, and their changing character.

Rhodes, R. A. W., and Paul 't Hart (eds) (2014) *The Oxford Handbook of Political Leadership* (Oxford University Press). A general survey of political leadership, including chapters on different kinds of executives.

LEGISLATURES

9

CONTENTS

- Legislatures: an overview
- The role of legislatures
- One chamber or two?
- Representatives and their work
- Legislatures in authoritarian states

PREVIEW

Legislatures lie at the foundation of democratic politics, the words used to name them reflecting their original purpose: assemblies gather, congresses congregate, diets meet, dumas deliberate, legislatures pass laws, and parliaments talk. Even if they do not always attract as much public attention as executives, they are the institutions of government that are closest to the citizens, since they are typically directly elected and are usually responsible for representing individual districts, rather than – as is the case with executives – the entire country. They also carry out multiple tasks that are essential to government, including the approval of legislation, the authorization of expenditure, the making of governments, deliberating over matters of public importance, and oversight of the executive.

This chapter begins with a review of these multiple roles, opinion on the dynamics of which is often divided. The chapter goes on to look at the structure of legislatures, including the differences between those with one chamber and those with two chambers. It then considers the members of legislatures, including the diversity of roles that they can and might play. It then discusses the problem of declining public trust in legislatures, made worse by the phenomenon of the career politician, and encouraging more voters to think about the pros and cons of imposing term limits on legislators. Finally, it looks at the role of legislatures in authoritarian states, pointing out that while they may appear weak, they have a number of uses for leaders and ruling elites.

KEY ARGUMENTS

- Legislatures are usually thought of as the focus of popular representation and law-making, but these are not their only functions.
- The extent to which legislatures are involved in making law depends on their relationship with executives and the balance of political parties.
- For most countries, a single-chamber legislature is enough. For others, a second chamber offers important benefits to the quality of representation.
- Not all representatives are equal, and several models have been developed – including the delegate, the trustee, and the partisan – to explain their work.
- Legislatures are often accused of being homes to career politicians, who collectively constitute a political class with a background and interests removed from the people it represents.
- Legislatures are found in most authoritarian regimes, where co-option lies at the heart of understanding their political role.

Brief profile

One of the world's oldest states, and birthplace of the parliamentary system, the United Kingdom of Great Britain and Northern Ireland and its four constituent parts (England, Scotland, Wales, and Northern Ireland) has undergone many changes since 1945 that have left troubling questions hanging over its future. The creation and now the decay of a welfare state, the end of empire, and the country's declining economic and military weight have forced a redefinition of the role of government, and of Britain's place in the world. A failed independence referendum in Scotland in 2014 has not ended the debate over the future of the union, and the shock decision by voters in a 2016 referendum to leave the European Union raised even more questions as the Conservative government of Theresa May struggled during 2017–18 to decide the best terms of the exit against a background of deep divisions in public opinion.

Form of government	Unitary parliamentary constitutional monarchy. Date of state formation arguably 1066; no codified constitution.
Executive	Parliamentary. The head of government is the prime minister, who is head of the largest party or coalition, and governs in conjunction with a cabinet. The head of state is the monarch.
Legislature	Bicameral Parliament: lower House of Commons (650 members) elected for renewable five-year terms, and upper House of Lords (about 790 members) consisting of a mix of hereditary and life peers, and senior members of the Church of England.
Judiciary	Based on the common law tradition. The creation in 2009 of a 12-member Supreme Court, albeit without the authority to veto legislation, strengthened the autonomy of the judiciary. Judges appointed for life, with mandatory retirement at 70 or 75, depending on date of appointment.
Electoral system	The House of Commons is elected using single-member plurality. A range of systems is used for elections to other bodies such as regional assemblies in Scotland, Wales, and Northern Ireland.
Parties	Multi-party, although traditionally dominated by Conservatives on the right and Labour on the left. Smaller parties and regional parties also significant.

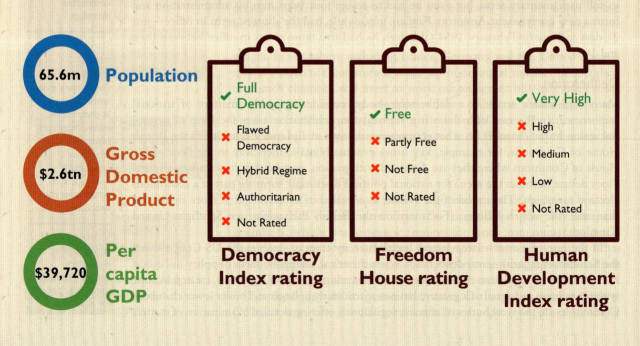

65.6m Population

$2.6tn Gross Domestic Product

$39,720 Per capita GDP

Democracy Index rating
- ✔ Full Democracy
- ✘ Flawed Democracy
- ✘ Hybrid Regime
- ✘ Authoritarian
- ✘ Not Rated

Freedom House rating
- ✔ Free
- ✘ Partly Free
- ✘ Not Free
- ✘ Not Rated

Human Development Index rating
- ✔ Very High
- ✘ High
- ✘ Medium
- ✘ Low
- ✘ Not Rated

The British Parliament

The British Parliament on the banks of the Thames in London. The parliamentary system was born in Britain, as a result of which most comparative studies of parliaments refer back to British precedent.
Source: Getty Images/Victor Cardoner.

The British Parliament is often known as the Mother of Parliaments, being the model upon which legislatures in parliamentary systems are based. Traditionally, it mixed omnipotence and impotence in a seemingly impossible combination; it was considered omnipotent because parliamentary sovereignty, allied to an uncodified constitution, meant there was no higher authority in the land, but it was considered impotent because the governing party exercised tight control over its Members of Parliament (MPs), turning Parliament into an instrument, rather than a wielder, of power.

Parliament's position is today less certain. It has lost powers to the regions thanks to the work of the Northern Irish, Scottish, and Welsh parliaments, and its loss of powers to the European Parliament was one of the complaints lodged by pro-Brexit campaigners in favour of the UK leaving the EU. Ironically, in the debate over Brexit, Parliament found itself in a fight with the administration of Theresa May that resulted in a greater assertion of parliamentary power.

MPs themselves have become more committed, they are increasingly drawn from professional and business backgrounds, they devote more time to an increasing amount of constituency casework, and the number of late sittings has been cut. The long-held view that Parliament was out of touch and old-fashioned has changed in recent years and it has become more assertive and effective, and more of a constraint on the government (Russell, 2016). At the same time, it has suffered from the same declining trust in government as many other legislatures, a problem pre-dating the current rise of anti-politics (Clarke et al., 2018).

The upper House of Lords occupies an uncertain position. Its nearly 800 members consist mainly of appointed life peers, but reform (if and when it is finally agreed) is likely to involve a substantial measure of election. Such a development may well make the Lords more assertive in challenging the executive. Yet, even as Britain's Parliament updates its skills, it will continue to do what it has always done best: acting as an arena for debating issues of significance to the nation, its government, and its leaders.

NORWAY

SCOTLAND
Edinburgh

NORTHERN
IRELAND

ENGLAND

Belfast

WALES

IRELAND

LONDON

Cardiff

North Atlantic
Ocean

FRANCE

Further reading

Griffiths, Simon, and Robert Leach (2018) *British Politics*, 3rd edn (Red Globe Press).

Heffernan, Richard, Colin Hay, Meg Russell, and Philip Cowley (eds) (2016) *Developments in British Politics 10* (Red Globe Press).

Leston-Bandeira, Cristina, and Louise Thompson (2018) *Exploring Parliament* (Oxford University Press).

Focus 9.1
Legislatures: does size matter?

It makes intuitive sense that the size of a legislature should reflect the size of a country's population. Thus China, the world's most populous country, has a National People's Congress with almost 3,000 members, while the Congress of the South Pacific island state of Micronesia (with a population of just 105,000) contains just 14 representatives.

However, size is a poor measure of strength and representation. Giant assemblies may seem powerful, but their sheer size makes it difficult for them to act cohesively, and they are in constant danger of being taken over by more coherent actors, such as political parties, or even their own committees. Ruling communist parties, as in China, prefer a large legislature precisely because it is easier to control. By contrast, a small chamber – numbering, say, under 100 – offers more opportunities for all deputies to have their say in a collegial environment.

A more telling statistic is the number of representatives per head of population (see Figure 9.4). The Chinese legislature may be large, but once its members are divided up among China's population, it turns out that each delegate represents about 460,000 people. By contrast, the Swedish Riksdag is much smaller, but its 349 members each represent only 28,400 people, leaving Swedes with more intensive representation at the national level than the Chinese.

At first glance, Indians may seem to have the worst level of political representation, with more than 2.3 million people per Member of Parliament. But India is a federal system (see Chapter 11), so Indians are also represented in state and local legislatures. The same point applies to other countries with relatively high numbers of people per representative, such as the United States and Nigeria. Conversely, Britain and Sweden appear to have the most generous levels of representation, but they have weaker units of government beneath the national than is the case with federations.

Institutionalism probably offers the most potentially productive theoretical approach to understanding the links between the overall size, the per capita size, and the representative qualities of legislatures. At the same time, and as the examples quoted here indicate, numbers are not the end of the story. In choosing cases, a researcher would have to be careful to note the context of politics in different countries.

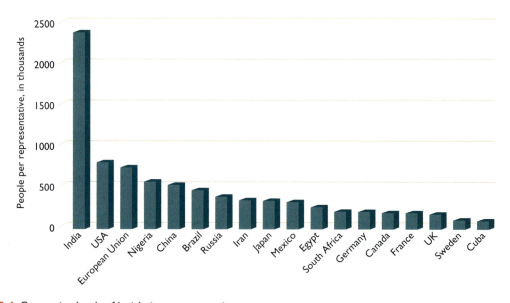

Figure 9.4 Comparing levels of legislative representation

Source: Calculated from data in Inter-Parliamentary Union (2018) (legislature size) and in World Bank (2018) (population). For bicameral legislatures, the size of the lower chamber only is used. Data are for 2016.

The dominance of the lower chamber can also be seen in other ways:

◆ It is usually the larger house, averaging 254 members compared with 95 in the upper house (Inter-Parliamentary Union, 2018).
◆ It often has special responsibility for the budget.
◆ It is the forum where major legislative proposals are introduced.
◆ It is entitled to override vetoes or amendments proffered by the second chamber.

In presidential systems, meanwhile, where presidents are directly elected and their continuation in office does not depend on keeping the confidence of the legislature, there is less need for the executive's accountability to focus on a single chamber. **Strong bicameralism** can emerge in these conditions, especially when combined with federalism (see Chapter 11). The US Congress is the best illustration of this more balanced arrangement. With its constitutional position as representative of the states, the Senate plays a full part in the country's governance.

A second question arises in bicameral legislatures: how to select the upper chamber. There is not much point in having a bicameral legislature unless the two chambers represent public interests differently; if they are the same size, are elected in the same way, and have the same powers, they will simply replicate one another. One means of avoiding this duplication is to select the two chambers in different ways, to which end there are three main options: direct election, indirect election, or appointment – see Figure 9.5.

Strong bicameralism
This occurs when the two chambers are more balanced, as in federations with presidential executives.

The enormous size and short meetings of the Chinese National People's Congress combine to leave it as little more than a rubber-stamp for the policies of the Chinese Communist Party.
Source: Getty Images/Zhang Peng.

authority, some professional support is available, and the Communist Party must anticipate the NPC's reaction to its proposals.

However, the NPC, still the world's largest legislature with members indirectly elected through sub-national governments and the military, remains strongly hierarchical. It meets only once a year for a session lasting about two weeks. Even more than in committee-based legislatures in democracies, the NPC's influence operates through smaller sub-groups. The most important of these is the Standing Committee, a group of about 150 members which meets regularly throughout the year; most also belong to the party, giving the party leadership an additional mechanism of control.

Of course, party domination of legislative proceedings is also found in parliamentary systems in liberal democracies, but there the party in command changes with the election results. Although the NPC and its sub-groups have become part of the Chinese power network, the party's supremacy is such that these bodies still cannot be understood through Western notions of the separation of powers and parliamentary sovereignty.

DISCUSSION QUESTIONS

◆ Which of the six roles carried out by democratic legislatures are (a) the most important, and (b) the most influential?

◆ Could a legislature made up entirely of heterosexual middle-class men of the same religion and ethnicity effectively represent a country? If not, why not?

◆ Other than in federal systems, do bicameral legislatures serve any real purpose?

◆ Which of the five models of representation outlined in this chapter do you find most compelling, either as an explanatory tool or as a guiding principle?

◆ Term limits: Good idea or bad?

◆ Are executives the only institutions that really count in authoritarian systems, or do the five roles associated with legislatures suggest that their roles are more important than we might at first assume?

KEY CONCEPTS

◆ Bicameral
◆ Committee
◆ Committee-based legislature
◆ Co-option
◆ Debating legislature
◆ Legislature
◆ Model of representation

◆ Plenary session
◆ Political class
◆ Strong bicameralism
◆ Term limits
◆ Unicameral
◆ Vote of confidence
◆ Weak bicameralism

FURTHER READING

Arter, David (ed.) (2013) *Comparing and Classifying Legislatures* (Routledge). A survey of the state of knowledge about legislatures, with chapters on European, Latin American, and African cases.

Blomgren, Magnus, and Olivier Rozenberg (eds) (2012) *Parliamentary Roles in Modern Legislatures* (Routledge). An edited collection on the different roles played by members of parliament, using cases in Europe, Australia, and New Zealand.

Fish, M. Stephen, and Matthew Kroenig (2011) *The Handbook of National Legislatures: A Global Survey* (Cambridge University Press). An extensive reference work assessing the powers of national legislatures by their autonomy, capacity, influence, and powers.

Loewenberg, Gerhard (2016) *On Legislatures: The Puzzle of Representation* (Routledge). A review of some of the puzzles and contradictions inherent in the way that legislatures work.

Martin, Shane, Thomas Saalfeld, and Kaare W. Strøm (eds) (2014) *The Oxford Handbook of Legislative Studies* (Oxford University Press). A comprehensive edited collection of essays on legislatures.

Olson, David M., and Gabriella Ilonszki (2012) *Post-Communist Parliaments: Change and Stability in the Second Decade* (Routledge). An edited collection looking at the way in which legislatures in post-communist Europe have improvised their transition to democracy.

BUREAUCRACIES

10

CONTENTS

- Bureaucracies: an overview
- Origins and evolution
- E-government
- How bureaucracies are organized
- How bureaucrats are recruited
- Bureaucracies in authoritarian states

PREVIEW

As the institutions responsible for implementing public policy, bureaucracies are a key part of the structure of government. Bureaucrats are the only employees of the government with whom most of us have much direct contact, whether we are applying for a driving licence or a passport, paying our taxes, or buying property. In spite of this familiarity, bureaucracies are routinely misunderstood, and just as routinely criticized for their failings as praised for their achievements.

Rarely formally studied in the West until Max Weber turned his attention to them in the early twentieth century, the stereotype of bureaucracies is that they are hierarchical, driven by procedure, and unresponsive to customer needs. Yet they are an essential part of government, and in order to understand their dynamics we need to understand how they are structured, the political and professional pressures that come to bear on the work of bureaucrats, and how bureaucracies are changing.

This chapter begins with a review of how bureaucracies evolved, taking the story through the rise of the new public management approach and onto the more recent growth of e-government. It then looks at how bureaucracies are organized in democracies, ranging from government departments down through the divisions within each department to the non-departmental public bodies that are increasingly used to deliver public services. The chapter then looks at how bureaucrats are recruited and kept accountable, and ends with a review of the dynamics of bureaucracies in authoritarian regimes, which show some surprising similarities to those of their democratic peers.

KEY ARGUMENTS

- Weber's traditional model of bureaucracy is the starting point for understanding the modern bureaucracy.
- New public management and outsourcing have changed the way in which bureaucracies work and relate to the public.
- E-government means easier access to government but also raises concerns about surveillance, privacy, and data protection.
- In democracies, the public sector is a complex network encompassing departments, divisions, and regulatory agencies.
- Two key factors determine the quality of public employees: how best to recruit them, and how best to keep them accountable.
- Bureaucracies are among the exceptions to the rule of marginal political institutions in authoritarian regimes. Dictators cannot dictate without officials to give effect to their will.

BUREAUCRACIES: AN OVERVIEW

The study of the **bureaucracy** (also known as the civil service) focuses on the networks of central departments and public agencies that underpin the political executive. These networks have two main functions: they give advice to politicians before policy is made, and they help to implement decisions once reached. The head of department offering advice to the government minister or secretary, the inspector checking tax returns, the engineer trying to work out the cause of a plane crash – all are part of the complex operation that is the public bureaucracy. The notion of bureaucracy can be extended further: the administrative staff of any large organization – such as a university, a political party, or a corporation – can be considered a bureaucracy, and the personality of the organizations of which they are a part gives them many of the same incentives, limitations, and motives as we find in the public bureaucracy.

Traditionally, studies of the bureaucracy focused on the permanent salaried officials employed in government departments. These elite officials, and the departments they occupy, remain of obvious importance, and the term bureaucracy is sometimes confined to them. However, attention increasingly focuses on the wider governance beyond: in semi-independent agencies, local governments, and even the non-governmental organizations and the private corporations to which the delivery of public programmes is increasingly outsourced. We refer here to all public networks as comprising the bureaucracy; others use such terms as *public administration* or *public management* to denote the study of the public sector in this wider sense. Whatever the labels, understanding the modern state, and following a career within it, requires a mental map of what are remarkably complex networks. Structural theory plays a useful role in helping us understand the networks, linkages, and interactions that bind bureaucracies to other parts of government.

In understanding bureaucracies, we need to review how they are internally structured, how their staff are recruited and held accountable, how best to achieve coordination across departments, and how to ensure that services are delivered efficiently in the absence of a normal market. Seeking out the best recruits and then giving employees of public agencies – particularly those at the less skilled and lower paid end of the spectrum – a sense of mission and a desire to serve is not easy. Professionals providing a key public service – such as doctors and nurses in a public health system – will have the highest sense of mission, but the stereotypical view of bureaucrats pushing paper (literally or metaphorically) and tying up services in **red tape** still often holds true.

Bureaucracies have undergone substantial changes in recent decades, however, pressed by efforts to reform the delivery of public services, and caught up in the transition to e-government. Two major themes in understanding the modern bureaucracy (in wealthier democracies at least) are the outsourcing that has led to many services being transferred to private contractors, and the switch to a reliance on the provision of information and services through the internet.

ORIGINS AND EVOLUTION

Ancient kingdoms and empires had some form of bureaucracy, perhaps the most famous being that of China. Based on principles set down by Confucius in the sixth century BCE, China established the first **meritocracy**, with bureaucrats earning their positions through examination and being used by emperors to run the country (a relationship that generally worked well in good times, but collapsed occasionally in bad times, as in the wake of war). In medieval Europe, meanwhile, clerical servants were originally agents of the royal household, serving under the personal direction of the monarch. Many features of modern bureaucracies – regular salaries, pensions, open recruitment – arose from a successful attempt to overcome this idea of public employment as personal service to the monarch.

Karl Marx (1818–83) was one of the first to theorize about the bureaucracy, arguing that its development was a natural counterpart to the development of the private corporation, and that the two were mutually reliant. The first systematic study of the bureaucracy, however, was undertaken by the German sociologist Max Weber (1864–1920), and many of his arguments continue to underpin our understanding of Western bureaucracy. Weber's model was based on the traditional institutional view of public administration as a disciplined hierarchy in which salaried officials

> **Bureaucracy**
> Literally, rule by officials. In the context of comparative politics, describes the people and organizations who form the public administration.

> **Red tape**
> The classic image of bureaucracies tied up in procedure and rules, deriving from the habit in some sixteenth-century European countries of binding administrative documents in red tape.

> **Meritocracy**
> A system in which career advancement and leadership is based on talent, qualifications, and achievement.

DISCUSSION QUESTIONS

◆ What images most immediately come to mind when you think of bureaucrats, and to what extent do you think those images reflect reality?

◆ Outsourcing: good idea or bad? Are there some services that cannot or should not be carried out by private contractors? If so, which ones and why?

◆ To what extent is e-government changing the personality of bureaucracy? Are the changes good or bad?

◆ Should senior bureaucrats be elected? What would be the implications of making such a change?

◆ Should more governments introduce the idea of allowing senior government ministers/ secretaries to have political advisory staff?

◆ What accounts for the looseness of the correlation between bureaucratic efficiency in democracies and authoritarian systems?

KEY TERMS

◆ Administrative capacity
◆ Affirmative action
◆ Bureaucracy
◆ Bureaucratic authoritarianism
◆ Crony capitalism
◆ Department
◆ Departmental recruitment
◆ Developmental state
◆ Division
◆ E-government

◆ Meritocracy
◆ New public management
◆ Non-departmental public body
◆ Ombudsman
◆ Outsourcing
◆ Red tape
◆ Regulatory agency
◆ Spoils system
◆ Unified recruitment

FURTHER READING

Hummel, Ralph P. (2015) *The Bureaucratic Experience: The Post-Modern Challenge*, 5th edn (Routledge). Argues that despite frequent talk of bureaucratic reform, its organizational structure continues to remain mainly unchanged.

Massey, Andrew (ed.) (2011) *International Handbook on Civil Service Systems* (Edward Elgar). A comparative assessment of the structure of bureaucracies, including chapters on Europe, the United States, China, Japan, India, and other countries.

Nixon, Paul G., Vassiliki N. Koutrakou, and Rajash Rawal (eds) (2010) *Understanding E-Government in Europe: Issues and Challenges* (Routledge). The mainly thematic chapters in this book examine the impact of information and communication technology on governance in Europe.

Peters, B. Guy (2018) *The Politics of Bureaucracy: An Introduction to Comparative Public Administration,* 7th edn (Routledge). A widely used comparative introduction to bureaucracy.

Van der Meer, Frits M., Jos C. N. Raadschelders, and Theo A. J. Toonen (eds) (2015) *Comparative Civil Service Systems in the 21st Century*, 2nd edn (Palgrave Macmillan). Includes chapters on bureaucracies in western and eastern Europe, Asia, and Africa.

Van der Wal, Zeger (2017) *The 21st Century Public Manager* (Red Globe Press). Although written for aspiring and current public managers, this is a useful assessment of the world of bureaucracies.

SUB–NATIONAL GOVERNMENTS

11

CONTENTS

PREVIEW

Comparative politics tends to focus mostly on activities at the national level, but it can just as easily compare government and politics at the regional, city, and local levels. The functional equivalents of national executives, legislatures, and courts can all be found at some or all of these levels, particularly in federal systems, meaning that no study of politics and government in a given state can afford to ignore them. Ironically, most voters tend to overlook the work of sub-national government: many of the services that most immediately impact their lives come from regional and local government, and local officials are usually more accessible than their national counterparts, and yet turnout at regional and local elections is much lower than at national elections.

This chapter begins with a review of the concept of multi-level governance, which describes the many horizontal and vertical interactions that often exist among different tiers of government. It then looks at the two most common models for the functioning of systems of national government: unitary and federal. Unitary systems are found in most countries, and work best in those that are both smaller and more homogeneous. Federal systems are rarer, but they are found in most of the world's larger countries, expanding their reach and global significance. The chapter then looks at the structures and functions of local government, touching on the growing importance of urban government, and ending with a review of the dynamics of sub-national government in authoritarian regimes, where traditional rulers sometimes still play a role.

KEY ARGUMENTS

◆ Multi-level governance is a framework for examining the relationships among different levels of administration (supranational, national, regional, and local).

◆ Most countries use a unitary form of government, in which regional and local units are subsidiary to national government.

◆ Other countries are federal, made up of two or more levels of government with independent powers.

◆ Unitary states are just as tiered as federal states, and often more so. The strengthening of regional government is a significant trend within unitary states.

◆ Local government is still the place where the citizen most often meets the state, and yet it is studied much less than it deserves.

◆ Sub-national government in authoritarian states has less formal power and independence than its democratic equivalent, but authoritarian rulers might rely on local leaders to sustain their grip on power.

SPOTLIGHT FRANCE

Brief profile

France is an important European state facing the challenge of adapting its unique traditions to a more competitive world. The country has a reputation for exceptionalism based on the long-term impact of the French Revolution of 1789, which created a distinctive ethos within France. As with other states built on revolution – such as the United States – France can be considered an ideal as well as a country. However, where American ideals led to pluralism, the French state is still expected to take the lead in implementing the revolution's ideals of liberty, equality, and fraternity. As the country became more modern, urban, and industrial after 1945, however, so French uniqueness declined: retreat from empire left France, as Britain, as a middle-ranking power with a new base in the European Union, its society made more complex by immigration from North Africa, and its economy and governing elites challenged by globalization.

Form of government	Unitary semi-presidential republic. Date of state formation debatable, and most recent constitution (the Fifth Republic) adopted 1958.
Executive	Semi-presidential. A president directly elected for no more than two five-year terms, governing with a prime minister who leads a Council of Ministers accountable to the National Assembly. There is no vice-president.
Legislature	Bicameral Parliament: lower National Assembly (577 members) elected for renewable five-year terms, and upper Senate (348 members) indirectly elected through local governments for six-year terms.
Judiciary	French law is based on the Napoleonic Codes (1804–11). The Constitutional Council has grown in significance and has had the power of judicial review since 2008. It has nine members serving single nine-year terms, with three each appointed by the incumbent president, the National Assembly, and the Senate. As many as three former presidents of France may also serve on the Council, although few actually do.
Electoral system	A two-round system is used for both presidential and legislative elections, with a majority vote needed for victory on the first round.
Parties	Multi-party, with the Socialists dominating on the left, backed by Greens, leftists, and radicals, while the Republicans (formerly Union for a Popular Movement) dominate on the right, and a new centrist party (En Marche!, or Forward!) was the base for the victory of President Emmanuel Macron in 2017. The far-right National Rally has also been making gains.

66.9m	Population
$2.6tn	Gross Domestic Product
$38,477	Per capita GDP

Democracy Index rating

- ✗ Full Democracy
- ✓ Flawed Democracy
- ✗ Hybrid Regime
- ✗ Authoritarian
- ✗ Not Rated

Freedom House rating

- ✓ Free
- ✗ Partly Free
- ✗ Not Free
- ✗ Not Rated

Human Development Index rating

- ✓ Very High
- ✗ High
- ✗ Medium
- ✗ Low
- ✗ Not Rated

Unitary government in France

France has seen much reorganization of its sub-national government in recent decades, leaving it with three levels: regions (16), *départements* (96), and *communes* (municipalities) (nearly 37,000). Adding to the complexity of the picture, it also has five overseas regions or counties (including French Guiana and Guadeloupe), and 'intercommunalities', which bring together *départements* and municipalities. Meanwhile, the three largest French cities – Paris, Lyon, and Marseille – are further subdivided into *arrondissements*.

France was once a highly centralized political system, with just two tiers of sub-national government: *départements* and *communes*. The network of *départements* was created by Napoleon early in the nineteenth century, and each is run by its own prefect and elected assembly. Napoleon called prefects 'emperors with small feet' but, in practice, the prefect must cooperate with local and regional councils, rather than simply oversee them. Prefects are now agents of *départements*, representing interests upwards as much as transmitting commands downwards. In 1972, the *départements* were grouped into 22 regions, each with their own elected councils, as well as regional economic and social committees that have an advisory role. (The number of regions was reduced in 2016 to 16.)

Meanwhile, the basic unit of government is the *commune*, governed by a mayor and a council based in the local city hall. *Communes* vary in size from a few dozen people to several tens of thousands, although most have populations of less than 1,500; a recent trend has been for the smallest *communes* to amalgamate with their neighbours. More pressures have been exerted on local government by the efforts of the French government to cut spending in order to control the national budget deficit. In spite of this, every *commune* has the same powers regardless of size.

In France, national politicians often become or remain mayor of their home town. This simultaneous occupancy of posts at different tiers is known in France as the cumul des mandats (accumulation of offices). Even after the rules were tightened in 1985 and 2000, the most popular cumul – combining the office of local mayor with membership of the National Assembly – is still allowed, reflecting the fused character of French public authority even in an era of decentralization.

The distinctive skyline of the French capital of Paris. Along with Lyon and Marseille, Paris has a separate status within the French system of local government.
Source: Getty Images/James Farley.

Further reading

Cole, Alistair (2017) *French Politics and Society*, 3rd edn (Routledge).
Cole, Alistair, Sophie Meunier, and Vincent Tiberj (eds) (2013) *Developments in French Politics 5* (Red Globe Press).
Elgie, Robert, Emiliano Grossman, and Amy G. Mazur (eds) (2016) *The Oxford Handbook of French Politics* (Oxford University Press).

Map 11.2 The regions of Belgium

this never happens, and the relationship changes with both time and place. It was usual in most federations during the twentieth century for national governments to steadily gain power, helped by the emergence of national economies and the flow of wealth to the centre as tax revenues grew with the expansion of economies and workforces. Since the 1980s, however, the trends have become less clear-cut, leading to different ideas about the relative powers of central and regional governments.

Where **dual federalism** provided the original inspiration for the United States, Europe (and especially Germany and Austria) has found more appeal in the contrasting notion of **cooperative federalism**. Where the US was based on a contract in which the states joined together to form a national government with limited functions, the European form rests on the idea of cooperation between levels, with a shared commitment to a united nation binding the participants together. In both cases, though, the operating principle is **subsidiarity**. The national government offers overall leadership but implementation is the duty of lower levels: a division, rather than a separation, of tasks.

Since its inception in 1949, Germany has been based on interdependence, not independence. All the *Länder* (states) are expected to contribute to the success of the whole, and in return are entitled to respect from the centre. The federal government makes policy but the *Länder* implement it, a division of administrative labour expressed in the constitutional requirement that 'the *Länder* shall execute federal laws as matters of their own concern'. But this cooperative ethos has come under increasing pressure from a growing perception that decision-making has become cumbersome and opaque. Constitutional reforms in 2006 were designed to establish clearer lines of responsibility between Berlin and the *Länder*, giving the latter – for example – more autonomy in education and environmental protection. Although this represented a move away from cooperative federalism towards greater subsidiarity, consultation remains embedded in German political practice.

It would also be helpful, for the sake of consistency and balance, if all the states within a federal union were similar in size, wealth and influence, but – again – this never happens. Historical circumstances have ensured that some states within a union have evolved to be bigger, wealthier, and more powerful than others. In India, for example, Uttar Pradesh in India is 182 times bigger in terms of population than the state of Mizoram, while the Brazilian

Dual federalism
National and local levels of government function independently from one another, with separate responsibilities.

Cooperative federalism
The layers are intermingled and it is difficult always to see who has ultimate responsibility.

Subsidiarity
The principle that decisions should be taken at the lowest feasible level.

Focus 11.1
The motives behind creating federations

The motives behind the creation of federations tend to be more often negative than positive; fear of the consequences of remaining separate overcome the natural desire to preserve independence. Rubin and Feeley (2008) suggest that federalism becomes a solution when, in an emerging state, 'the strong are not strong enough to vanquish the weak and the weak are not strong enough to go their separate ways'.

Historically, the main incentive for coming together has been to exploit the economic and military bonus of size, especially in response to strong competitors. Riker (1996) emphasizes the military factor, arguing that federations emerge in response to an external threat. The 13 original American states, for example, joined together partly because they felt vulnerable in a predatory world. However, US and Australian federalists also believed that a common market would promote economic development.

A more recent motivation has been ethnic federalism, as with the Belgian case. Further south, Switzerland integrates 26 cantons, four languages (German, French, Italian, and Romansh), and two religions (Catholic and Protestant) into a stable federal framework. But the danger with federalizing a divided society is that it can reinforce the divisions it was designed to accommodate. The risk is particularly acute when only two communities are involved, because the gains of one group are the losses of another. Federations are more effective when they cut across (rather than entrench) ethnic divisions, and when they marginalize (rather than reinforce) social divisions.

The challenges faced by Nigeria are illustrative. It became independent in 1960 with three regions, added a fourth in 1963, replaced them with 12 states in 1967, and has since cut the national cake into ever smaller pieces in an effort to prevent the development of states based around particular ethnic groups. There are now 36 states and a federal capital territory, and yet regionalism and ethnic divisions continue to handicap efforts to build a sense of Nigerian unity.

Table 11.3 The strengths and weaknesses of federalism

Strength	Weakness
A practical arrangement for large or divided countries.	May be less effective in responding to national security threats.
Provides stronger checks and balances.	Decision-making is slower and more complicated.
Allows for the recognition of diversity.	Can entrench internal divisions.
Reduces overload at the centre.	The centre finds it more difficult to launch national initiatives.
Encourages competition between states or provinces and allows citizens to move between them.	How citizens are treated depends on where they live.
Offers opportunities for policy experiments.	Complicates accountability: who is responsible for addressing problems?
Allows small units to cooperate in achieving the economic and military advantages of size.	May permit majorities within a province to exploit a minority.
Brings government closer to the people.	Basing representation in the upper chamber on states violates the principle of one person, one vote.

state of São Paulo is 88 times bigger than the state of Roraima. In Mexico, meanwhile, more than 15 per cent of the population lives in and around Mexico City, which is also by far the wealthiest part of the country when measured by per capita GDP. Another kind of imbalance is sometimes found in cultural differences, as in the case of Quebec nationalists who have long argued for special recognition for their French-speaking province within Canada, which they view as a compact between two 'equal' communities (English- and French-speaking, the former outnumbering the latter by 4:1) rather than as a contract between ten equal provinces.

Focus 11.2
The government of cities

With a majority of the world's people now living in urban areas, the question of how cities are best governed has become more pressing, as has the question of how best to treat the interdependence of cities and suburbs. The argument that they should be treated as single metropolitan areas – as city regions – has proved difficult to address given traditional boundaries. To complicate matters, cities have distinctive problems, not least because they are more diverse than rural areas; their boundaries contain rich and poor, natives and immigrants, black and white, gay and straight, believers and atheists, and almost every other combination known to human society.

Not all countries have made a success of metropolitan governance, as the case of Australia shows (Gleeson and Steele, 2012). It is a nation of cities, with the five largest state capitals – Adelaide, Brisbane, Melbourne, Perth, and Sydney – being home to nearly two-thirds of the country's people (see Map 11.4). These urban areas are inadequately governed in the existing three-tier (national, state, local) federation. National involvement in running cities is limited by the constitution; state administrations must also confront other pressures (including those from rural areas); and local government itself is subordinate and fragmented, with 34 local authorities operating in Sydney alone. A federal structure does not mesh well with a population concentrated in a few large cities.

Global city
A city that holds a key place within the global system via its financial, trade, communications, or manufacturing links. Examples include Dubai, London, Moscow, New York, Paris, Shanghai, and Tokyo.

In the governance of cities, the national capital occupies a special place. As an important component of the national brand, the capital's leaders merit regular communication with the central government. But the capital's international connections (and even those of major non-capital cities such as Frankfurt, New York, Hong Kong, Mumbai, and São Paulo) mean it can become semi-detached from its national moorings, as implied by the notion of a **global city**. Even though they are located in the same country, the interests of the centre and the capital can diverge. Inevitably, the capital is treated differently from other cities, providing further complexity to the idea of multi-level governance.

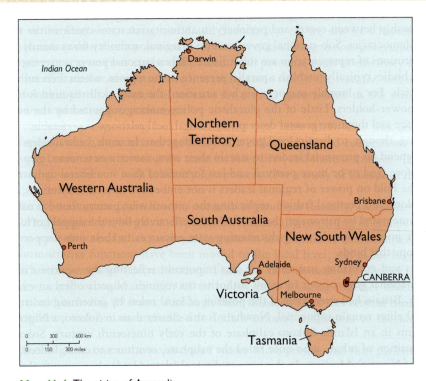

Map 11.4 The cities of Australia

Traditional political units in Nigeria have the advantages over modern, postcolonial units of deep roots in local culture. By contrast, elected legislatures and competing political parties based far off in state capitals or the national capital of Abuja are alien, and have difficulty establishing firm foundations. Nigerian federal governments face a dilemma: should the special place of traditional leaders in the community be exploited to extend the reach of federal government and to support programmes of modernization and democratization (thereby perhaps weakening the authority of the federal government), or should traditional leaders be bypassed and their powers reduced (thereby risking the anger of local Islamic communities and reducing the credibility of the federal government)?

In some of the least stable authoritarian states, the institutions of sub-national government are supplanted by opportunistic and/or informal control in the form of **warlords**. While much has been made of warlords' recent role in Afghanistan and Somalia, they are far from a new phenomenon, and in some ways are perhaps the oldest form of political domination. Basing their control on military power, they are found sprinkled through the history of Europe, China, Japan, and Mongolia, and have been a more recent phenomenon in several parts of Africa and Asia. Many, argue Felbab-Brown *et al.*, (2018), are the consequence of a breakdown in domestic governmental institutions, step in to the resulting vacuum, and develop popularity and support among local populations. They even sometimes develop their own enduring institutions, often undermining the legitimacy of the national state.

Warlords
Informal leaders who use military force and patronage to control territory within weak states with unstable central governments.

Field research on warlords is by definition dangerous, but our understanding of their motives and methods has improved thanks to their new prominence in several parts of the world. In one early study of their role in Liberia, Sierra Leone, and the Democratic Republic of the Congo, Reno (1997) made the link between warlords and weak states with rich resources such as diamonds, cobalt, and timber. For Marten (2012), warlords are not state-builders, like some of their feudal Asian and European predecessors, but instead rely on private militias to extract resources,

General Germain Katanga (left foreground) – a warlord with the nickname Simba the lion – appears before a military court in Kinshasa, capital of the Democratic Republic of Congo, charged with crimes against humanity.
Source: Getty Images/Papy Mulongo/ Stringer.

enforce support, and threaten state officials. They thrive on their capacity to provide brutal political control in situations where the formal institutions of state have failed to develop or simply failed.

In larger authoritarian states, such as China and Russia, sub-national government is more developed. Personal links remain important but institutional arrangements cannot be dismissed. Instead, sub-national government is actively exploited so as to ensure the continued power of the centre. China, for example, is a massive unitary state whose regions (with exceptions such as Hong Kong and Tibet) are ruled in imperial fashion from Beijing. Sub-national government takes the form of 22 provinces, six of which – Guangdong, Shandong, Henan, Sichuan, Jiangsu, and Hebei – each contain more than 70 million people, making them bigger than most countries. There are further subdivisions into either counties and townships, or cities and districts.

The Communist Party adds to this by providing a means of integrating centre and periphery. In particular, the circulation of party leaders between national and provincial posts helps to connect the two tiers, creating China's equivalent to the French *cumul des mandats*. Several provincial leaders serve on the party's central politburo, and most members of this key body have worked in top provincial posts at some point in their career. It is these party linkages that provide the key channel through which Beijing maintains a measure of control over the country.

However, recent research suggests that the balance between the centre and the parts has changed. Zhong (2015) shows that after more than a decade of administrative and economic reform, central government has become increasingly remote and less important for many localities, and that the centre's mobilization capacity has weakened. Increasingly, central government policies are ignored and local officials are often more interested in local or even personal projects than in centrally directed economic plans. This effective decentralization allows provinces to become laboratories for new policies but simultaneously accentuates inequalities between them, leading to occasional expressions of concern about the possibility of the country disintegrating.

Chinese leaders want to keep control, a goal that is more easily achieved in a unitary system than in a federal system. It might be logical to assume, then, that most hybrid and authoritarian states would avoid either maintaining or creating a federal system. And yet about half the world's federations are either hybrid or authoritarian states, including Ethiopia, Iraq, Nigeria, Pakistan, Russia, Sudan, and Venezuela. Assuming that the divided powers inherent in a federal system are not clearly helping move each of them towards democracy, how have they made this work? The short answer is that they have worked out a means for remaining federations while ensuring centralized control over key political issues.

This is certainly true of Russia, which is a federation, to be sure, but one in which the parts have less independence from the centre than is usually associated with federalism. Although Russia saw a decentralization of power under Boris Yeltsin (President, 1991–99), Vladimir Putin has since overseen a recentralization of power, providing a contrast to the decline of central control in China. Putin's success is based on several developments (Slider, 2014):

◆ Setting up an administrative system that allowed him to better monitor the work of regional executives without having to depend on information those executives provided.
◆ Dividing Russia into seven new extra-constitutional federal *okrugs* (districts) to oversee lower-level units. Each *okrug* is overseen by a 'representative' of the president, whose first job is to work to bring regional law back into line with federal law. The representatives also ensure that branches of the federal government in the regions remain loyal to Moscow.
◆ Obliging all regional governors to give up their previous party affiliations and to join the ruling United Russia party, and working to win majorities for United Russia in every regional assembly.
◆ Reducing the powers of the Federation Council, the upper chamber of the national legislature, by giving the president the authority to appoint its members.

Through these devices, Putin has increased the capacity of the central state to govern the Russian people, so much so that Ross (2010) concludes that 'Russia is now a unitary state masquerading as a federation'. Certainly, Putin's reforms contributed to his project of creating what he termed a 'sovereign democracy' in Russia. In Putin's eyes, a sovereign democracy is not built on the uncertain pluralistic foundations of multi-level governance. Rather, it gives priority to the interests of Russia, which include an effective central state capable of controlling its population. On that foundation, the Russian state seeks to strengthen its position in what it still sees as a hostile international environment.

While Russia is a large and diverse country, perhaps best thought of as the product of an empire rather than of a more conventional process of state-building, Venezuela is a much smaller and more homogeneous country, that also happens to be authoritarian. Why, then, is it a federation? It became one immediately upon independence in 1821, and remains one today, even though it has a population of just 31 million people concentrated in its coastal regions. To a large extent, though, Venezuelan federalism is nominal. A combination of political instability, oil wealth (see discussion on the resource curse in Chapter 20) and populist military dictatorship has prevented devolution, and while the constitution argues that the states are given all the powers not reserved to the federal government or to municipalities, the federal government has the lion's share of those powers, including control of elections, education, health, agriculture, and labour. Even where states have the authority to make their own laws, they must use federal laws as a framework (Brewer-Carías and Kleinheisterkamp, 2013). The division of powers, then, does not amount to much, and Venezuela is mainly federal in name alone.

DISCUSSION QUESTIONS

◆ In what circumstances is a unitary system a more appropriate form of government, and in what circumstances is a federal system more appropriate?

◆ Why is there no exact template for a unitary or a federal system, and does it matter?

◆ Should all local governments replicate national governments and be headed by elected legislatures and executive mayors?

◆ Does your country have any global cities? If so, how do they relate to the rest of the country? If it has none, does this matter to national or local politics?

◆ Why is local government studied so much less than national government?

◆ Does the experience of authoritarian states, where local government is often important, suggest that power in democracies has become too centralized?

KEY CONCEPTS

◆ Confederation
◆ Cooperative federalism
◆ Deconcentration
◆ Delegation
◆ Devolution
◆ Dual federalism
◆ Federal system
◆ Global city

◆ Local government
◆ Multi-level governance
◆ Quasi-federation
◆ Regional government
◆ Subsidiarity
◆ Unitary system
◆ Warlord

FURTHER READING

Bache, Ian, and Matthew Flinders (eds) (2004) *Multi-level Governance* (Oxford University Press). Examines multi-level governance and applies the notion to specific policy sectors.

Haider-Markel, Donald P. (2014) *The Oxford Handbook of State and Local Government* (Oxford University Press). An edited collection of essays on state and local political institutions and public policies.

Hueglin, Thomas O., and Alan Fenna (2015) *Comparative Federalism: A Systematic Inquiry*, 2nd edn (University of Toronto Press). A survey of the meaning of federalism, comparing how it works in theory and in practice in different societies.

Parker, Simon (2011) *Cities, Politics and Power* (Routledge). A study of the government of cities and the way in which their power is structured and used, illustrated by cases from Europe, the Americas, and China.

Pierre, Jon (2011) *The Politics of Urban Governance* (Red Globe Press). Assesses four models of governance in light of the challenges facing cities.

Watts, Ronald J. (2008) *Comparing Federal Systems*, 3rd edn (McGill-Queen's University Press). Considers the design and operation of a wide range of federations.

POLITICAL CULTURE 12

CONTENTS

PREVIEW

Political culture describes the beliefs, values, attitudes, and norms that characterize political systems. What do people expect of government, how much do they trust (or distrust) it, how do values vary in space and time, and how do attitudes compare in democratic and authoritarian systems? The answers to these questions are all essential to an understanding of government and politics in its many varieties. Reviewing the structure, rules, and dynamics of institutions – as we have done in the preceding chapters – is important, but in order to compare effectively, we need also to understand the 'personalities' of different political systems.

Offering a key point of reference, this chapter begins with a discussion of the idea of civic culture, a particular form of political culture based on an acceptance of the authority of the state and a belief in civic participation; in other words, probably the ideal when it comes to understanding how democracies should work. After looking at identity politics, multiculturalism, and post-materialism, it goes on to look at the causes and effects of the decline in political trust in democracies. It then reviews the controversial arguments made by Samuel Huntington in his book *The Clash of Civilizations*, and considers what this analysis might tell us about political culture at the global level. Finally, the chapter looks at the particular challenges of understanding political culture in authoritarian regimes, where there have been fewer substantive studies, and it is sometimes difficult to distinguish between indigenous and imported political values.

KEY ARGUMENTS

◆ The concept of political culture is attractive, but can be misused: cultures do not always coincide with states, and we should avoid the pitfalls of stereotypes about national cultures.

◆ Ideas such as civic culture, identity politics, and political trust have all been used in an effort to identify the attitudes most supportive of stable liberal democracy.

◆ The drift to post-materialism is an interesting attempt to understand how political cultures change.

◆ Political trust has been decaying in many democracies, but at different rates and for different reasons.

◆ The idea of conflict between transnational civilizations is a controversial attempt to apply cultural analysis to a post–ideological world.

◆ Much of the evidence suggests that there is more support in authoritarian regimes for strong leaders than for freedom and self-expression.

Brief profile

Germany provides a fascinating case study for comparative politics. Created in 1871, it went on to play a key role in two world wars, was then divided into separate democratic and communist countries, was reunited in 1990, and has played a key role as a leader and paymaster of European integration. Because Germany naturally views European developments through the lens of its own system of government, the country's political institutions are of continental significance. Within a parliamentary framework, Germany offers a distinctive form: a chancellor democracy in which the nation's leader determines government policy, appoints cabinet ministers, heads a large staff, and can be removed from office only when the legislature can agree a named successor. Germany boasts the largest economy in Europe, and its skilled employees, working in capital-intensive factories, produce premium manufactured goods for export. Its military influence in the world, however, is distinctly limited.

Form of government	Federal parliamentary republic consisting of 16 Länder (states). Modern state formed 1871, and most recent constitution (the Basic Law) adopted 1949.
Executive	Parliamentary. The chancellor leads a cabinet of between 16 and 22 ministers, while a president (elected to five-year terms – renewable once – by a special convention of the Bundestag and Länder) serves as mainly ceremonial head of state.
Legislature	Unicameral: a 631-member Bundestag elected for renewable four-year terms. Although it functions like an elected upper house, the 61-member Bundesrat consists of delegates drawn from the Länder.
Judiciary	The Federal Constitutional Court has proved to be highly influential as an arbiter of the constitution. It has 16 members, half elected by the Bundestag and half by the Bundesrat for single 12-year terms with mandatory retirement at age 68.
Electoral system	The Bundestag is elected through a complex mixed member proportional representation system, with half elected using single-member plurality, half using Länder party list proportional representation, and adjustments made to ensure that the number of seats for each party reflects the extent of their support. Members of the Bundesrat are nominated by the Länder.
Parties	Multi-party. The leading parties are the Christian Democratic Union (CDU), with its Bavarian partner the Christian Social Union (CSU), and the Social Democratic Party (SPD). Other significant players are the Green Party and the right-wing Alternative for Germany.

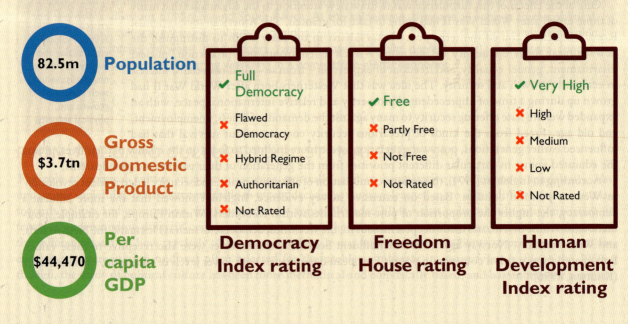

82.5m Population

$3.7tn Gross Domestic Product

$44,470 Per capita GDP

Democracy Index rating
- ✔ Full Democracy
- ✖ Flawed Democracy
- ✖ Hybrid Regime
- ✖ Authoritarian
- ✖ Not Rated

Freedom House rating
- ✔ Free
- ✖ Partly Free
- ✖ Not Free
- ✖ Not Rated

Human Development Index rating
- ✔ Very High
- ✖ High
- ✖ Medium
- ✖ Low
- ✖ Not Rated

The Bundestag in Berlin, symbolic of the political reconstruction of Germany, a country that still struggles to define its political culture in the wake of reunification.
Source: John McCormick.

Political culture in Germany

Political culture is shaped in large part by a country's history, and the post-war division of Germany provides a rare natural experiment, allowing us to gauge how these developments affected popular thinking.

Two main processes can be observed. The first is the positive impact of post-war economic recovery on political culture in western Germany. Between 1959 and 1988, the proportion of West Germans expressing pride in their political institutions increased from 7 to 51 per cent. Over a similar period, support for a multi-party system grew from 53 to 92 per cent. This experience showed that economic growth could deliver political legitimacy, and offered hope to other transitional countries seeking to build a democratic culture on an authoritarian history.

The second process is the impact of reunification. At the time of German reunification in 1990, people in the east were significantly less trusting of the legislature, the legal system, and each other than were people in the west. The experience of living under a communist regime, particularly one which engaged in such close surveillance of its population, had left its mark (Rainer and Siedler, 2009).

There has since been evidence of declining contrasts between east and west, but considerable differences remain: disposable income and the percentage of younger people are both higher in the west, while unemployment and support for right-wing political parties is higher in the east. Easterners tend to perceive westerners as bourgeois, patronizing, materialistic, and individualistic, while many westerners seem to look down on easterners, and certainly are perceived to do so by easterners themselves. Ironically, a 2014 poll found that 75 per cent of easterners considered reunification to have been a success, but only 50 per cent of westerners felt the same way (Noack, 2014).

It is reasonable to suppose that cultural contrasts will continue to weaken if (and this is a big If) living standards in the east converge on those in the west. In such circumstances, the more materialistic culture in the east is likely to acquire the post-material tinge long found in the west. For now, though, unification without unity remains a common theme in discussions of German political culture.

Further Reading

Langenbacher, Eric, and David P. Conradt (2017) *The German Polity*, 11th edn (Rowman & Littlefield).

Padgett, Stephen, William E. Paterson, and Reimut Zohlnhöfer (eds) (2014) *Developments in German Politics 4* (Red Globe Press).

Roberts, Geoffrey K. (2016) *German Politics Today*, 3rd edn (Manchester University Press).

When Inglehart began his studies in the early 1970s, materialists outnumbered post-materialists by about four to one in many Western countries. By 2000, the two groups were more even in size, a change that represented a major transformation in political culture. Globalization plays a key role in spreading post-materialist values even more widely, as does the expansion of education. In fact, experience of higher education (especially in the arts and social sciences) is the best single predictor of a post-material outlook. Liberal values acquired or reinforced at college are then sustained through careers in expanding professions where knowledge, rather than wealth or management authority, is the key to success. In France, surveys conducted between 2005 and 2008 showed that 56 per cent of those with at least some university education were post-materialists, compared with only 25 per cent among those with lower educational achievement (Dalton, 2013).

The reach of post-materialism should not be overstated, though. Not only have many conservative parties continued to prosper in the post-material age, but extreme right-wing and populist parties have emerged in several European democracies, partly as a reaction against post-material values. The distinctive challenges of the twenty-first century include issues such as terrorism, energy supply, climate change, immigration, youth unemployment, and social security. These problems have encouraged a renewed focus on the value of security and survival, forcing themselves onto the political agenda with an energy that has offset some of the cultural change that had emerged generationally.

Even if opinion is divided on the value of post-materialism as an analytical tool, its advent was indicative of the continued sophistication of approaches to measuring and understanding values, including those at the foundation of political culture. In 1981, the European Values Study was founded in the Netherlands with the goal of better measuring and understanding values in selected European countries. This was followed soon afterwards by the World Values Survey (in which Ronald Inglehart was involved), which has gone on to carry out several waves of survey research, the most recent in 2017–19, covering more than half the countries in the world. The US-based Pew Research Center has also generated a considerable body of survey research on political values and attitudes that can be usefully used to compare political culture in many different countries.

The results of one recent Pew survey – asking people whether or not they consider life in their country to have improved in the last 50 years – is shown in Figure 12.1. Even a glance at the results is enough to reveal that there is little correlation between rich countries and poor countries, or democracies and authoritarian regimes. For example, the group of countries where large majorities feel that life is better include two wealthy and politically stable democracies (Germany and Sweden), an emerging democracy with widespread poverty (India), and a country whose politics has recently stumbled towards authoritarianism (Turkey). Meanwhile, and more predictably, three

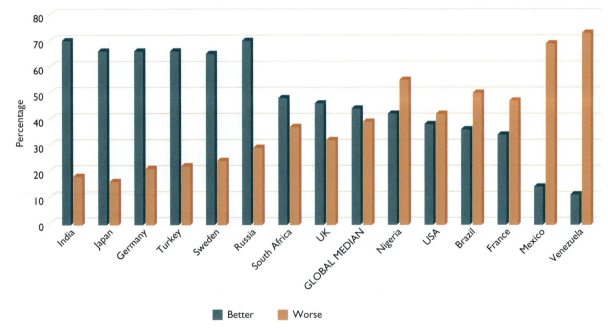

Figure 12.1 Is life better or worse than 50 years ago?

Source: Pew Research Center (2017a).

Note: Responses to the statement: 'Life in our country today is _____ than it was 50 years ago for people like me.'

flawed democracies (the United States, Brazil, and France) have more negative results, while the greatest numbers of people who see life as worse are found in a flawed democracy (Mexico) and an authoritarian system (Venezuela).

POLITICAL TRUST

When Almond and Verba were undertaking their research, it was widely assumed that one of the hallmarks of a successful liberal democracy was a high degree of **political trust**. Such trust exists when there is a belief that political systems and the institutions of government will generate competent decisions which reflect the concern of leaders for those they govern. Hardin (2006) makes a distinction between trust and trustworthiness, suggesting that if the former is on the decline, then so must be the latter. 'The value of trustworthiness', he argues, 'is that it makes social cooperation easier and even possible, so that its decline would entail losses of cooperativeness … [and] might even lead us to avoid interactions with most others'.

> **Political trust**
> The belief that rulers are generally well-intentioned and effective in serving the interests of the governed.

Particularly in the 1990s and 2000s, the conventional wisdom was that political trust was decaying in many Western democracies. However, the trend was by no means consistent across countries, and it was driven more by public confidence in the performance of democratic institutions than on the principle of democracy itself. These conclusions, though, tended to be based on the study of a select few democracies. More recently, Dalton and Welzel (2014) – taking Almond and Verba's study as their base – undertook a wider study of multiple countries around the world and found that many people had turned away from allegiance, adopting a newly assertive attitude towards politics. They had become more distrustful of electoral politics, institutions, and representatives and were more ready to confront elites with their demands.

These results are confirmed by surveys undertaken for the Trust Barometer by Edelman, a US-based marketing consultancy, which has been researching levels of trust in four sets of institutions (government, business, media, and non-governmental) since 2001. It has found those levels changing according to economic and political circumstances, with – for example – trust in business overtaking government and the media in 2007–8, but then falling in the wake of the global financial crisis. Trust in all four institutions reached a new post-crisis peak in 2016, before falling again in 2017–18. Its surveys have also revealed quite different levels of trust comparatively, as reflected in the data for 2018 shown in Figure 12.2.

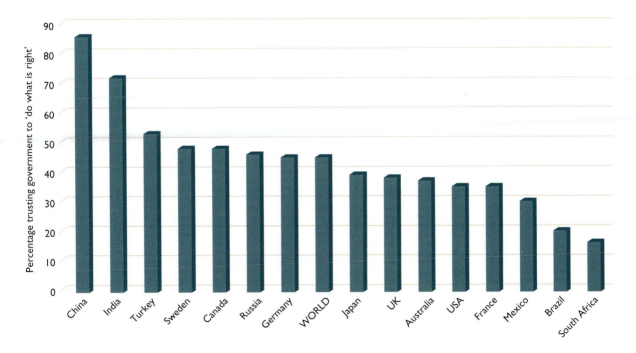

Figure 12.2 Comparing trust in government
Source: Edelman (2018).
Note: Based on fieldwork in 28 countries.

Figure 12.3 Trust in government in the United States
Source: Various, compiled by Pew Research Center (2017b).

Such data are helpful and interesting, but it is often left to others to provide the explanations. Are the record levels of trust in China an indication of true faith in the political system, for example, or a reflection of Chinese concerns about being critical of the authoritarian regime under which they live? For all its years of stability, Sweden comes in surprisingly low; it ranks high on the Democracy Index, *Freedom in the World*, and the Corruption Perceptions Index, yet less than half of Swedes trust their government. (For Linde and Erlingsson (2012), one cause of this is a suspicion among Swedes that corruption is a wider problem in their country than usually supposed.) The Russian figure is a reflection of the country's political uncertainties, and yet it stands in contrast to the high approval ratings recently enjoyed by Vladimir Putin – see later in this chapter. The low British figure, meanwhile, can be explained in part by the disruptions caused by Brexit, while the low numbers in Mexico, Brazil, and South Africa are unsurprising, not least because corruption is such a problem in all three countries.

The United States is an interesting case (see Figure 12.3). In the late 1950s and early 1960s, about three-quarters of Americans felt that they could trust the federal government most or all of the time. By 1994, that number had fallen to just one-fifth. It then improved somewhat, with Americans rallying around the flag in the fallout from the attacks of September 2001. Then, with the intelligence failings exposed by 9/11, mixed opinions about the wisdom of invading Iraq in 2003, and the financial crisis that broke in 2007, trust fell back to new lows. More deeply, many Americans – particularly those in rural parts of the country – were beginning to feel threatened by the changes they saw around them, with jobs lost or transformed by globalization, a growing gap between the rich and poor, doubts about the rise of a political class, and concerns among working white men about the effects of immigration and social change and about their 'traditional' political and economic role (Wuthnow, 2018).

A CLASH OF CIVILIZATIONS?

Political culture is not only a national or a local phenomenon, but can also be understood at the global level. A key example of global-scale analysis is offered by the best-selling (and controversial) study by the American political scientist Samuel Huntington titled *The Clash of Civilizations* (Huntington, 1996). It was particularly influential in introducing the issue of religion into the discussion about political culture.

Writing before the September 2001 terrorist attacks, Huntington suggested that cultures, rather than countries, would become the leading source of political conflict in the twenty-first century. The end of the Cold War would not mean the end of cultural divisions, he said. Instead, he predicted that the focus would shift from a battle of ideologies to a clash of civilizations. Since such groupings were supranational, Huntington claimed that political culture had escaped its national moorings to embrace wider identities: civilizations were the broadest cultural entities in the world, he argued, or 'cultures writ large'.

Huntington saw seven or eight of them in all: Western, Japanese, Islamic, Hindu, Slavic-Orthodox, Latin American, Chinese, and (possibly) African. Between the contradictory worldviews of these civilizations, he argued,

Table 12.1 Huntington's states and civilizations

Type	Qualities	Example
Core state	The most powerful and culturally central state in a civilization.	India (Hindu)
Member state	A state fully identified with a particular civilization.	UK (Western)
Lone state	A state lacking cultural commonality with other societies.	Japan (Japanese)

Source: Huntington (1996).

there was little room for compromise, and while economic conflicts could be bargained away, cultural differences carried no easy solutions. Huntington noted, for example, how cultural kinship influenced the choice of sides in the wars of the 1990s: in the conflicts in Yugoslavia, 'Russia provided diplomatic support to the Serbs, not for reasons of ideology or power politics or economic interest but because of cultural kinship.' Later, cultural kinship was the excuse for takeover of the Crimean Peninsula by Russia's Vladimir Putin in 2014 and his subsequent efforts to destabilize eastern Ukraine, a country long torn between Europe and Russia.

How do states relate to Huntington's civilizations? He provided an intriguing classification of core, member, and lone states – see Table 12.1. Huntington also discussed mixed or torn states whose leaders try to move their country from one civilization to another, an effort about which Huntington was sceptical. Australia had failed to reinvent itself as an Asian country, he said, simply because – in cultural terms – it was not Asian. Cultural differences also explain why Turkey has had such problems with its application to join the European Union; there has always been a question of whether the country is primarily European or Asian, and of how an Islamic state (even if it is traditionally a secular one) can integrate with Christian states (even ones where church attendance has declined).

Huntington's thesis has drawn considerable criticism, with many scholars either rejecting the idea of distinct civilizations, or at least questioning the evidence of clashes between them. The thesis has been particularly criticized for its assessment of the relationship between Islam and the West, which Huntington had portrayed as a permanent conflict of civilizations:

> The underlying problem of the West is Islam, a different civilization whose people are convinced of the superiority of their culture and are obsessed with the inferiority of their power. The problem for Islam is the West, a different civilization whose people are convinced of the universality of their culture and who believe that their superior, if declining, power imposes on them the obligation to extend that culture throughout the world.

Many critics rejected such ideas. In an article titled 'The Clash of Ignorance', for example, the scholar Edward Said (2001) referred to 'unedifying' labels such as Islam and the West, arguing that 'they mislead and confuse the mind, which is trying to make sense of a disorderly reality that won't be pigeonholed or strapped down as easily as all that'. For his part, Stepan (2001) interpreted Islam as multi-vocal, capable of varying its voice across place and time. Consider the contrasts offered by Turkey and Saudi Arabia: both are Muslim countries, but Turkey's traditionally secular state has become more explicitly Islamic under Recep Tayyip Erdoğan (President since 2014). Meanwhile, Saudi Arabia's authoritarian regime was historically guided by a severe form of Islam but has recently made modest moves in a more liberal direction. Such contrasts show the value of Gregorian's description (2004) of Islam as 'a mosaic, not a monolith'. The reaction to 9/11 confirmed Islam's multi-vocal character: the hijackers undoubtedly drew on one anti-Western dialect within Islam but most Muslims, as most Christians, regarded the attacks as morally unjustified (Saikal, 2003).

Furthermore, the idea of a monolithic Islam is invalidated by the tensions that have long existed between Sunni and Shia Muslims, and by the increasingly overt expression of this divide within Middle Eastern societies following the Arab Spring of 2011. (Sunnis make up about 80 per cent of all Muslims, and found their practices on the actions of Muhammad, while accepting some separation of political and religious authority, while Shia Muslims advocate a more direct political role for religious leaders, and form a majority in Iran and Iraq.) The monolithic nature of Christianity is also a myth; for centuries, the major cause of war in Europe was religious differences, and even today there are tensions between Protestants, Catholics, and the myriad other doctrines to be found within the broad label of Christianity.

In spite of the criticisms, Huntington's thesis of a divide succeeded in stimulating badly needed research into the cultural differences between Muslim and Western countries, which have mainly revealed only limited differences

It is revealing that in spite of the criticism that has been directed at Putin from abroad since Russia injected itself into Georgian affairs in 2008 (ostensibly to protect Russian interests in the breakaway region of South Ossetia), and that moved into even higher gear as Russia injected itself into Ukrainian affairs in 2014, Putin has enjoyed remarkably high approval ratings in Russia (Taylor, 2014). Polls from both state-run and independent sources found that he had the approval of 72 per cent of Russians in March 2014, a three-year high. (President Obama meanwhile had 43 per cent approval and President Hollande of France less than 20 per cent approval.) His approval subsequently slipped in the wake of concerns about the economy and the persistence of corruption, but was still at levels rarely found in the case of liberal democratic leaders. Clearly, Russians are rejecting the old regime, but they still admire strong and decisive leadership, even – seemingly – if it involves breaking international law.

One objection to the position that non-democratic regimes are supported by political culture is that the relationship is really the other way round. As we have already suggested, culture can reflect rather than sustain the nature of a regime. In the case of Russia, the lack of political trust there may well reflect the country's non-democratic history and the corrupt nature of its contemporary governance. Were a secure liberal democracy to take root in Russia, by whatever means, the nation's political culture would probably also shift in a democratic direction. In other words, over the longer-term political culture reflects the nature of the regime, rather than vice versa.

Interestingly, Welzel and Inglehart (2009) reject this idea. They insist, as did Gabriel Almond a generation earlier, that political culture is an independent force. In rejecting the view that it is merely a mirror of the current political system, they suggest that 'high levels of intrinsic support for democracy emerged in many authoritarian

Focus 12.2
Revolutions and political culture

Earlier in this chapter, we saw that there is a common inclination to equate the dominant political culture of a country with its national culture, and to define the dominant culture in terms of the values of political elites. This, as we also saw, would be a mistake. It is particularly mistaken in the case of authoritarian states where rule is often by a political elite whose membership is narrower and smaller than is the case in democracies, where the values of elites are often counterbalanced by the capacity of multiple groups in society to make themselves heard.

Occasionally in authoritarian systems, we find elites being removed – whether through popular uprisings or through electoral upsets – and being replaced by new regimes that go about redefining what might be regarded as 'normal' in regard to beliefs, attitudes, and values as they pertain to politics and the political system. This has happened, for example, in almost every case of a revolution that has toppled an old regime, whether in the case of France in 1789, Mexico in 1910–20, Russia in 1917, Egypt in 1952, Cuba in the 1950s, or Iran in 1979. More recently, a similar story of change has come to Venezuela, albeit by different means; rather than overthrowing an existing regime, Hugo Chávez came to power in 1998 by winning an election, at which point he launched his Bolivarian revolution.

Named for Venezuelan revolutionary leader Simón Bolívar (1783–1830), the revolution came in the wake of austerity measures imposed in Venezuela and several other Latin American countries in their effort to recover from the regional debt crisis of the mid-1980s. Its core features are described by Strønen (2017) as an effort to challenge a political culture shaped by the country's history as a major oil producer, and to break the hegemony of the middle and upper classes by mobilizing the poor and reforming state institutions. But Chávez died in office in 2013, leaving behind a deeply divided society, a chaotic economy, many unmet promises for change, and widespread disillusion with continuous political reform. His personalist rule weakened rather than strengthened state institutions, and the independent force of political culture that was identified by Welzel and Inglehart cannot be reshaped so quickly.

Placed within its wider context, it is important to note that relatively little is known about political culture in Latin America, making it more difficult to assess the meaning of the Venezuelan case. Booth and Richard (2015) point out that electoral democracy has long been scarce in the region, tends to break down when it emerges, and that while much progress has been made as Latin American countries have thrown off military dictatorships, the staying power of electoral democracy is uncertain at best. The Venezuelan case, they conclude, raises questions about the commitment of elites and masses alike to democracy.

Supporters celebrate the 2014 victory of Egyptian president Mohammed el-Sisi, who had reinvented himself as a civilian candidate soon after coming to power in a military coup.
Source: Getty Images/NurPhoto.

societies *before* they made the transition to democracy', citing such examples as South Korea and Taiwan. Their view is that, as societies modernize, so their better-educated segments give more emphasis to self-expression and post-material values. This cultural shift then leads to pressure to democratize. The case of Venezuela, however, would seem to suggest otherwise given the extent to which its middle and upper classes held on to power and have resisted change in recent years – see Focus 12.2.

In many non-democratic Islamic countries, authoritarian rulers seek to draw from the well of Islamic culture in a way that supports their hold on power. They present democracy as an alien Western concept which in practice leads to licence rather than freedom, to an emphasis on material rather than spiritual values, and to the pursuit of individual self-interest rather than social harmony. For example, Mahathir bin Mohamad, Prime Minister of Malaysia (1981–2003, and again from 2018), condemned Western democracies in which 'political leaders are afraid to do what is right, where the people and their leaders live in fear of the free media which they so loudly proclaim as inviolable'. Through such statements, authoritarian rule can be presented as expressing an indigenous cultural tradition inherently opposed to Western liberalism.

But how should we explain the recent story of Egypt? First we see its people standing at the forefront of the Arab Spring, with massive public demonstrations in early 2011 that led to the toppling in February of the Mubarak regime, in office for nearly 30 years. Egyptians then embraced democracy, taking part in competitive elections in 2011–12, and electing the government of Mohammed Morsi, who was notable not just for heading the first Islamist government in Egypt's history, but also for being the only civilian among the five leaders that Egypt has had since the overthrow of the monarchy in 1952. When Morsi began to show signs of authoritarianism, he was removed by the military in July 2013, and eventually replaced by the then little-known head of the Egyptian military, Abdel Fattah el-Sisi.

For Maghraoui (2014), the dynamics behind el-Sisi's rise are 'a mystery when abstracted from the general context of Egypt's authoritarian past. He is a man with no charisma, no political experience, no warrior's aura, no distinct ideology, and no clear plan of how to tackle Egypt's chronic social and economic problems.' It seems that in spite of the support that Egyptians gave to democratic change in 2011, many still hold on to the idea of strong leadership, suggesting that there is still a core streak of authoritarianism within Egyptian political culture, at least among older Egyptians if not the mainly younger protestors who were at the forefront of the protests against Mubarak and Morsi. El-Sisi made the 'war on terror' a cornerstone of his government, an idea that appealed to many Egyptians and that helped strengthen his base of support. In the view of Cambanis (2015), el-Sisi needed 'just enough power to stay in charge, and enough international support to ignore the outrage of Egyptians who want civil rights, political freedom, and genuine economic development'. How long he can make this last, however, remains to be seen.

When it comes to much of sub-Saharan Africa, one of the key challenges faced by political scientists is to distinguish indigenous political values from those created by the fallout from the colonial experience. When the borders of European states were formed, it was as a result of conflict and competition among Europeans themselves. The borders of African (and Middle Eastern) states were, by contrast, imposed from outside, by European colonial powers, paying no heed to political, cultural, or religious realities. The result was the creation of contrived political units in which ethnic communities with different histories were expected to work together and to build a sense of national unity while also ruling with partly formed political systems and underdeveloped economies.

Nigeria is a case in point of the resulting problems. In pre-colonial times, ethnic groups in the region such as the Hausa and Yoruba had worked out a balance between themselves that protected them from too much interference. The creation of Nigeria by British colonialism forced these groups to live and work together and to build shared systems of government and administration, setting them on a path of mutual hostility as they competed for power and resources and struggled to preserve their identity. Lacking a state tradition, Nigerians continue to find it hard to trust government officials, so they look instead to their communities for stability, and they believe that loyalty to the community is the paramount virtue. So persistent have Nigeria's ethnic divisions become that they once led a frustrated Wole Soyinka (1997) – the Nigerian novelist and 1986 Nobel laureate for literature – to dismiss the idea of a Nigerian nation as a 'farcical illusion'.

One of the consequences is a tradition of systemic corruption, which has become so normal that many locals call it 'the Nigerian factor'. As well as reflecting all the obvious and standard features discussed in Chapter 6, the Nigerian brand of corruption has gone international via the multiple emails sent from Nigeria to Western recipients offering millions of dollars to help settle the affairs of people who have allegedly died and left no successors. Named 419 scams after the section of the Nigerian penal code dealing with fraud, they have been so successful that they have become Nigeria's second biggest source of foreign revenues after oil (Smith, 2007).

How much of the Nigerian experience with political culture is truly Nigerian, and how much is a consequence of Nigeria's difficulties in building a sense of national unity? Can modernization make a difference in such circumstances? Does Nigeria even have discernible political cultural trends that have roots in Nigerian society and that are subject to the same kinds of pressures and influences as the trends we find in more democratic Western states with a longer history of relatively stable national identity? Or is the best that we can say about political culture in authoritarian systems that it exists, but that it is fundamentally negative in nature?

DISCUSSION QUESTIONS

- ◆ How healthy is the civic culture in today's democracies?
- ◆ What can be done to reverse the decline in political trust?
- ◆ Does post-materialism still make sense as a way of understanding political culture in the West?
- ◆ Is there a clash of civilizations between the Muslim and Western worlds?
- ◆ Is there such a thing as a Western political culture, and – if so – what are its features?
- ◆ Can revolutions change political culture, or does change take much longer?

KEY CONCEPTS

- ◆ Civic culture
- ◆ Elite political culture
- ◆ Identity politics
- ◆ Political culture
- ◆ Political trust
- ◆ Post-materialism

FURTHER READING

Dalton, Russell, J., and Christian Welzel (eds) (2014) *The Civic Culture Transformed: From Allegiant to Assertive Citizens* (Cambridge University Press). A reassessment of the concept of civic culture, noting the shift in many countries towards a distrust of government that has encouraged more confrontation with political elites.

Fukuyama, Francis (2018) *Identity: The Demand for Dignity and the Politics of Resentment* (Farrar, Straus and Giroux). A controversial author tackles the subject of identity politics, arguing that liberal democracy is being challenged by narrower forms of recognition based on nation, religion, sect, race, ethnicity, or gender.

Inglehart, Ronald (2018) *Cultural Evolution: People's Motivations are Changing, and Reshaping the World* (Cambridge University Press). A new assessment of post-materialism by the originator of the idea, arguing that diminishing job security and rising inequality have led in recent decades to an authoritarian reaction.

Norris, Pippa (2011) *Democratic Deficit: Critical Citizens Revisited* (Cambridge University Press). Based on extensive survey analysis, this book challenges the claim that liberal democracies have experienced a continuously rising tide of public disaffection since the early 1970s.

Uslaner, Eric M. (ed.) (2018) *The Oxford Handbook of Social and Political Trust* (Oxford University Press). An edited collection of studies of the sources and outcomes of social and political trust, including several comparative chapters.

Wiarda, Howard J. (2014) *Political Culture, Political Science, and Identity Politics: An Uneasy Alliance* (Ashgate). An assessment of the fall and rise of political culture as an explanatory paradigm in political science.

POLITICAL PARTICIPATION

13

CONTENTS

- Political participation: an overview
- Who participates, and why?
- Public opinion
- The dynamics of public opinion
- Women in government and politics
- Political participation in authoritarian states

PREVIEW

The quality of democracy depends to a high degree on the extent to which citizens are willing or able to take part in the process of governing. There are many different channels available for participation, ranging from the conventional to the unconventional, but no guarantees that people will want to use them. Two points will become clear in this chapter. First, the quantity and the quality of participation vary not only between regime types but also within individual countries over time and among different social groups. Even in democracies, rates of participation are far from equal. Second, even as the variety of forms of participation expands, many people still choose not to express themselves, or are poorly informed about the issues at stake. In authoritarian systems, of course, their views and opinions are not usually entertained to begin with.

This chapter begins with an assessment of who participates and why, looking in particular at the problem of political exclusion, and reviewing the distinctions between conventional, unconventional, and illegal forms of participation. It then ties participation to public opinion, explaining how opinion is measured, and discusses the implications of variable levels of knowledge about political affairs. The chapter then considers the particular place of women in politics, looking at barriers to their participation and asking why government is still often dominated by men. The chapter ends with a discussion of how participation is managed and limited in authoritarian states, pointing out that levels of participation are often higher than might be expected.

KEY ARGUMENTS

- We know who participates in democracies, and who does not, but the reasons behind patterns of participation vary by time and place.
- Studies of participation in democracies show a bias towards privileged social groups, reflecting inequalities of resources and interest.
- While political participation may seem to be declining in many parts of the world, it may be that more people are choosing a wider variety of means to express themselves.
- The science of measuring public opinion has improved dramatically, but the political and technological challenges it faces have grown.
- While political engagement by women has increased substantially, inequalities in their access to positions of power continue.
- In authoritarian regimes, clientelism and mobilized participation are important phenomena, but gauging public opinion is often difficult.

POLITICAL PARTICIPATION: AN OVERVIEW

Political participation
Actions by individuals intended to influence who governs or the decisions taken by those who do.

Conventional participation
Takes place within formal politics and the law.

Unconventional participation
Takes place outside formal politics or even the law.

Political participation describes the ways in which people actively seek to influence the composition or policies of government. **Conventional** forms of participation include voting in elections, citizens contacting their representatives, activists campaigning for their favoured candidate, and – increasingly – engagement via social media. But participation can also take **unconventional** forms – such as taking part in a demonstration – and may even involve breaking the law or turning to violence, as in the case of terrorist acts against the state. The distinctions between conventional and unconventional types are becoming less clear as the options for political participation widen and change, leading Theocharis and van Deth (2018) to ask how we can any longer recognize participation when we see it.

In a liberal democracy, people can choose whether to be involved in politics, to what extent, and through what channels. Participation is also found in authoritarian regimes, even if it is only to create a facade of engagement, manipulated so as to support, rather than threaten, the existing rulers. The forms and the costs of participation are somewhat different.

What expectations should be brought to the study of participation? One perspective, dating back to the ancient Greeks, is that involvement in collective decision-making is both an obligation owed to the community and an exercise in personal development, widening individual horizons and providing political education. From this standpoint, participation benefits both the political system and the individual, and non-participants are free-riders who gain from the efforts of others.

A second perspective, rooted in practical realities more than high ideals, sets a lower bar. This suggests that people are not naturally political animals, and that extensive participation is less a sign of a healthy democracy than of unresolved tensions within a political system. Demonstrations, protests, and even high voter turnout may be indicative of a system that is overheating, rather than one that is in good health. In normal times, limited participation may indicate the system's success in meeting popular demands, freeing citizens to pursue more fulfilling activities.

In these two accounts, all that matters in a liberal democracy is that citizens monitor political events, and become involved as necessary; that the channels are open, not that they are in constant use. Schudson (1998) suggests that, even when citizens appear inactive, they remain poised for action, like parents watching their children play in a swimming pool. Especially in an age when some conventional forms of participation have declined, such surveillance can even be seen as a central mechanism of democracy: 'To be watchful, alert, and on guard are essential attributes of citizenship', suggests Rosanvallon (2008), who argues that monitoring should be understood as a form of participation, and vigilance as 'a mode of action'.

A third perspective argues that many of those who fail to participate do so because they feel marginalized or alienated, or think that their involvement will make no difference, or see government as a set of institutions dominated by elites. Humans may not be political animals, but they routinely make cost–benefit calculations, and some make the rational calculation that participating is not worth the time or the trouble. This is a view that has become more evident as levels of trust in government have fallen.

WHO PARTICIPATES, AND WHY?

Rates and types of participation have been the subject of much study over recent decades, with concerns expressed about declining political participation and the implications of different levels of engagement by different social groups, and what the numbers tell us about satisfaction, cynicism, and alienation. For democracy to work, a sufficient number of people must engage with government and believe that their engagement matters. As we will see in Chapter 17, turnout at elections in many countries is declining, which would seem – at first glance – to be a sign of a problem. Another sign of a potential problem, as we will also see in Chapter 17, is that support for political parties is declining. But voting and party activities are only two parts of the overall picture, rates and trends vary from one country to another (and even within countries), and while trends may be downwards in terms of certain kinds of activities, they are heading upwards in other kinds, particularly those associated with social media.

For decades, the most striking result of studies of participation in democracies was how little most people involved themselves other than through voting; only a small minority engage themselves activity in politics, while a large minority chooses not to engage at all, or only rarely. In an influential comparative analysis of participation

Jacinda Arden, the third woman to hold the position of prime minister in New Zealand, a country that has been a global leader in removing barriers to the engagement of women in government and politics.
Source: Getty Images/AFP.

engagement and participation, but also to election or appointment to political office (Henderson and Jeydel, 2013). Part of the explanation lies in the relatively late arrival of women to politics: New Zealand may have been the first country in the world to allow women to vote (in 1893), and Finland may have been the first country to have a woman elected to its national legislature (in 1907), but women's suffrage only spread more widely after World War II in tandem with the creation of new states.

Taking voter turnout as a simple indicator, data generated by the World Values Survey (WVS) (see Solijonov, 2016) finds that – in 59 countries surveyed – men and women turned out in 2010–14 in approximately similar numbers: 61 per cent of men and 59 per cent of women claimed that they 'always' voted, and 22/23 per cent respectively claimed that they 'sometimes' voted. When broken down by country, though, significant differences were found: women were more active than men in about one-third of the countries surveyed (including Russia, New Zealand, Brazil, South Africa, and Sweden), while men were more active in the Middle East, North Africa, and Asia (notably Pakistan, Egypt, Nigeria, and Japan).

Having said this, though, the WVS data are based on opinion polls, and hard data on gender turnout is difficult to find for the simple reason that – because of voting secrecy laws – it is rarely collected. One of the few countries with such data over an extended period of time is the United States. There, in presidential elections, the gender gap has grown steadily in favour of women, who are now regularly outvoting men by about four percentage points – see Figure 13.2. There are several possible reasons for this: women often deal with government more directly in their daily lives than men (through welfare, education, and health care, for example), social norms are changing as more active younger women supersede their less-involved mothers and grandmothers, and women's issues (such as abortion, gender rights, child care, and equal pay) have achieved a new prominence on the political agenda (Rampell, 2014).

In most forms of formal political participation beyond voting, though, men still hold the lead; they tend to dominate political party activities, making direct contact with politicians and bureaucrats, and protest activities.

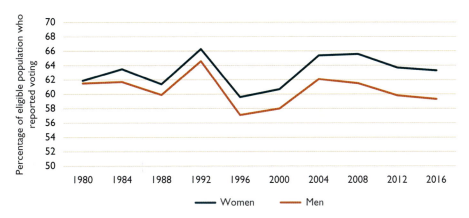

Figure 13.2 Voter turnout by gender in United States presidential elections
Source: Center for American Women and Politics (2017).

When it comes to holding political office, women are found disproportionately at the local rather than the national level (Stokes, 2005: Part V), and the higher the political office, the more likely it will be that a man will hold the post. The number of women elected as legislative representatives is growing, to be sure (see Figure 13.3), but high-level politics continues to be dominated by men. There are several possible reasons for this, some specific to particular countries and cultures, others more universal:

◆ Many men (particularly outside Europe) are not ready to vote women into office.
◆ Women face more obstacles in accessing the resources needed to run for office, or in being selected by major political parties.
◆ Women are less likely than men to think they are qualified to run for office, and are also less competitive and more risk averse than men (Lawless and Fox, 2012).
◆ In some countries (mainly in the Middle East) women are barred from running for elective office. It was only in 2015 that the first women in Saudi Arabia were elected into public office, for example. As Figure 13.3 indicates, there are no women members in the Yemeni legislature, the Majlis.
◆ Legislatures in particular are **gendered institutions**, meaning that they still advantage men over women by, for example, having working hours that are unwelcoming to women with more than their fair share of family responsibilities (Kittilson and Schwindt-Bayer, 2012).

Gendered institution
A body that operates with formal rules and informal conventions which, intentionally or unintentionally, advantage men over women.

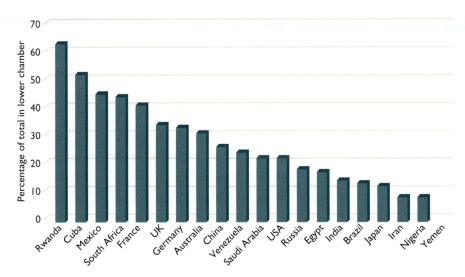

Figure 13.3 Comparing women in legislatures
Source: Inter-Parliamentary Union (2018).

Numerous intriguing questions are raised by the impact of women on politics, whether as voters or politicians. Several are posed by Paxton and Hughes (2017: Chapter 8): Are women in power more likely to see women constituents as a distinctive group? Do women differ from men in their attitudes towards policy priorities, and do they prioritize different issues? To what extent can we say that some policy issues – such as domestic violence or abortion – are more distinctly women's rather than men's issues? Are women in power taking the initiative to act on behalf of women? Do women have a different legislative style from men, and are they changing the rules of the political game? It may be premature to assume that the increase in office-holding by women will be enough by itself to transform the policy agenda or predominant political style. Where party systems are strong, the behaviour of both male and female legislators may continue to be shaped more by party than by gender.

Many countries have adopted formal means to increase the number of women in legislatures, but this is a relatively recent development, with the 1995 UN-sponsored Beijing Platform for Action providing new momentum. Three main methods are used, the oldest and rarest of which is *reserved seats*, by which a party selects women members for special seats granted in proportion to its share of the vote; the more seats a party wins in the general election, the more reserved seats it is allocated. In Pakistan, where this format is well established, 60 of the 342 seats in the National Assembly are reserved for women. The method is also used in Rwanda, which has the world's highest proportion of female legislators. There, 24 of 80 seats in the lower Chamber of Deputies are reserved for women; other female candidates are elected directly.

The second and by far the most common method is the *party quota*. Introduced and prevalent in Europe, this occurs when one party adopts a quota (typically 25–50 per cent) for women candidates (or, more neutrally, for candidates from each gender) and others follow in order to avoid being seen as falling behind. To forestall a token effort, additional stipulations may require some women to be placed high on a party's list (in party list electoral systems), or to be selected for winnable districts (in plurality systems).

The third and most recent method, which is particularly common in Latin America, is the *legal mandate*. This operates in a similar way to the party quota except that it is mandated by law and applies to all parties. Argentina was the first country in the world to adopt such a law, in 1991, since when almost every other Latin American country has followed suit. The requirements range from 50 per cent in Bolivia, Costa Rica, Ecuador, Mexico, and Panama to 30 per cent in Argentina and Brazil, and 20 per cent in Paraguay (Piscopo, 2015). Setting a target, though, does not necessarily mean achieving that target. Mexico established its 50 per cent mandate in 1996, for example, but only 37 per cent of its Senators were women after the 2012 election. The problem stems from loopholes (closed in 2014) such as women placed on the ballot being encouraged to cede their place to male reserve replacements (often their husbands), or being placed too low down the list of candidates in the proportional representation element to stand much chance of winning (Glover, 2014). Brazil has fared even worse: while its 30 per cent mandate was set in 1997, only 15 per cent were women in the Senate in 2014 and only 11 per cent were women in the House of Representatives.

Quotas are no cure-all, not least because they can be seen as a remedy that fails to address the underlying causes of unequal representation. Also, they do not always work, thanks to the kinds of loopholes found in cases such as Mexico, or to the failure of political parties to deliver on the quotas to which they have subscribed. Even so, they are a widely used device for influencing patterns of participation and have rapidly become a global standard (Krook, 2009).

Even though more than half the countries in the world now have gender quotas, remarkably little is understood about their impact on the number of women elected or appointed to higher political office. Critics have argued that quotas undermine women, because they might be seen as a form of political stigma that compromises the ability of women to be treated in government as the equal of men, and to undermine the idea of leadership based on merit. A study by O'Brien and Rickne (2016), however, using Sweden as a case, finds that quotas increase not just the number of women in legislatures, but also the supply of female politicians able to use this as a launch pad for higher office.

The number of women being elected to the highest offices has only grown, such that when a woman is elected as a president or prime minister it is much less noteworthy than it once was. Since the election in July 1960 of the world's first female head of government of the modern era – Sirimavo Bandaranaike, prime minister of Ceylon (now Sri Lanka) – more than four dozen countries have had women as national executives – see Table 13.2 for some examples.

Globally, the number of women holding cabinet positions has also grown, with several countries – including Finland, France, Iceland, Norway, Spain, South Africa, Sweden, and Switzerland – having achieved, or coming close to achieving, an equal number of women as men in cabinet. While many women ministers are still found in

Table 13.2 Women executives (selected)

Country	Name	In office
Sri Lanka	Sirimavo Bandaranaike	1960–65, 1970–77, 1994–2000
India	Indira Gandhi	1966–77, 1980–84
Israel	Golda Meir	1969–74
Britain	Margaret Thatcher Theresa May	1979–90 2016–
Dominica	Eugenia Charles	1980–95
Norway	Gro Harlem Brundtland	1981, 1986–89, 1990–96
Pakistan	Benazir Bhutto	1988–90, 1993–96
Philippines	Corazon Aquino	1986–92
New Zealand	Jenny Clark Jacinda Arden	1999–2008 2017–
Indonesia	Megawati Sukarnoputri	2001–04
Mozambique	Luisa Diogo	2004–10
Germany	Angela Merkel	2005–
Liberia	Ellen Johnson Sirleaf	2006–18
Iceland	Jóhanna Sigurðardóttir[1] Katrín Jakobsdóttir	2009–13 2017–
Australia	Julia Gillard	2010–13
Brazil	Dilma Rousseff	2011–16
South Korea	Park Geun-hye	2013–16
Poland	Ewa Kopacz Beata Szydło	2014–15 2015–17

Note: [1] World's first openly lesbian head of government.

the 'soft' areas of education and social policy, they have also moved into more powerful fields such as defence, finance, and foreign policy (Paxton and Hughes, 2015). Despite this progress, it is as well to remember that the glass of participation remains well over half empty. In a large majority of countries, most ministers and legislators – as well as most top business executives – are still men.

POLITICAL PARTICIPATION IN AUTHORITARIAN STATES

The argument is sometimes made that political participation, at least as understood in liberal democracies, is an empty concept in non-democratic settings. After all, the nature of authoritarian regimes is that they must seek to control popular activity in order to ensure their own survival and retention of power. Yet the evidence suggests that while rates of participation vary more widely than is the case in democracies (they are generally higher in the Middle East and Africa, and lower in Asia – see Figure 13.4), some of the patterns of participation found in hybrid and authoritarian states are not that different from those found in democracies: older people are more likely to vote, for example, while younger people are more likely to participate in less conventional ways, and more educated citizens are more likely to participate generally.

Having said that, the limits and nature of participation in authoritarian regimes are often subject to an implicit dialogue as opponents and activists test the boundaries of the acceptable: see Spotlight Russia. Authoritarian rulers may allow free speech in those areas such as local politics which do not directly threaten the central leadership. They may permit the expression of opinion on the internet even as they censor television broadcasts. Further, as

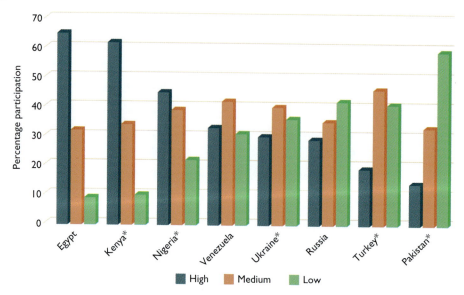

Figure 13.4 Political participation in hybrid and authoritarian states

Source: Pew Research Center (2014).

Note: Participation is measured by frequency of voting, participation in protests, signing petitions, and other forms of engagement.

* Hybrid regimes; all others are authoritarian.

societies grow more complex, rulers often come to realize that responding to popular pressure on non-sensitive issues can limit dissent and enhance political stability. They will only allow this to go so far, however.

China offers an example of these tensions. Against the background of a long history of authoritarianism, the Communist Party has opened some social space in which sponsored groups can operate with relative freedom. For example, more than 150,000 civic associations were registered in 2007, providing an opportunity for citizen-to-citizen communication under the party's watchful eye in such areas as education and the environment (Guo, 2007). Explicit opposition to the party, however, remains forbidden. The topic may go unmentioned, but memories remain of the Tiananmen Square massacre of 1989, when the army's tanks turned on pro-democracy demonstrators in Beijing. At the local level, sometimes violent protests continue against corruption, unemployment, pollution, illegal levies, or non-payment of wages or pensions. Demonstrations by ethnic minorities aside, these local protests do not threaten the party's dominance but are directed at local failures to implement national policies.

Elsewhere, a common technique for channelling, but also controlling, participation in authoritarian states is **clientelism**, or patron–client relationships. These are traditional, informal hierarchies fuelled by exchanges between a high-status patron and clients of lower status. The colloquial phrase 'big man/small boy' conveys the nature of the interaction: patrons are landlords, employers, party leaders, government ministers, ethnic leaders, or anyone with control over resources, and around whom clients – lacking resources of their own – gather for protection and security.

Clientelism
Politics based on patron–client relationships. A powerful figure (the patron) provides protection to lower-status clients in return for their unqualified allegiance and support.

Although patron–client relationships are found to some extent in all political systems, including democracies, they are of greatest political significance in authoritarian regimes. Particularly in low-income countries, and unequal societies with weak governing institutions, personal networks of patrons and clients can be the main instrument for bringing ordinary people into contact with formal politics, and are often the central organizing structure of politics itself (Figure 13.5). Despite their informality, these networks underpin, and often overwhelm, more formal channels of participation such as political parties.

Political patrons control the votes of their clients and persuade them to attend meetings, join organizations, or simply follow their patron around in a deferential manner. Participation by clients is controlled and mobilized, but the patron–client relationship is based on personal exchange rather than a political party or a shared political outlook. The patron's power, and its inhibiting effect on democracy, is illustrated in this comment by Egypt's President Abdul Nasser (in power 1956–70), interviewed in 1957 when he was still a reforming leader (Owen, 1993):

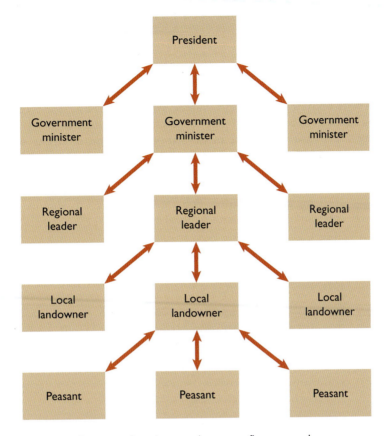

Resources flow downwards, support flows upwards.

Figure 13.5 A patronage network linking centre and periphery

> We were supposed to have a democratic system between 1923 and 1953. But what good was this democracy to our people? You have seen the landowners driving the peasants to the polling booths. There they would vote according to the instructions of their masters. I want the peasants to be able to say 'yes' and 'no' without this in any way affecting their livelihood and daily bread. This in my view is the basis for freedom and democracy.

Participation through patronage appeals in authoritarian settings because it links elite and mass, centre and periphery, in a context of inequality. Although inequality provides the soil in which patronage networks flourish, these relationships still act as political glue, binding the highest of the high with the lowest of the low.

By linking people across social levels, patron–client relationships limit the expression of solidarity among people of the same class, such as peasants. For the elite, they are a useful tactic of divide and rule. The decay of such hierarchical networks of dependence can be an indication of a transition to a more modern society in which people have acquired sufficient resources to be able to participate in an autonomous fashion. Put bluntly, security means people no longer need to trade their vote. Poverty and authoritarian rule provide a setting in which patron–client relationships flourish; affluence and democracy generate a climate in which they decay.

One phenomenon unique to authoritarian states is **mobilized participation**. In contrast to the autonomous participation found in liberal democracies, where citizens make their own choices as it suits them, mobilized participation is managed, manipulated, and obligatory. Although the term was originally used mainly in the context of communist countries, and still reappears in discussions about participation in China, it actually has wider application, usefully describing any instance where people may be encouraged to take part in political events or rallies in return for rewards such as food, entertainment, or just a cash payment, or may be induced to do so by threats. (It might even appear occasionally in democracies, when mass events such as conferences are organized by political parties and stage-managed for maximum media coverage.)

Mobilized participation
Elite-controlled involvement in politics designed to express popular support for the regime.

SPOTLIGHT RUSSIA

Brief profile

Russia has undergone dramatic changes in recent decades. For nearly 70 years, it was the dominant partner in the Union of Soviet Socialist Republics (USSR), a state that most Westerners feared and misunderstood. The USSR collapsed in 1991, but its state socialist political and economic system still casts a shadow over modern Russia. For democrats, the challenge has been to build a multi-party democracy in a culture unfamiliar with and unsympathetic to democracy. Its leaders have never lost sight of the national tradition of strong executive authority, and understanding Russia today is as much a question of assessing the actions and motives of President Vladimir Putin, and the clique around him, as of comprehending the country's governing institutions. Putin served two terms in office between 2000 and 2008, then stepped down as required by the constitution, winning re-election in 2012 and 2018. Despite a static economy and population, Putin seeks to reassert what he sees as Russia's rightful position as a leading power confronting a hostile international system.

Form of government	Federal semi-presidential republic consisting of 83 'subjects', including republics, provinces, and territories. Date of state formation debatable, and most recent constitution adopted 1993.
Executive	Semi-presidential. The president is directly elected, and limited to two consecutive six-year terms. The prime minister comes out of the Duma, heads the Council of Ministers, and succeeds the president if needed (there is no vice-president).
Legislature	Bicameral Federal Assembly: a 450-member State Duma elected for five-year terms, and a relatively weak 166-member Federation Council with two members appointed by the president from each federal unit.
Judiciary	Based on civil law and the constitution of 1993. Headed by a 19-member Constitutional Court (members nominated for 12-year terms by the president and confirmed by the Federation Council) and, for civil and administrative cases, a Supreme Court.
Electoral system	Direct elections for the president, with the possibility of two rounds if no one wins a majority in the first ballot. Party list proportional representation is used for the State Duma.
Parties	Multi-party, but parties are weak and unstable – reflecting, rather than shaping, power. The leading party, United Russia, provides a foundation for the authoritarian rule of Vladimir Putin.

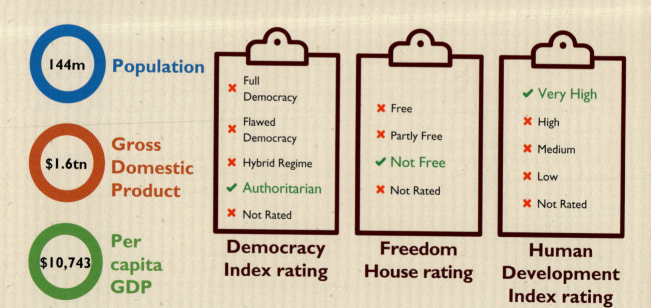

144m Population

$1.6tn Gross Domestic Product

$10,743 Per capita GDP

Democracy Index rating
- ✗ Full Democracy
- ✗ Flawed Democracy
- ✗ Hybrid Regime
- ✔ Authoritarian
- ✗ Not Rated

Freedom House rating
- ✗ Free
- ✗ Partly Free
- ✔ Not Free
- ✗ Not Rated

Human Development Index rating
- ✔ Very High
- ✗ High
- ✗ Medium
- ✗ Low
- ✗ Not Rated

Participation in Russia

Russia offers a case of the limits of political participation in an authoritarian regime. On the one hand, it is an intensely political society with an educated people interested in domestic and international affairs. On the other hand, political participation is shallow, held back by pervasive cynicism about the capacity of ordinary people to make a difference, and handicapped by government control of the media, and the manipulation of elections. The authoritarianism of the past and the present pervades political attitudes, creating a country with an unusually passive majority. According to a 2017 survey, 48 per cent of Russians still supported the view that a strong leader who could make decisions without interference from the legislature or the courts was a good thing. Globally, only 26 per cent of people had the same view, sinking to 13 per cent in most European countries (Pew Research Center, 2017c).

Supporters of the Putin government march in Moscow during the annual celebration of National Unity Day, marking the anniversary of the expulsion of Polish forces from the Kremlin in 1612.
Source: iStock/NickolayV.

Suspicion of organizations is endemic, with more people distrusting than trusting even the highest-rated institutions (the army and the Church), and placing most of their trust in personal networks of friends and family. Political parties languish near the bottom of the trust list, being mainly the creatures of politicians and the president, and proving themselves to be unstable, with an insecure social base.

Few people belong to any voluntary public organizations, membership of trade unions is low, and regular church attendance is uncommon. Few social organizations have lasted long or built large memberships, while others have been incorporated into the regime, and any with foreign links are charged by the Putin administration with being engaged in espionage. With few organizations standing between citizen and state, mass political participation is concentrated on national elections, and Russia remains a distinctly uncivil society. The Russian people are subjects first and participants second.

Public protest in Russia against Putin's manipulation of parliamentary elections in 2011, and of the presidential contest of 2012, represented an important development. Younger, better-educated people in the largest cities, notably Moscow, showed their dissatisfaction with their country's highly managed politics. At least in the short term, however, the most concrete outcome was a new law restricting (but not banning) such protests.

Further reading

Colton, Timothy J. (2016) *Russia: What Everyone Needs to Know* (Oxford University Press).

Monaghan, Andrew (2016) *The New Politics of Russia: Interpreting Change* (Manchester University Press).

White, Stephen, Richard Sakwa, and Henry E. Hale (eds) (2019) *Developments in Russian Politics 9* (Red Globe Press).

POLITICAL COMMUNICATION

14

PREVIEW

Mass communication lies at the heart of political discourse. It informs governments and citizens, it defines the limits of expression, and it provides us with 'mental maps' of the political world outside our direct experience. The technology of mass political communication has changed dramatically over the past century, taking us from a time when newspapers dominated to the era of broadcasting (first radio and then television), and bringing us to the current age of the internet, with instant information in unparalleled quantities from numerous sources. As that technology has changed, so have the dynamics of political communication: consumers now play a critical role in defining what constitutes 'the news', changing the relationship between the governed and the government, and the nature of political communication.

This chapter begins with a brief survey of the evolution of the mass media and political communication, ending with an assessment of the not-yet-entirely understood implications of digital media. It then looks at how the political influence of mass media is felt, reviewing the key mechanisms of that influence: reinforcement, agenda-setting, framing, and priming. After considering the content and effect of recent trends in political communication (commercialization, fragmentation, globalization, and interaction), the chapter ends with an assessment of political communication in authoritarian states. There, the marketplace of ideas is more closely controlled, though the internet in general, and social media in particular, have created more space for free communication among some citizens.

KEY ARGUMENTS

◆ A free flow of political information provides a key test of the difference between democracies and authoritarian regimes.

◆ The impact of the internet and social media on political communication has been substantial, but is not yet fully understood.

◆ The internet has made more political information more widely available, but it has also exacerbated the problems of the echo chamber and fake news.

◆ There are four main classes of media effects (reinforcement, agenda-setting, framing, and priming), whose dynamics are changing thanks to the internet.

◆ The shift to more commercial, fragmented, global, and interactive media is reshaping political communication.

◆ Studies find that the differences in the quality of political communication between democracies and authoritarian states are not as clear as they might at first seem.

POLITICAL COMMUNICATION: AN OVERVIEW

Society – and, with it, government and politics – is created, sustained, and modified through communication. Without a continuous exchange of information, society would not exist, and political participation would be impossible. Efficient and responsive government depends on such an exchange, without which leaders would not know what citizens needed, and citizens would not know what government was doing (or not doing). Mass communication is also a technique of control: 'Give me a balcony and I will be president', said José Maria Velasco, five times president of Ecuador. It is, in short, a core political activity, allowing meaning to be constructed, needs transmitted, and authority exercised.

Assessments of the quality of **political communication** are key to the process of understanding political systems. Democracies are characterized by a free flow of information through open and multiple channels, with Dahl (1998) arguing that a liberal democracy must provide opportunities for what he calls enlightened understanding: 'each member [of a political association] must have equal and effective opportunities for learning about relevant alternative policies and their likely consequences'. In hybrid regimes, by contrast, the dominance of media outlets is a tool through which leaders maintain their ascendancy over potential challengers. For their part, authoritarian regimes typically allow no explicit dissent. Media channels are limited and manipulated, and citizens must often rely more on unofficial channels, including the rumour mill, for their political news.

> **Political communication**
> The means by which political information is produced and disseminated, and the effects that it has on the political process.

Even though much recent research in political communication focuses on the messages sent and the meanings embedded within them, the danger of focusing solely on content is that we learn nothing about the receivers and even less about the political effect of those messages. Blaming media bias for why others fail to see the world as we do can be tempting, but is usually superficial and unenlightening. The transmission model is – as we will see – a helpful way of understanding the process of communication via mass media. This takes into consideration the sender of the message, the nature of the message itself, the channel used, the user, and the impact of the message.

At the same time, media technology has never been static, even if we moved at a snail's pace from the first printed book to the advent of mass communication (a process that took the best part of 1,300 years). The speed of change has since greatly accelerated, notably during the digital age as media have gone online and the means and methods of political communication have had to change to keep up. The shape, the effects, the reach, and the power of political communication have all changed; it has become more globalized, networked, interactive, and participatory (McNair, 2018), and these dramatic developments continue to evolve at a speed that makes it hard to keep up and adapt. We understand some of the effects of those changes, but not others, and much that we once thought of as fairly predictable has become highly volatile and unpredictable. The media remain our primary point of connection to political information, but while 'the news' has always been exploited and distorted to political ends, the extent of that distortion has grown and the means used to change the message have become more sophisticated. No one can yet be certain of the long-term impact on the political process.

THE EVOLUTION OF MASS MEDIA

The political significance of the media is famously encapsulated in the quip attributed (depending on the source used) either to Edmund Burke or to Thomas Macaulay, both British politicians. Noting the existence of three existing political 'estates' (the nobility, the clergy, and commoners), Burke or Macaulay referred to the reporters sitting in the gallery of the House of Commons as the **fourth estate**, a term that has since been used to denote the political significance of journalists. That significance has evolved with the changing technology of media, whose structure and content matters because, as Chaffee (2001) notes, 'the structure of communication shapes the structure of politics, both because so much of political activity consists of communication and because constraints on communication limit the exercise of power'.

> **Fourth estate**
> A term used to describe the political role of journalists.

> **Mass media**
> Channels of communication that reach a large number of people. Television, radio, and the internet are examples.

Although we take access to a variety of **mass media** for granted, their rise has been a relatively recent development, dating back no more than two centuries (see Figure 14.1). The first printed book dates from China in 686, the Gutenberg press started printing with moveable

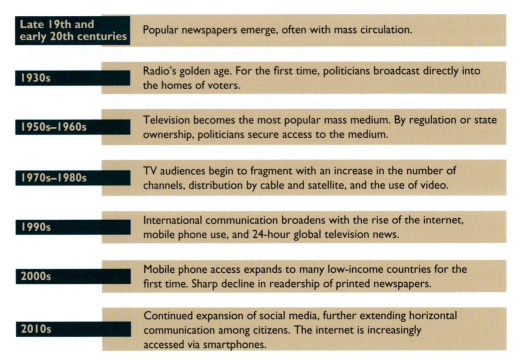

Late 19th and early 20th centuries	Popular newspapers emerge, often with mass circulation.
1930s	Radio's golden age. For the first time, politicians broadcast directly into the homes of voters.
1950s–1960s	Television becomes the most popular mass medium. By regulation or state ownership, politicians secure access to the medium.
1970s–1980s	TV audiences begin to fragment with an increase in the number of channels, distribution by cable and satellite, and the use of video.
1990s	International communication broadens with the rise of the internet, mobile phone use, and 24-hour global television news.
2000s	Mobile phone access expands to many low-income countries for the first time. Sharp decline in readership of printed newspapers.
2010s	Continued expansion of social media, further extending horizontal communication among citizens. The internet is increasingly accessed via smartphones.

Figure 14.1 The evolution of mass media

type in 1453, and the first newspaper appeared in 1605. But most of what we now consider mass media came with developments in technology in the nineteenth and twentieth centuries, allowing communication to the mass level. This, in turn, facilitated the emergence of common national identities and the growth of the state. For the first time, political communication meant a shared experience for dispersed populations, providing a glue to connect the citizens of large political units.

Newspapers

The key development in political communication during the nineteenth and early twentieth centuries was the emergence of popular newspapers in Western states, encouraged by widespread literacy in shared languages. Advances in printing and distribution opened up the prospect of transforming party journals with a small circulation into populist and profitable papers funded by advertising. By growing away from their party roots, newspapers became not only more popular but also, paradoxically, more important to politics.

In compact countries with national distribution, such as Britain and Japan, newspapers built enormous circulations, and owners became powerful political figures. In interwar Britain, for example, four newspaper barons – Lords Beaverbrook, Rothermere, Camrose, and Kemsley – owned papers with a combined circulation of over 13 million, amounting to half of all daily papers sold. Stanley Baldwin, a prime minister of the time, famously described such proprietors as 'aiming at power without responsibility – the prerogative of the harlot throughout the ages' (Curran and Seaton, 2019).

Broadcasting

Although newspapers remained significant channels of political communication, their primacy was supplanted in the twentieth century by broadcasting. Cinema newsreels, radio, and then television enabled communication with the mass public to take place in a new form: spoken rather than written, personal rather than abstract, and – increasingly – live rather than reported. Communication also went international, beginning in the 1920s with the development of shortwave radio, used by Britain and the Netherlands to broadcast to their empires. Nazi Germany, the United States, the Soviet Union, and other major Western states followed.

Domestically, broadcasting's impact in Western liberal democracies was at first relatively benign. A small number of national television channels initially dominated the airwaves in most countries after World War II, providing a shared experience of national events and popular entertainment. By offering some common ground to societies which were, in these early post-war decades, still strongly divided by class and religion, these new media initially served as agents of national integration.

Donald Trump is swamped by national and international media during his presidential campaign in 2016, once again emphasizing the extent to which broadcasting and politics have become intertwined.
Source: Getty Images/Joe Sohm/Visions of America.

More dramatic was the impact of broadcasting on politicians themselves. While a public speech to a live audience encouraged expansive words and dramatic gestures, a quieter tone was needed for transmission from the broadcasting studio direct to the living room. The art was to talk to the millions as though they were individuals. President Franklin Roosevelt's fireside chats, broadcast live by radio to the American population in the 1930s, exemplified this new approach. The impact of his folksy idiom was undeniable, and he talked less *to* the citizens than *as* a citizen, thereby earning his country's trust. In this way, broadcasting – and the medium of radio, specifically – transformed not only the reach, but also the style, of political communication.

This was even more true of television, where candidates and leaders had to think not just about what they were saying, but also about how they looked while they were saying it. This was first brought home forcefully with the televised Nixon–Kennedy debates during the 1960 presidential election in the United States. The debates marked the first time that candidates had faced off against each other on television, and although there were four, it was the first of the debates that went on to receive the most analysis. Kennedy appeared healthy and relaxed on television, while Nixon appeared nervous and unwell, but while a majority of those who watched the debate on television felt that Kennedy had performed best, a majority of those who listened on radio thought that Nixon had performed best. Thereafter, television moved to the centre of political campaigning, and how candidates and leaders presented themselves on television became central to their communication strategy.

Broadcasting also made a substantial contribution to political communication in most low-income countries, thanks to its two major advantages over print media: it does not require physical distribution to users, and it is accessible to the 15 per cent of the world's population who cannot read. These factors initially encouraged the spread of radio, with distant villagers being able to gather around the shared set to hear the latest news, not least on the price of local crops. Satellite television and mobile phones have since become accessible to many of the world's poor, expanding opportunities not only for downward communication from the elite, but also for horizontal communication between ordinary people.

In Kenya, for example, internet access was expensive and slow until 2002, when the government opened up the mobile phone market. This sparked a fierce war for market share among carriers, leading to a simultaneous reduction in prices and a broadening of options. Safaricom became a successful local provider, and many Kenyans now have access to M-Pesa, a mobile banking platform that allows bills to be paid and funds moved online.

INTO THE DIGITAL AGE

The birth and growth of digital technology has had the effect of throwing a series of rocks into the pond of political communication: it has created splashes and ripples, but also much disturbance, making it difficult to see into the reaches of the pond in order to establish the effects. This has all happened in a remarkably short period of time: the first commercial internet providers date back only to the 1980s, the World Wide Web was invented only in 1989, Google was founded in 1998, Wi-Fi emerged a year later, and most of the sites, habits, and expectations that we associate with **social media** are barely into their second decade of existence; see Table 14.1.

The rise of the internet has brought the fastest and most widespread changes ever seen in mass communication, meaning that scholars are today at least as busy simply documenting the changes as they are trying to understand those changes. At first, argue van Dijk and Hacker (2018), it was presumed that digital communication would have many positive political effects, such as improved information retrieval, more public debate, and even higher rates of political participation. While some of this has indeed happened, there have also been many negative effects.

The good news is that copious new amounts of information have been made available via the internet, while social media in particular have changed the ways in which governments and citizens communicate, and in which citizens communicate with one another. Political leaders and parties can communicate more often and more directly with citizens via social media, and social media connects people who would not previously have been able to communicate with one another, helping bring like-minded groups of people together in coordinated political events or demonstrations to a degree that was previously impossible.

The bad news takes several parts. First, there are now so many sources of information that users can become overwhelmed, and might be tempted to exert control by seeking out (and being reinforced by) sources and information that align with their existing values and preferences. Before the internet, there was more chance of people being exposed to contrasting ideas; now, they are more likely to feel the effects of the **echo chamber**. The quality of political debate has also been undermined by the manner in which internet users can be dragged into exchanges with ubiquitous and uncivil **internet trolls**. The result: interference with the free marketplace of ideas, the reinforcement of biases and closed minds, and the promotion of myths and a narrow interpretation of events. It should be no surprise, argues Sustein (2017), that people of different political views find it increasingly difficult even to understand one another.

Second, users of social media in particular can have their opinions manipulated by the use of automated **bots** or robo-tweets, or by increasingly sophisticated algorithms that feed users with stories based on past habits. A study by Bessi and Ferrara (2016) into the use of bots in US elections finds that they have been used to support some candidates, oppose others, point internet

Table 14.1 Forms of social media

Type	Features	Examples
Social networking	Allows people to connect with one another and to share information and ideas.	Facebook (created in 2004), LinkedIn, MySpace, Instagram, Snapchat, VK (Russia), and Google+.
Media sharing	Allows users to upload pictures, videos, and other media.	YouTube (created 2005), Reddit, and Pinterest.
Collaborative sites	Allows users to post content.	Wikipedia is the best known, created in 2001.
Blogs and microblogs	Allows users to share ideas and hold online conversations on matters of shared interest.	Twitter (created 2006), Tumblr, and Weibo (China).

Focus 14.1
The problem of fake news

The advent of the Trump administration in the United States drew new attention to an old problem: the accuracy of the news we read, hear, or watch (and of the claims made by leaders). As long as it has been shared, whether by word of mouth from one villager to another, or on a global scale via television or the internet, news has always been subject to manipulation and distortion. Outright lies might be told, inaccuracies may be passed on, subtle efforts may be made to selectively shape facts to create a false impression, or such facts may simply not be reported. Authoritarian states, including communist governments such as China's, are adept at such manipulation. The bigger the lie, implied Adolf Hitler in *Mein Kampf*, the more people are likely to believe it.

Yet fake news is also a growing problem in democracies. In the United States, Donald Trump has proved particularly sensitive to what he considers to be false reporting of his administration, often referring to 'fake news', describing reporters at his press conferences as 'unbelievable liars' and 'the most dishonest people', and dismissing the news media (as once did Joseph Stalin) as 'enemies of the people'. Early in his administration, one of his advisers – in taking issue with reports of the number of people who attended Trump's inauguration – even went so far as to say that his administration had 'alternative facts' to offer on the subject.

It was all the more ironic, then, when the *Washington Post* reported in May 2018 that, during his first 466 days in office, President Trump had made just over 3,000 verifiably false or misleading assertions (Kessler *et al.*, 2018). These included claims about the size of the crowds at his inauguration, about the size of a tax cut he had signed into law, about the number of jobs created since he had come to office, about the amount spent by the US on wars in the Middle East, and about the size of the US trade deficit with China.

Among the effects of the internet is that hackers can break in to websites and alter information, that social media can be manipulated to introduce falsehoods to potentially large audiences, and that ordinary people can engage in distortion by posting comments online. The old adage that a lie can travel around the world in the time is takes for the truth to get its boots on has taken on new meaning thanks to lies and misrepresentations that can be subject to 'rumour cascades' as they are copied and spread online. In looking at several thousand such cascades, Vosoughi *et al.* (2018) came to the conclusion that falsehoods spread 'significantly farther, faster, deeper and more broadly than the truth in all categories of information', that fake news was a particular problem with political news, and that the actions of ordinary humans were at least as much involved as were automated internet bots.

users to websites with fake news (see Focus 14.1), automatically retweet messages on Twitter containing key words or phrases, trawl search engines and post news stories meeting specified criteria, and post tweets automatically. Few skills are needed to do this, it is often unknown who is involved, and the bots are difficult to block.

The third problem accentuated by the internet is that of fake news. Studies find that while most people agree that the internet offers access to a far wider range of views than is the case with traditional media, it has also increased the influence of more extreme views, and poses new challenges to users in separating truth from fiction. The internet was once described as an information superhighway, but perhaps it is better regarded as a series of gated information communities, and those communities are often not what they seem: as users seek out fewer sources of news and are subjected more to the influence of bots, algorithms, and echo chambers, so the problems of fake news and the **post-truth** society grow – see Focus 14.1.

It is also important to note that access to the internet is far from equal. Many people have no access at all (because they have no access to electricity and/or computers and/or smart phones and/or broadband services), authoritarian regimes such as China and Iran continue to censor the internet, even in wealthy countries there are still many older citizens who remain unconnected, and there are many people who do not use the internet for news, or use it only in a selective manner.

Post-truth
The idea that appeals to emotions and personal beliefs have become more influential in shaping public opinion and public policy than objective facts.

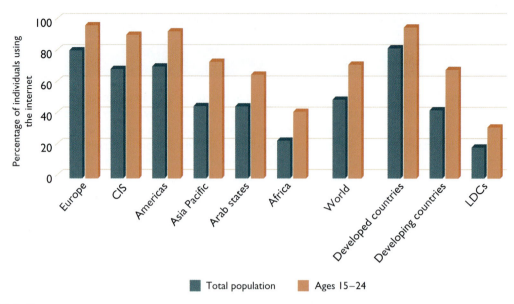

Figure 14.2 Comparing internet access
Source: International Telecommunication Union (2017).
Note: CIS = Commonwealth of Independent States (former USSR). LDCs = least developed countries.

As of 2017, just over half the people in the world still did not have internet access, with rates of connection ranging from 80 per cent in Europe to 66 per cent in the Americas, 44 per cent in Asia and the Pacific, and 22 per cent in Africa (see Figure 14.2). Younger people are more connected to the internet than older people, though, hinting at broader generational changes yet to come. It might also be suggested that the Western dominance of the internet has created a new form of information imperialism, but the balance has changed with the rise of Chinese equivalents (Jin, 2015). These include Baidu (a search engine), Weibo (equivalent to Twitter), Taobao (an online market), and Youku (YouTube).

As to the long-term effect of social media on mass media in general, we will have to wait and see. Frame (2015) notes that the past development of new media has routinely led to proclamations of the imminent demise of pre-existing media, but that these predictions never came true. Instead, society adopts the new form of communication while the 'old media' specialize and adapt. Radio and television were once seen to threaten the existence of print media, for example, and yet all three learned to coexist, and this pattern might happen also with social media.

MEDIA INFLUENCE

Transmission model
A model that distinguishes between five different elements or components in any communication, of which the message itself is only one.

Much political communication seeks to persuade rather than to inform. Whether we are receiving information directly from political leaders and parties, or via the mass media, that information is subject to value judgements and biases that create – according to Kaid *et al.* (1991) – at least three different 'realities':

◆ The *objective* political reality of events as they actually occurred.
◆ The *subjective* reality of events as they are perceived by governments, politicians, and citizens.
◆ The *constructed* reality of events as they are covered and presented by the media.

In seeking to understand how the mass media help shape these realities, we can use the **transmission model** as a guide. This distinguishes five components in any act of political communication: who says what to whom, through which medium, and with what effects (see

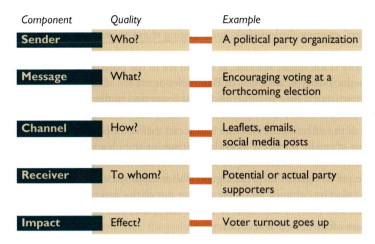

Component	Quality		Example
Sender	Who?		A political party organization
Message	What?		Encouraging voting at a forthcoming election
Channel	How?		Leaflets, emails, social media posts
Receiver	To whom?		Potential or actual party supporters
Impact	Effect?		Voter turnout goes up

Figure 14.3 The transmission model of political communication

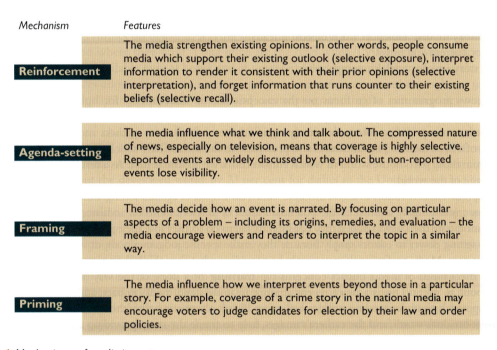

Mechanism	Features
Reinforcement	The media strengthen existing opinions. In other words, people consume media which support their existing outlook (selective exposure), interpret information to render it consistent with their prior opinions (selective interpretation), and forget information that runs counter to their existing beliefs (selective recall).
Agenda-setting	The media influence what we think and talk about. The compressed nature of news, especially on television, means that coverage is highly selective. Reported events are widely discussed by the public but non-reported events lose visibility.
Framing	The media decide how an event is narrated. By focusing on particular aspects of a problem – including its origins, remedies, and evaluation – the media encourage viewers and readers to interpret the topic in a similar way.
Priming	The media influence how we interpret events beyond those in a particular story. For example, coverage of a crime story in the national media may encourage voters to judge candidates for election by their law and order policies.

Figure 14.4 Mechanisms of media impact

Figure 14.3). Working our way through these components, it soon becomes clear that the media offer a structure within which many people can live their entire political lives. Just how they do that, though, is a matter of debate, the thinking having evolved with changes in the technology of delivery, and the impact of those changes on four mechanisms: reinforcement, agenda-setting, framing, and priming (see Figure 14.4).

In the 1950s, before television became pre-eminent, the **reinforcement** thesis – also known as the 'minimal effects model' – held sway (Klapper, 1960). The argument here was that party loyalties initially transmitted through the family acted as a political sunscreen protecting people from media effects. People saw what they wanted to see and remembered what they wanted to recall. In Britain, for example, where national newspapers were strongly partisan, many working-class people brought up in Labour households continued to read Labour newspapers as adults. The correlation between the partisanship of newspapers and their readers reflected **self-selection**

Self-selection
The choice of media sources made by an individual. For example, people who are already conservative will most likely choose conservative sources of news.

SPOTLIGHT VENEZUELA

Brief profile

Venezuela should by all rights be a Latin American success story, but a combination of political and economic difficulties has resulted in its recent downgrading in the Democracy Index from a hybrid to an authoritarian regime. It is rich in oil (as well as coal, iron ore, bauxite, and other minerals) but most of its people live in poverty. The wealth of the rich, displayed through imported luxury cars, manicured suburbs, and gated communities, coexists with public squalor. Much of the failure can be attributed to Hugo Chávez, elected president in 1998 on a populist left-wing platform. His supporters, known as *chavistas*, claim that his policies of economic nationalization and expanded social programmes helped the poor, but his critics charge that they contributed to inflation and unemployment. He died in 2013, but his successor Nicolás Maduro has built on the Chávez legacy, continuing to distort the economy, demonize opponents, and over-politicize the country's culture.

Form of government	Federal presidential republic consisting of 23 states and a Capital District. State formed 1811, and most recent constitution adopted 1999.
Legislature	Unicameral National Assembly of 165 members elected for fixed and renewable five-year terms.
Executive	Presidential. A president elected for an unlimited number of six-year terms, supported by vice-president and cabinet of ministers.
Judiciary	Supreme Tribunal of Justice, with 32 members elected by the National Assembly to 12-year terms.
Electoral system	President elected in national contest using a plurality system. National Assembly elected using mixed member proportional representation, with 60 per cent elected by single-member plurality and the balance by proportional representation.
Parties	Multi-party, with a changing roster of parties currently dominated by the United Socialist Party of Venezuela.

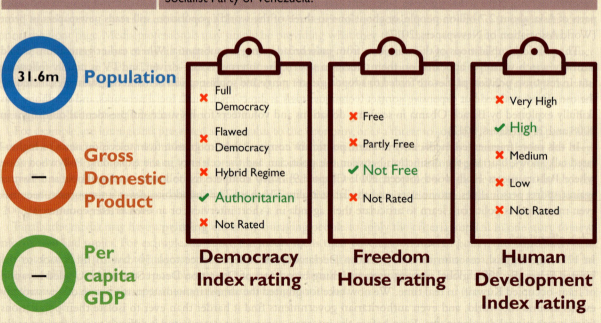

Note: No data available for GDP and per capita GDP.

A newspaper vendor in Caracas, the capital of Venezuela, with newspapers headlining the re-election victory of President Nicolás Maduro, leader of a regime that has seen growing limits on media freedom.
Source: Getty Images/Luis Robayo.

Political communication in Venezuela

One of the sources of Venezuela's low ranking in indices of democracy is its poor record on media freedom. As elsewhere in Latin America, the media establishment is privately owned, but this status does not prevent chronic intervention by government. In its *Freedom of the Press* report, Freedom House (2017) ranks Venezuela as Not Free, and the annual reports published by Reporters Without Borders (a French-based group that promotes press freedom) charge the government with imposing pressure on independent media. The means used include a travel ban on editors and media executives, the biased adjudication of court cases involving journalists, a reduction in access to newsprint, and even death threats against journalists.

The Venezuelan constitution guarantees freedom of expression, but a 2004 law includes wording that limits expression; for example, news that could 'incite or promote hatred' or foment the 'anxiety' of Venezuelan citizens can be banned, as can media coverage considered to 'disrespect authorities'. Regulations also allow the president to interrupt regular television programming to deliver what are known as *cadenas*, or live official broadcasts that can include attacks on the opposition.

The constitution guarantees the rights of citizens to access public information, but journalists find it hard to implement these rights. The government actively bars access to information that would reflect poorly on its policies. For example, when reports broke in 2014 of the possible outbreak of a mosquito-borne disease in a coastal province of Venezuela, President Maduro accused journalists who wanted to issue public warnings of practising 'terrorism', and issued orders for their prosecution.

The political style of former president Hugo Chávez provides a good example of a populist leader using broadcast media to influence the poorer voters who are his natural support base. Many callers to his lengthy Sunday morning broadcast show, *¡Aló, Presidente!*, petitioned the president for help in securing a job or social security benefit, usually citing in the process the callousness of the preceding regime. The president created a special office to handle these requests. In Chávez's governing style, we saw how the leader of an authoritarian regime could strengthen his authority through dominance of the broadcast media even against the opposition of many media professionals themselves.

Further reading

Derham, Michael (2010) *Politics in Venezuela: Explaining Hugo Chávez* (Oxford University Press).

Matos, Carolina (2012) *Media and Politics in Latin America: Globalization, Democracy and Identity* (London: I B Tauris).

Tinker Salas, Miguel (2015) *Venezuela: What Everyone Needs to Know* (Oxford University Press).

ELELCTIONS

15

CONTENTS

PREVIEW

Elections lie at the heart of representative democracy. They are the primary means by which most voters connect with government, they provide the brief moment during which politicians and parties are supplicants rather than supervisors, and they serve as a competition for office and a means of holding the government to account. But election campaigns also provide an opportunity for a dialogue between voters and parties, and between society and state: 'no part of the education of a politician is more indispensable than the fighting of elections', claimed Winston Churchill. Competitive elections endow office-holders with authority (contributing to the effectiveness with which leaders can perform their duties), and facilitate choice, accountability, dialogue, and legitimacy.

This is all well and good, but ensuring that elections result in fair and accurate representation is easier said than done. Multiple electoral systems have been developed, ranging from plurality to majority and proportional systems, but none has yet resulted in the perfect form of representation. This chapter begins by looking in turn at each of these systems and at their use in legislative and presidential elections. The results differ according to the methods used, reflecting contrasting ideas of representation and of democracy itself. The chapter then looks at the particular effects of referendums, initiatives, and recalls. It ends with a discussion of the role of elections in authoritarian regimes, where – despite active manipulation of outcomes – elections still perform several key political functions.

KEY ARGUMENTS

◆ There are many different electoral systems in use, but all of them fall short of the core goal of accurately translating votes into seats.

◆ Legislative and executive elections differ in both their mechanics and their implications; voting for a multi-member legislature requires different rules than electing a one-person chief executive.

◆ Election campaigns are less important for the result they produce than for their role as learning opportunities for voters, candidates, and parties.

◆ The political impact of an election depends on the narrative established about it after the results are in, with exaggeration often being the order of the day.

◆ Referendums, initiatives, and recalls make voters into decision-makers, but questions remain about how desirable they are for democracy.

◆ Numerous controls are imposed on elections in authoritarian regimes, but the effect is usually to curb rather than to eliminate political choice.

ELECTIONS: AN OVERVIEW

Elections lie at the heart of the democratic process, their purpose being to ensure that the preferences of voters are reflected in the make-up of legislatures and governments. The quality of representation is directly related to the quality, regularity, and arithmetic of elections, and one of the most telling distinctions between democracies and authoritarian systems is that elections in the former are generally free and fair, while in the latter they are not. An electoral system cannot be expected by itself to resolve underlying social conflicts, but it can be considered to be doing its job if it is both widely acceptable and stable over time, if the winners do not try to alter the system to their own advantage, and if the losers do not blame the election rules for their defeat.

In terms of the mechanics of elections, the manner in which votes are computed into choices for executives and legislatures varies: the major alternatives are plurality, majority, proportional, and mixed systems. Whatever the system, voter preferences are rarely exactly reflected in who wins the executive or how legislatures are made up, but the extent of the bias varies greatly. Elections also vary in terms of their significance; where the stakes are higher in **first-order elections**, **second-order elections** include less significant mid-term and local elections.

In parliamentary systems, for example, general elections are clearly first-order elections because they might result in a change of government. Hence they draw much more attention, and usually attract much higher voter turnout, than do local elections. Meanwhile, local elections – usually held at a different time from general elections – are clearly second-order elections: they attract less voter interest and turnout, and voters often use them to comment on national government. They weaken the link between the performance of representatives and the response of voters, such that a competent local administration might find itself dismissed for no other reason than the unpopularity of its party at the national level.

In understanding elections, we also need to consider their scope: while American government includes more than 500,000 elected posts (a figure reflecting a strong tradition of local self-government), European voters have traditionally been limited to voting for their national legislatures and their local governments, with regional and European elections added more recently. To illustrate the contrast, Dalton and Gray (2003) calculated that between 1995 and 2000 a resident of Oxford in England could have voted just four times, while a resident of Irvine, California, could have cast more than 50 votes in 2000 alone.

There are dangers in too many elections, not least of which is voter fatigue, leading to a fall in interest, turnout, and quality of choice. In authoritarian systems, a different dynamic is at work: levels of interest and turnout are often exaggerated, and there is no real choice. The question, then, is not about the structure of the electoral system so much as it is about how elections are manipulated and exploited to keep the ruling elite and/or the ruling party in power.

First-order elections
Elections in which the stakes are highest, usually involving the possibility of a change of government.

Second-order elections
Elections in which the stakes are lower, such as local or mid-term elections.

LEGISLATIVE ELECTIONS

Who governs? At various time during the nineteenth century, a Belgian lawyer, a French mathematician, an English lawyer, a Danish mathematician, and an American architect all wrestled with this question, working to develop an **electoral system** that accurately reflected the wishes of voters. For Victor d'Hondt and André Sainte-Laguë, the solution lay in a list proportional representation (PR) system. For Thomas Hare and Carl George Andrae, it lay in a single transferrable vote. For W. R. Ware, it lay in the alternative vote. While PR went on to be a popular option in much of Europe, none of these men fully solved the problem; all methods of converting votes to seats have their own set of strengths and weaknesses.

At first glance, the subject of elections might seem fairly simple: elective offices need to be filled, there will usually be competing candidates, voters are asked to make a choice, and the person with the most votes is declared the winner. However, even a cursory glance at the arithmetic involved reveals numerous problems; in spite of the core claims of a representative democracy, votes are not equal in their effects, and the **electoral formula** employed rarely translates the share of votes won by a party into exactly the same percentage share of seats in a legislature. For executives meanwhile, those who vote for losing candidates have little to show for their efforts.

Electoral system
A general term for the rules governing an election, including the structure of the ballot (e.g. how many candidates are listed per party), the **electoral formula** (how votes are converted to seats), and districting (the division of the territory into separate constituencies).

Numerous electoral systems have been proposed or used, but in this section we boil them down to the four options most often used for legislative elections (summarized in Table 15.1), followed in the next section with a discussion about executive elections. The simplest system – single-member plurality – has one of the best records at producing majority governments, but one of the worst records in turning share of the vote into the same share of seats. Meanwhile, the systems that do best at reflecting voter preferences – notably proportional representation – are more complex in their mechanics and often yield coalition governments that are determined by post-election bargaining between the parties represented in the legislature.

Table 15.1 Comparing legislative electoral systems

System	Procedure	Examples
PLURALITY SYSTEM		
Single-member plurality (SMP)	Parties contest single-member districts, with the candidate winning the most votes (not necessarily a majority) winning the seat.	Bangladesh, Canada, India, Malaysia, Nigeria, Pakistan, UK, USA
MAJORITY SYSTEMS		
Two-round system	If no candidate wins a majority, the leading candidates face a second, runoff election. Used more often for executive elections.	Belarus, France, Haiti, Iran, Vietnam
Alternative vote (AV)	All candidates are ranked by voters. Anyone winning a majority of first preference votes is declared the winner. Failing this, lowest-placed candidates are eliminated and their votes reassigned until one person has won a majority.	Australia, Papua New Guinea
PROPORTIONAL REPRESENTATION		
List system	Parties contest multi-member districts and publish lists of candidates. Votes are cast for a party, and seats in the district are divided up among parties in proportion to their shares of the vote.	Most of Europe and Latin America, South Africa, Turkey
Single transferable vote (STV)	Similar to AV in that voters rank candidates, but winners are determined by a quota based on a formula and a series of counts.	Australia (upper house), Ireland, India (upper house), Malta
MIXED SYSTEMS		
Parallel, or mixed member majoritarian (MMM)	Some seats are determined by PR and others by SMP or two-round elections. Effectively two separate elections.	Egypt, Hungary, Japan, Mexico, Philippines, Russia, South Korea, Ukraine, Venezuela
Mixed member proportional (MMP)	Much like MMM except that PR seats are used to adjust the total share of seats.	Bolivia, Germany, New Zealand

In most cases, the examples refer to the lower chamber of the legislature (in bicameral systems) or the only chamber in unicameral systems. For a full list of electoral systems and the countries that use them, see International Institute for Democracy and Electoral Assistance (IDEA) at www.idea.int.

Plurality system

In the **single-member plurality** (SMP) format (also known as 'first-past-the-post' (FPTP) or 'winner-take-all'), territories are divided into districts (or constituencies) that are each represented by a single member of the legislature. Each district is contested by multiple candidates, and the winner is the one receiving the greatest number of votes, whether this is a plurality (more than anyone else) or a majority (more than 50 per cent). Despite its antiquity, the plurality system is becoming less common, surviving mainly in Britain and British-influenced states. However, because several are so populous (such as India, Pakistan, the United States, and Nigeria), more people living in democracies vote using this method than any other (Farrell, 2011).

The main advantages of SMP are its simplicity and the fact that it produces a single district representative, but its critical disadvantage is the prospect of unbalanced results: for example, parties with strong blocks of support in parts of a country tend to win more seats than parties whose support is spread more thinly. Consider the following examples:

> **Single-member plurality**
> An electoral system based on districts that each have one representative, and in which the winner is the candidate with the most votes.

◆ In 17 of the 20 general elections held in Britain between 1945 and 2017, a single party won a majority in the House of Commons, even though no party ever won a majority of votes.
◆ In the 2014 general election in India, the Bharatiya Janata Party won only 31 per cent of votes but nearly 52 per cent of seats in the national parliament.
◆ In the 2015 elections in Canada, the Liberals won 54 per cent of seats with less than 40 per cent of votes, while the other parties combined won more than 60 per cent of votes but only 46 per cent of seats (see Figure 15.1).

Majority systems

As the label implies, majority electoral systems require the winning candidate to earn a majority of votes, the democratic argument being that no candidate should be elected to office without proving themselves acceptable to most voters. There are two usual ways of doing this: through a two-round election (also known as a runoff election), or – more uncommonly – using an alternative vote (AV) arrangement.

In the case of the former, all candidates run against each other in a district, and if one wins more than 50 per cent of the vote they are declared the winner. But if no one passes the 50 per cent mark, the top two candidates from the first round compete in a second round held soon afterwards, thereby ensuring that one wins a majority. (In France, any candidate winning more than 12.5 per cent of the vote in the first round can run in the second, although deals are often brokered in order to clear the way for the leading candidates to compete in the second and decisive round.)

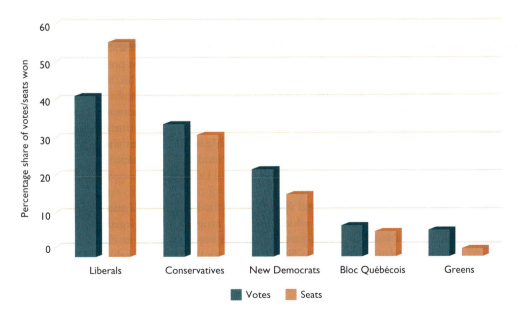

Figure 15.1 The Canadian federal election, 2015

Table 15.2 The German federal election, 2017

Party	Direct vote			Party list		Total seats
	% share votes	Seats	% share seats	% share votes	Seats	
Christian Democrats	30.2	185	62.9	26.8	15	200
Social Democrats	24.6	59	19.7	20.5	94	153
Alternative for Germany	11.5	3	1.0	12.6	91	94
Free Democrats	7.0	0	0	10.7	80	80
The Left	8.6	5	1.7	9.2	64	69
Alliance 90/the Greens	8.0	1	0.3	8.9	66	67
Christian Social Union	7.0	46	15.4	6.2	0	46
Other parties	3.1	0	0	5.1	0	0
TOTAL	100	299	100	100	410	709

casting a 'party' ballot to choose among parties running in Germany's 16 *Länder* (states) on the basis of PR. The ideal is that each party wins the same proportion of SMP seats and PR seats, but this rarely happens, so some topping up is done using 31 'balance' or 'overhang' seats. Parties that win more district seats than PR seats will be given the fewest of the balance seats, while parties that win fewer district seats than PR seats will be given more of the balance seats (see Farrell, 2011).

The result is not an exact correlation between votes cast and seats won, as the 2017 election results reveal (see Table 15.2), but it allows for adjustments to be made. The PR element particularly helped the smaller parties: the right-wing Alternative for Germany, the centrist Free Democrats, the Left party and the Greens, which among them won just nine district seats, but 301 party list and balance seats. The system is not easy to describe or to understand, but it has proved influential because it seems to provide a fairly accurate reflection of voter preferences while retaining a representative for each district.

EXECUTIVE ELECTIONS

While the electoral systems used for legislatures are varied and often complex, those used for presidents are relatively straightforward, since a one-person presidency cannot be shared between parties. This eliminates PR as an option, leaving the main choice between plurality and majority systems.

Mandate

A commission to act on another's behalf in a specific area. An election mandate is an authorization from the people for the government to follow a particular course.

While plurality systems tend to be the simplest, they can also fail to produce a convincing **mandate** (see Focus 15.2): the more candidates contesting the election, the more this is likely to happen. Presidents who win office without a majority will have less credibility and less ability to pursue their policy agendas. This problem is particularly acute when the victorious candidate secures only a small plurality of the total vote. For example, Fidel Ramos became president of the Philippines in 1992 with just 24 per cent of the vote – hardly a resounding endorsement with which to send the winner to the highest executive office in the land. Rodrigo Duterte won in 2016 with 39 per cent of the vote; better, but still far short of a majority. In Mexico, since electoral reforms in the 1990s, winning candidate have rarely done well: Felipe Calderón's winning share of the vote in 2006 was just 36 per cent, and Enrique Peña Nieto's share in 2012 was just 38 per cent. It was not until 2018 that Andrés Manuel López Obrador was able to win a more convincing 53 per cent share.

For this reason, most presidential electoral systems require a majority by using a two-round system. In the first round, all eligible candidates compete, and if one wins more than half the vote, that candidate is declared the winner. If no one wins more than half the vote, then a second

Focus 15.2
Electoral messages and mandates

An election does not end when the results are declared. Far from it. After the declaration comes the interpretation, which plays a large part in shaping the impact of an election on the politics that follow. Was it a mandate for change? A repudiation of the government? A referendum on the economy? Have 'the people' indeed spoken? If so, what have they said? Here we can see the relevance of an interpretive approach to politics (see Chapter 2); the election narrative can influence later politics, even if vote shares or the party composition of the government remain unchanged.

The primary focus is usually on the winner, or on a small party that has done surprisingly well; losers tend to be quickly forgotten unless the scale of the loss is dramatic. The larger and more unexpected the winner's margin, the greater the demand for a narrative giving positive reasons for the victor's triumph. Claiming that Party X won because of Party Y's unpopularity, or that Candidate A won because Candidate B performed poorly, rarely fits the bill. One benign effect of this search for the winning party's merits is to add to its authority as it begins to govern.

Interpretations of election results focus on the opaque notion of a mandate. Winners routinely claim that their victory is a repudiation of the former government and confirmation of the changes they propose to make, and the media can often be persuaded to agree. Only individual voters, not the electorate as a whole, have reasons for their decisions. Even so, editorials and blogs can be found after every campaign explaining what the electorate intended by its collective judgement.

The case of the 2015 British general election offers an example. For five years, the Conservative party of David Cameron had been governing in a troubled coalition with the much smaller Liberal Democrats, and faced three major issues: the economy, a Scottish independence movement, and a debate over membership of the UK in the European Union. The polls had the Conservative and Labour parties tied in votes but in fact the Conservatives won a majority of seats, enabling them to form a single-party government. The result was greeted with terms such as *surprising*, *stunning*, and *astonishing*, and was interpreted both as a mandate for the Conservatives to continue with their pro-market policies and as a rejection of Labour's more radical approach. But the Conservative majority was just 12 seats on just 37 per cent of the vote (a modest 0.7 per cent increase over 2010), and Labour's defeat probably reflected doubts about its governing capacity more than its left-wing policies. Still, the story was written, the message was transmitted, and the mandate was secured. And all (or mainly) because the polls underestimated Conservative support.

round is held between the two top-placed candidates, usually within two to three weeks of the first contest. As well as ensuring that the winner attracts the support of the majority of voters, the two-round system also encourages the two runoff candidates to reach out to unsuccessful candidates from the first round, which may be helpful in promoting more broadly based politics. On the other hand, two-round elections extend the campaign season and its associated costs, run the danger that turnout may fall in the second round, and open the door to tactical voting in the first round.

France is an influential case (see Lewis-Beck *et al.*, 2011). French voters, it is said, vote with their hearts in the first round and with their heads in the second, which creates the possibility of unexpected surprises, as in the case of the 2002 presidential election (see Table 15.3). The incumbent, Jacques Chirac, was running for a second term, but had lost popularity and the election was held against a background of concerns about law and order. It was expected that the two major contenders would be Chirac and his socialist opponent, Lionel Jospin, but many voters expressed their displeasure with Chirac by voting for minor candidates in the first round. While Chirac came out top, it was by only a small margin (just over three percentage points), and Jospin was knocked into third place by the right-wing National Front candidate Jean-Marie Le Pen. Shocked by the result, most voters determined to block Le Pen at the second round, turnout grew to nearly 80 per cent, and Chirac won more than 82 per cent of the vote, the biggest winning margin for a president in the history of democratic France.

Table 15.3 The French presidential election, 2002

Candidate	Party	First round (%)	Second round (%)
Jacques Chirac	Rally for the Republic	19.88	82.21
Jean-Marie Le Pen	National Front	16.86	17.79
Lionel Jospin	Socialist	16.18	–
François Bayrou	Union for French Democracy	6.84	–
Arlette Laguiller	Workers' Struggle	5.72	–
11 other candidates		34.52	–
Votes cast		28.5 million	31.0 million
Percentage turnout		71.6	79.7

Distribution require-ments
Rules specifying how a winning candidate's votes must be arranged across different regions or social groups.

As an interesting side-note, three countries – Indonesia, Kenya, and Nigeria – go beyond a simple runoff by requiring winning candidates to meet additional **distribution requirements** proving the breadth as well as the depth of their support. In the case of Nigeria, which has substantial ethnic, regional, and religious divisions, a victorious president must demonstrate regional as well as national support. In the first round, the winning target is a majority of all votes cast and at least 25 per cent of the vote in at least two-thirds of Nigeria's 36 states. If no candidate crosses this barrier, a second round is held with the same requirements. If the barrier is still not crossed, a third round is held between the two top finishers, a simple majority sufficing.

Indirect election is still used in several countries to elect the president. Examples include several parliamentary systems where the president possesses few meaningful executive powers, such as Germany and India. The United States is now highly unusual in using an Electoral College to elect an executive president (see discussion in Bugh, 2016). The College was originally designed to filter the voice of the people through an assembly of 'wise men'; votes were cast for members of the College, rather than directly for presidential candidates. Opinion is divided today on whether it should be kept or abolished. Complicating matters, all but two states use a winner-take-all formula where the candidate with the biggest popular vote in the state wins all the College votes from that state.

The folly of this system has been on clear display in recent presidential elections. In 2000, the winner of the popular vote (Al Gore) lost the Electoral College vote to George W. Bush, against a background of deeply flawed vote recording and rules on access to voting booths. In 2008, Barack Obama won 68 per cent of the votes in the Electoral College, despite winning just 53 per cent of the popular vote. In 2016, Hillary Clinton won 2.8 million more votes than Donald Trump (48.3 per cent of the popular vote to Trump's 46.1 per cent), and yet she lost the Electoral College vote – and the election – to Trump by a margin of 304 votes to 227. (See also Spotlight United States.)

Three other features of presidential elections, whether direct or indirect, are worth noting. First, presidential terms are sometimes longer, but rarely shorter, than those for legislators. The longer the term, the easier it is for presidents to adopt a broad perspective free from the immediate burden of re-election. With terms of just four years, first-term presidents in Argentina, Brazil, and the United States are likely to find themselves building experience during their first year and campaigning during their fourth year, leaving only the middle phase for real accomplishments.

Second, presidents are more likely than legislators to be subject to term limits; it is usual to restrict an incumbent to just one or two terms in office, or to require a cap of no more than two consecutive terms (see Table 15.4). The fear is that without such constraints presidents will be able to exploit their unique position to secure endless re-election. But term limits can have unintended consequences: a president who cannot be re-elected is no longer directly accountable to the voters, a reality which constitutes a limitation on democracy. Also, such presidents often lose political clout as their term nears its end. At the same time, term limits prevent popular and effective presidents from continuing to bring their experience to bear. One of the more stringent sets of limits is found in Mexico, where neither presidents nor state governors can serve more than one term, and legislators are barred from serving consecutive terms.

Table 15.4 Comparing presidential elections

Country	Method	Term (years)	Limits
Argentina	Two round	4	Maximum two consecutive terms
Nigeria	Up to three rounds	4	Two terms
Brazil, Colombia, Egypt, Iran	Two round	4	Two terms
Chile	Two round	4	No consecutive terms allowed
United States	Electoral college	4	Two terms
South Africa	Elected by legislature	5	Two terms
China	Elected by legislature	5	Unlimited
France, Turkey	Two round	5	Two terms
Russia	Two round	5	Maximum two consecutive terms
Peru	Two round	5	No consecutive terms allowed
Mexico, Philippines	Plurality	6	One term
Finland	Plurality	6	No consecutive terms allowed
Venezuela	Plurality	6	Unlimited

Third, the timing of presidential elections matters. When they occur at the same time as elections to the legislature, the successful candidate is more likely to be drawn from the largest party in the legislature. Without threatening the separation of powers, concurrent elections limit fragmentation, increasing the likelihood that the president and the legislature will be of similar mind. Such thinking lay behind the decision in 2000 to reduce the French president's term from seven years to five years, the same tenure as that of the National Assembly.

REFERENDUMS, INITIATIVES, AND RECALLS

Elections may be instruments of representative democracy, but the role of the people is only to decide who will decide. By contrast, devices such as the referendum, the initiative, and the recall make voters into decision-makers; they cast votes on focused issues that usually result directly in forming policy. But while they are good examples of direct democracy, are they necessarily good for democracy?

Referendums

The **referendum** is the most important form of direct democracy. Referendums may be mandatory (meaning that they must be called on specified topics, such as constitutional amendments), optional, or even constitutionally forbidden on a few reserved subjects such as taxation and public spending. Their outcome may be binding, as with constitutional amendments requiring popular approval, or merely advisory, as with Britain's vote in 2016 on continued membership of the European Union (which came down opposed).

> **Referendum**
> A vote of the electorate on a limited issue of public policy such as a constitutional amendment.

Referendums are growing in frequency (see Figure 15.3). Switzerland heads the list, holding nearly 500 referendums between 1940 and 2017 on a range of issues including nuclear power, same-sex partnerships, and immigration. Australia, too, makes use of state and national referendums, but only in relation to changes to the constitution: more than 40 have been held since the creation of the federation of Australia in 1901, although less than a quarter have resulted in a Yes vote. One of the more notable was the 1999 referendum on whether or not Australia should cut its last links with the British crown and become a republic; nearly 55 per cent of voters said No, but the issue has not gone away. Few other countries have made more than occasional use of the device, although they have become more common in the European Union, where they have been used for decisions on joining the EU or the euro, and for adopting new EU treaties.

SPOTLIGHT UNITED STATES

Brief profile

As the world's pre-eminent economic and military power, the United States has both driven and been deeply affected by the global changes of the last few decades. During the Cold War, it led the Western alliance against the Soviet Union and its clients, and was seen as the political, economic, and military leader of the 'free world'. Today it must use its continuing strengths to confront a more complex set of international challenges: it is caught up in the struggle against global terrorism and faces economic competition on an unprecedented level. Domestically, it suffers the effects of social divisions, a record national debt, persistent racial tensions, decaying infrastructure, an expanding gap between rich and poor, and concerns over immigration. Problems in the functioning of government recently earned the United States a downgrading on the Democracy Index from a full to a flawed democracy.

Form of government	Federal presidential republic consisting of 50 states and the District of Columbia. State formed 1776, and most recent constitution adopted 1787.
Executive	Presidential. A president elected for a maximum of two four-year terms, supported by a vice-president, an Executive Office of the President, a White House Office, and a federal cabinet.
Legislature	Bicameral Congress: lower House of Representatives (435 members) elected for renewable two-year terms, and upper Senate (100 members) containing two senators from each state, elected for renewable six-year terms.
Judiciary	A dual system of federal and state courts headed by the federal Supreme Court with nine members appointed by the president (and confirmed by the Senate) for lifetime terms.
Electoral system	One of the few large countries still employing the single-member plurality method. Formally, the president is elected indirectly through an electoral college.
Parties	Multi-party, but dominated by the moderately conservative Republican Party and the moderately liberal Democratic Party.

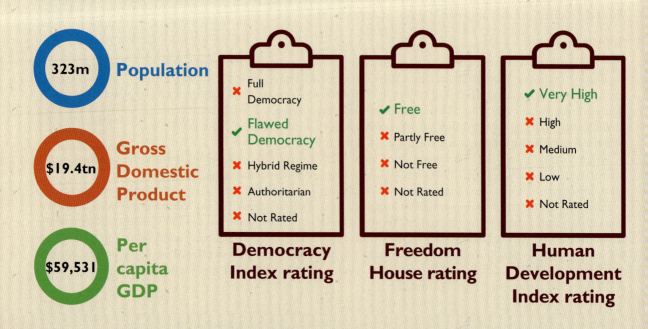

323m Population

$19.4tn Gross Domestic Product

$59,531 Per capita GDP

Democracy Index rating
- ✗ Full Democracy
- ✓ Flawed Democracy
- ✗ Hybrid Regime
- ✗ Authoritarian
- ✗ Not Rated

Freedom House rating
- ✓ Free
- ✗ Partly Free
- ✗ Not Free
- ✗ Not Rated

Human Development Index rating
- ✓ Very High
- ✗ High
- ✗ Medium
- ✗ Low
- ✗ Not Rated

Elections in the United States

Elections in the United States are unusual (or even unique) in at least three ways: in the sheer number of elected offices, in the astonishing amounts of money that are spent on campaigns, and in the extent to which their democratic qualities are undermined by the use of an Electoral College for the presidential election, and by the manipulation of electoral districts for Congressional elections.

The large number of elected posts – ranging from the president down through state governments to local judges and sheriffs – reflects not only the practical requirements of governing a large and one-time frontier society, but also a culture that emphasizes equality and accountability. In addition, the distinctly American institution of primary elections opens up the selection of a party's candidates to the general population.

A national political party convention in the United States. The time and money spent on US elections contrasts with the growing cynicism that many Americans show towards party politics.
Source: Getty Images/Jessica Kourkounis/Stringer.

While the large amounts spent on campaigning are no guarantee of electoral success, it is all but impossible to make a mark on the electorate without having access to large advertising budgets. The numbers have snowballed in recent elections, from $3 billion in the 2000 election season (all offices), to more than $5 billion in 2008, nearly $6.2 billion in 2012, and nearly $6.5 billion in 2016 (Center for Responsive Politics, 2017). In the name of free speech, a 2010 Supreme Court ruling overturned some previous limits on campaign financing and allowed all but unlimited spending, often by groups protected by anonymity.

The undemocratic results produced by the Electoral College are troubling, but even more consistently troubling is the quintessentially American problem of **gerrymandering**. With the majority political parties in most states allowed to design Congressional electoral districts, many have chosen to manipulate the lines in their favour, producing often strangely shaped districts based on the distribution of party supporters or voters from ethnic minorities. The result is skewed and manipulated election results, in which – it is often said – legislators choose voters rather than vice versa. Legal challenges are being mounted to gerrymandering, a test case occurring in the state of Pennsylvania in 2018 when it was ordered to redraw its districts so as to make them less partisan.

Gerrymandering

A phenomenon (associated mainly with the United States) involving the deliberate redrawing of electoral districts to favour one political party over another.

Further reading

Barbour, Christine, and Gerald Wright (2017) *Keeping the Republic: Power and Citizenship in American Politics: The Essentials*, 8th edn (Sage).

Duncan, Russell, and Joe Goddard (2018) *Contemporary United States*, 5th edn (Red Globe Press).

Wasserman, Harry (2015) *The Basics of American Politics*, 15th edn (Pearson).

POLITICAL PARTIES

16

CONTENTS

◆ Political parties: an overview
◆ Origins and roles
◆ Party systems
◆ Party organization
◆ Political parties in authoritarian states

PREVIEW

For most residents of democracies, political parties are the channel through which they most often relate to government and politics. Parties offer them competing sets of policies, encourage them to take part in the political process, and are the key determinant of who governs, and who does not. It is all the more ironic, then, that while parties are so central to the political process, they are not always well regarded by citizens. They are often seen less as a means for engaging citizens than as self-serving channels for the promotion of the interests of politicians; as a result, support for parties is declining as people seek other channels for political expression. In authoritarian regimes the story is even unhappier: parties have routinely been the means through which elites manipulate public opinion, and have been both the shields and the instruments of power.

This chapter begins with a survey of the origins and changing roles of parties, before looking at the variety of party systems around the world, ranging from states where parties are not allowed through single-party, dominant party, and two-party systems to the multi-party systems found in most democracies. It reviews the different dynamics of parties in these different systems, then looks at the manner in which parties are organized, and at how leaders and candidates are recruited. After discussing the ways in which parties are financed, and reviewing the pros and cons of public funding, it concludes with an examination of the roles parties play in authoritarian systems.

KEY ARGUMENTS

◆ Political parties were once key agents of society and forces for political mobilization, but disillusion with their impact and political role has grown.

◆ Political parties have six core roles, including guiding and mobilizing voters, aggregating political interests, and providing a foundation for governments.

◆ Party systems come in several different forms, the major theme being the decline of dominant party and two-party systems, and the rise of multi-party systems.

◆ The selection process for party leaders and candidates has been changing, but the effects on candidate quality are unclear.

◆ The growth in public funding of parties has changed their political role and their character.

◆ Parties in authoritarian regimes are a means for resolving conflict, balancing threats, managing elections, extending influence, and educating voters.

POLITICAL PARTIES: AN OVERVIEW

It would be hard to imagine political systems functioning without **political parties**, and yet their history is shorter than most people might imagine. The nineteenth-century Russian-born political thinker Moisei Ostrogorski was one of the first to recognize their growing importance in politics. His study of parties in Britain and the United States was less interested, as he said, in political forms than in political forces; 'wherever this life of parties is developed,' he argued, 'it focuses the political feelings and the active wills of its citizens' (1902). His conclusions were fully justified: in Western Europe, mass parties were founded to battle for the votes of enlarged electorates; in communist and fascist states, ruling parties monopolized power in an attempt to reconstruct society; in the developing world, nationalist parties became the vehicle for driving colonial rulers back to their imperial homeland.

> **Political party**
> A group identified by name and ideology that fields candidates at elections in order to win public office and control government.

Parties were a key mobilizing device of the twentieth century, drawing millions of people into the national political process for the first time. They jettisoned their original image as private factions engaged in capturing, and even perverting, the public interest. Instead, they became accepted as the central representative device of liberal democracy. Reflecting this new status, they began to be mentioned explicitly in new constitutions, some countries even banning non-party candidates from standing for the legislature, or preventing members from switching parties once elected. Such restrictions were deemed necessary for ensuring party-based elections. By the century's end, parties had become part of most political systems, providing functions ranging from being the very foundations of government, to aggregating interests, mobilizing voters, and recruiting candidates for office. Most liberal democracies even offered some public funding to support party work.

Therein rests the problem. No longer do parties seem to be energetic agents of society, seeking to bend the state towards their supporters' interests. Instead, they appear to be at risk of capture by the state itself. They also often seem to be less concerned with offering voters alternatives than with promoting their own interests, and competing for power for its own sake. As a result, parties have lost much of their attraction to the politically engaged, who seem to be increasingly disillusioned with achieving democracy through competing political parties.

In authoritarian states, meanwhile, parties are either non-existent (in a few cases) or else are operated as a tool of the ruling elite. The notion of competitive parties does not fit with the idea of non-democratic control, and parties are not so much the representatives of groups or interests as tools by which authoritarian leaders can build, keep, and express their power. Excepting the enormous power of ruling communist parties, they tend to be weak, lacking autonomy from the national leader, and reinforcing elite control of society. In countries that are poor and ethnically divided, parties typically lack the ideological contrasts that provided a base of party systems in most liberal democracies, and are instead come to be identified with the interests of one social group over another.

ORIGINS AND ROLES

Political parties are neither as old nor as central to government as we might think. They might seem to be the lifeblood of democratic politics, and yet governments and states have long been wary of their potentially harmful impact on national unity, which is one reason why parties – unlike the formal institutions of government – went unmentioned in early constitutions.

In looking at the origins of parties, we can distinguish between two types:

◆ Cadre (or elite) parties were formed by members within a legislature joining together around common concerns and fighting campaigns in an enlarged electorate. The earliest nineteenth-century parties were of this type; they include the conservative parties of Britain, Canada, and Scandinavia, and the first American parties (the Federalists and the Democratic-Republicans). Cadre parties are sometimes known as 'caucus' parties, the caucus denoting a closed meeting of the members of a party in a legislature. Such parties remain heavily committed to their leader's authority, with ordinary members playing a supporting role.

◆ Mass parties – which emerged later – originated outside legislatures, formed around **political cleavages** and designed, for example, to help social groups achieve representation as a way of achieving their policy objectives. The working-class socialist parties that spread across Western Europe around the turn of the twentieth century epitomized this type. Mass parties acquired an enormous membership organized in local branches, and – unlike

> **Political cleavage**
> The practice by which voters are divided into like-minded voting groups based on national ethnic, religious, linguistic, or social differences.

Brazil has developed a particularly colourful multi-party system since its return to civilian government in 1985. No fewer than 28 parties won seats in the 2014 elections to the Chamber of Deputies, representing a wide range of opinions and interests that coalesced into a pro-government coalition, two opposition coalitions, and a cluster of stand-alone parties. Twelve parties each had less than ten members, and the pro-government coalition contained nine parties that together controlled 59 per cent of the seats. The picture in Brazil is complicated by a widespread aversion to right-wing parties (stemming from the heritage of the military years), weak discipline within many of the smaller parties, and the powerful role played by other actors, such as state governors. The result is a system that has been labelled 'coalition presidentialism', describing presidents who must rely on large and unstable coalitions to pass legislation (Gómez Bruera, 2013).

Two important elements of multi-party systems in several countries are niche parties that operate outside traditional party divisions (see Focus 16.1), and parties that operate only at the regional level, or at the state level in federations. In the latter case, Britain – for example – has parties that represent the interests of Scotland, Wales, and Northern Ireland, while the German Christian Democratic Union is in a sustained coalition with the Christian Social Union, which operates only in the state of Bavaria. Few countries offer a more varied array of regional parties than India, where such parties now play an expanded role in national politics. For example, the Congress-led United Progressive Alliance relied heavily after the 2009 elections on regional parties in the states of West Bengal, Tamil Nadu, and Maharashtra. The

Focus 16.1
The rise of niche parties

Niche party
A political party that appeals to a narrow section of the electorate, usually highlighting non-economic issues.

A recent phenomenon in many European countries has been the rise of the **niche party**, which is one that appeals to a narrower part of the electorate. These have been defined in several different ways: non-centrist or extremist, limited-issue, or even single-issue parties, as parties that focus on non-economic issues, and as parties that cut across traditional social cleavages and partisan alignments (see discussion in Wagner, 2012). For many European countries, the niche is often ideological, producing parties with far right, nationalist, and/or populist agendas. Unlike main mainstream parties, they rarely prosper by moderating their position, instead achieving most success from exploiting their natural but limited support group (Meguid, 2008). Several of these parties – including Austria's Freedom Party and Switzerland's People's Party – have participated in coalitions, while others (such as the UK Independence Party in Britain) have succeeded in influencing the agenda of mainstream parties.

Niche parties of the far right are an exception to the thesis that parties emerge to represent well-defined social interests. Evidence suggests that they draw heavily on the often transient support of less educated and unemployed young men. Disillusioned with orthodox democracy and by the move of established conservative parties to the centre, this constituency is attracted to parties that blame immigrants, asylum seekers, and other minorities not only for crime in general, but also for its own economic and cultural insecurity in a changing world (Akkerman, et al., 2016).

It is tempting to identify a new cleavage here: between the winners and losers from contemporary labour markets. In the winner's enclosure stand well-educated, affluent professionals, proudly displaying their tolerant post-material liberalism. Outside the enclosure we find those without qualifications, without jobs, and without prospects in economies where full-time unskilled jobs have been exported to lower-cost producers. In this context, the perceived economic success of immigrants, especially those of a different colour, is easily regarded with resentment.

Matters are not quite that simple, though. This is not a cleavage in the usual sense, because far-right parties are supported by alienated individuals whose concerns are overlooked by mainstream parties. Many protest voters might cease to vote for niche parties if they became leading parties, thus creating a natural ceiling to their support. Even joining a coalition dilutes the party's outsider image. In the long term, niche parties lack the resilience of those based on a more secure and traditional cleavage (McDonnell and Newell, 2011).

2014 election resulted in an 11-seat majority for the Bharatiya Janata Party, but it continued to be part of a coalition originally formed in 1998, in which it worked with nearly 30 regional parties with nearly 60 seats in the Lok Sabha, the lower chamber of the Indian parliament.

PARTY ORGANIZATION

Large political parties are multi-level organizations, ranging from the party leadership, major funders, and research departments down through different strata to volunteers working at national, regional, and local levels. This complexity means that any large party is decentralized, and that while references to 'the party' as a single entity are unavoidable, the idea of party 'organization' is sometimes too grand a term. Below the centre, and especially in areas where the party is electorally weak, the party's organization may be little more than an empty shell, and coordination between levels is often weak. Some authors even draw a comparison between parties and franchise organizations such as McDonald's (Carty, 2004). In a franchise structure, the centre sets policy priorities, manages the brand, runs marketing campaigns, and supports the operating units. Local agents, whether McDonald's outlets or local party branches, are left to get on with key tasks. Local parties, for example, are charged with selecting candidates and implementing election strategy at local level.

The thinking about party organization was long dominated by the arguments made by the German scholar Robert Michels (1875–1936). In *Political Parties* (1911), he argued that even organizations with democratic pretensions become dominated by a ruling clique of leaders and supporting officials. He suggested that leaders developed organizational skills, expert knowledge, and an interest in their own continuation in power, while ordinary members – aware of their inferior knowledge and amateur status – accepted their own subordination as natural. Michels's pessimism was expressed in his famous **iron law of oligarchy**: 'to say organization is to say a tendency to oligarchy' (often reproduced as 'who says organization, says oligarchy').

Much has since changed. Recruitment to elected office continues to be a vital and continuing function of parties, which – even as they decline in other ways – continue to dominate elections to the national legislatures from which, in democracies, most political leaders are drawn. Given that candidates nominated for **safe districts**, or appearing near the top of their party's list, are virtually guaranteed a place in the legislature, it is the '**selectorate**', not the electorate, which makes what Rahat (2007) calls 'the choice before the choice'. At the same time, there is evidence of a growing role for ordinary party members in the selection of leaders as well as candidates, a finding which suggests that Michels's iron law is corroding as parties seek to retain members by giving them a greater voice in party affairs (Cross and Katz, 2013).

Party leaders

The method of selecting the party leader deserves more attention than it usually receives (Pilet and Cross, 2014), for the obvious reason that major party leaders in most parliamentary systems stand a good chance of becoming prime minister. In some countries, to be sure, including many in continental Europe, the chair of the party is not allowed to be the party's nominee for the top post in government (Cross and Blais, 2012). In Germany, for example, the party's candidate for chancellor is appointed separately from the party leader and need not be the same person. In the United States, the presidential candidate and chair of the party's national committee are different people; indeed, the former usually chooses the latter. Otherwise, it is important to review the mechanics and implications of the selection of the party's leaders.

There are several different options, the traditional method being election by members of the party in the legislature, as still used in several parliamentary systems, including Australia, Denmark, and New Zealand. Interestingly, some parties give a voice both to members of parliament and ordinary members, either through a special congress or a two-stage ballot. For example, the British Conservatives offer ordinary members a choice between two candidates chosen by the parliamentary party. Although this would appear to be a more democratic option, it can lead to problems when the rank-and-file membership is out of step with the national party, resulting in the triumph of local over national interests.

A vote of the party's members of the legislature alone is, of course, a narrow constituency. And the ability of potential leaders to instil confidence in their parliamentary peers may say little about their capacity to win a general election fought through television and social media. Even so, colleagues in the legislature will have a close knowledge of a candidate's abilities; they provide an expert constituency for judging the capacity to lead not only the party, but

Iron law of oligarchy
States that the organization of political parties – even those formally committed to democracy – becomes dominated by a ruling elite.

Safe district
An electoral district in which a political party has such strong support that its candidate/s are all but assured of victory.

Selectorate
The members who nominate a party's candidates for an election.

Cartel party
A leading party that exploits its dominance of the political market to establish rules of the game, such as public funding, which reinforces its own strong position.

for themselves, a process captured by Katz and Mair's idea (1995) of **cartel parties**: 'colluding parties become agents of the state and employ its resources to ensure their own survival'. The danger of cartel parties is that they become part of the political establishment, weakening their historic role as agents of particular social groups and inhibiting the growth of new parties in the political market.

POLITICAL PARTIES IN AUTHORITARIAN STATES

'Yes, we have lots of parties here,' says President Nazarbaev of Kazakhstan. 'I created them all' (quoted in Cummings, 2005). This quote reflects the secondary character of parties in most authoritarian regimes. Rather than being a channel for guidance, aggregation, mobilization, and recruitment, the party is a means of governing, and neither a source of power in itself nor a channel through which elections are contested, won, and lost. As Lawson (2013) says of parties under dictatorships, 'the party is a shield and instrument of power. Its function is to carry out the work of government as directed by other agents with greater power (the military or the demagogue and his entourage).' In doing this, it often presents itself as pursuing a national agenda based on a key theme such as anti-imperialism, national unity, or economic development, but such messages are often a means of legitimizing power rather than a substantive commitment.

Geddes (2006) argues that in spite of the risks potentially posed to authoritarian regimes by allowing parties and elections, there are several roles they can fulfil that dictators find useful, ranging from conflict resolution to public education – see Figure 16.4. The longer-term result is that what she describes as 'support parties' can prolong the political life not just of individual leaders but also of the regimes themselves. Of course, many of these functions are also performed by parties in democracies, but the latter provide additional value: they were often founded as a result of social cleavages, and continue today to appeal to groups of voters based on competing views about economic and social issues. In many poorer authoritarian states, politics is driven more by differences of identity and interest rather than policy. Ethnic, religious, and local identities matter more than policy preferences.

Nigeria illustrates these points. It has a long history of political party activity, pre-dating its independence from Britain in 1960. Its first party – the National Council of Nigeria and the Cameroons – was founded in 1944 on a platform of Nigerian nationalism, but was quickly joined (in 1948 and 1949 respectively) by two regionally based parties: the Action Group in the west and the Northern People's Congress in the north. Following independence, parties continued to work along ethnic lines, leading to the collapse of two civilian governments in 1966 and 1983. A still-born effort was made by the military government in 1987 to invent two national political parties named the Social Democratic Party and the National Republican Convention. Concerns remain that in a strongly regional country, parties will continue to drift towards identification with the different ethnic groups. However, a peaceful election

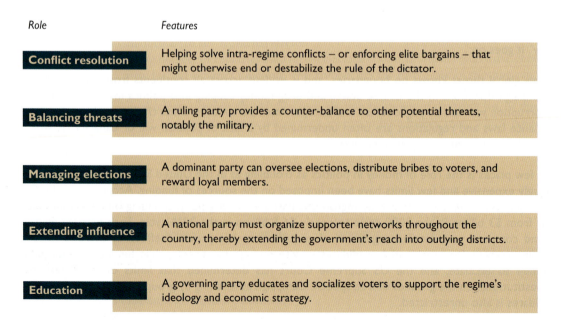

Role	Features
Conflict resolution	Helping solve intra-regime conflicts – or enforcing elite bargains – that might otherwise end or destabilize the rule of the dictator.
Balancing threats	A ruling party provides a counter-balance to other potential threats, notably the military.
Managing elections	A dominant party can oversee elections, distribute bribes to voters, and reward loyal members.
Extending influence	A national party must organize supporter networks throughout the country, thereby extending the government's reach into outlying districts.
Education	A governing party educates and socializes voters to support the regime's ideology and economic strategy.

Figure 16.4 Five roles of political parties in authoritarian states

in 2015 did witness the first-ever defeat for an incumbent president standing for re-election, suggesting a maturing of the country's party system and a transition to a more democratic order. Nonetheless, it remains a hybrid regime.

Political parties in sub-Saharan Africa are a puzzle, in the sense that many seemingly similar countries have had very different records. Following independence in the 1950s and 1960s, the heroes of the nationalist struggle routinely put a stop to party competition, and one-party systems were established; the official party was often justified in terms of the need to build national unity, even if it only served as the leader's personal vehicle. The tradition of the benevolent chief was skilfully exploited by dictators such as President Mobutu Sese Seko (leader of Zaire, now the Democratic Republic of the Congo, between 1965 and 1997):

> In our African tradition, there are never two chiefs; there is sometimes a natural heir to the chief, but can anyone tell me that he has known a village that has two chiefs? That is why we Congolese, in the desire to conform to the traditions of our continent, have resolved to group all the energies of the citizens of our country under the banner of a single national party. (quoted in Meredith, 2006)

But these single parties proved to be weak, they lacked autonomy from the national leader, and rather than building unity they merely entrenched the control of the elites. As with government itself, they had an urban bias, lacking a strong presence in the rural areas, and showed little concern with policy. True, the party was one of the few national political organizations and proved useful in recruiting supporters to public office, but these functions could not disguise a lack of cohesion, direction, and organization. Indeed, when the founder-leader eventually departed, his party would sometimes disappear at the same time. This was what happened, for example, with the United National Independence Party (UNIP) in Zambia, another hybrid regime. Founded in 1959, UNIP formed the first government of an independent Zambia in 1964, and stayed in power – as did Zambian president Kenneth Kaunda – until 1990. Following riots and a coup attempt that year, free elections were held in 1991 at which Kaunda was defeated. He retired from politics and UNIP sank into obscurity: his son Tiljenyi ran as the party's presidential candidate in 2011 and 2016, but won less than 1 per cent of the vote, and the party has no seats in the Zambian National Assembly.

Supporters of the governing ZANU-PF party in Zimbabwe celebrate the victory of Emmerson Mnangagwa in the 2018 presidential election, a result that ensured continued control by a party that has been in power since 1980.
Source: Getty Images/Luis Tato.

Despite recent economic growth, many African states still experience poverty, cultural heterogeneity, and centralized political systems that would seem to pose severe handicaps to democracy. Even so, Riedl (2014) finds that nearly two dozen have achieved a measure of democratic competition since the early 1990s; these include South Africa, Botswana, Ghana, Tanzania, and Mozambique. She suggests that the nature of the democratic transition shapes its success (see Chapter 5). In what might seem to be a counter-intuitive conclusion, she argues that where authoritarian incumbents are strong, they tightly control the democratic transition, leading to a stronger party system. Where the ruling party is weak, it loses control of the transition, allowing others to enter the process, resulting in a weaker party system.

The difficulties of establishing party competition in hybrid regimes is illustrated by recent events in Tanzania, yet another hybrid regime. Dominated for decades by a single party – Chama Cha Mapinduzi (CCM), or Party of the Revolution, which has won 70–75 per cent of the seats in the country's recent legislative elections – Tanzania has been led since 2015 by President John Magufuli. Chosen by the party as an outsider who was untainted by allegations of corruption, he at first seemed to be a reformer, paying unannounced visits to government offices to make sure that bureaucrats were at their desks, and firing officials on live television. But he also cracked down on political opposition, and exploited his dual powers as president of the country and chair of the party to remove opponents and appoint supporters to key positions. A recent tendency towards pluralism in Tanzania appears to have become undone, notes *The Economist* (2018), because CCM is the most stable and powerful institution in Tanzania, and too little has been done to strengthen other institutions and limit the powers of the presidency.

Moving the focus to Latin America, there is a wide variation in the nature of party systems, both across countries and within countries over time. Many explanations have been proposed for this, including the strength of executives, and different social circumstances. A historical study by Frantz and Geddes (2016) looks at the impact of dictatorship on party systems, and at what happens when dictators leave office and countries work to restore democracy. It begins by suggesting that dictators usually have three choices when taking power:

1. Repressing all parties, as in the case of Venezuela.
2. Allying themselves with a traditional party and using it to help them govern, as in the cases of Colombia, Nicaragua, and Paraguay.
3. Repressing pre-existing parties and creating a new one to support themselves, as in the case of the Dominican Republic.

The study found that when options 1 or 2 were chosen, the effect – when the dictator left office and the country began to re-democratize – was to contribute to a stable new political system. This has even been the case in instances of long-term repression of parties, which tend to go underground and then to re-emerge – as if from a freezer – when allowed to function again. Options 1 and 2 tend to preserve the old party system, preventing the rise of new parties. When option 3 was chosen, however, long-term party stability was undermined. This is because the new party has only shallow roots, and once the dictator leaves office, all institutions created to support the regime tend to fall by the wayside.

It will be interesting to see what happens in Venezuela if and when it returns to democracy. An earlier phase of dictatorship saw the outlawing in 1948 of multiple parties, only for them to re-emerge almost as soon as the military regime fell in 1958. Two pre-existing parties – the centrist Democratic Action (AD) and the moderately conservative Copei – became active again, producing every president until 1993. A new party was formed in 1997 to support the presidential campaign of Hugo Chávez, and has since gone on – as the United Socialist Party – to dominate Venezuelan politics, with the AD and Copei joining other parties in opposition, and often refusing to take part in what they see as deeply flawed elections.

A quite different set of circumstances can be found in Russia, which had no history of competitive party politics when the Soviet Union came to an end in 1991. At first glance, Russia would now seem to have a wide range of political parties from which its voters can choose. However, few of these have been able to develop either permanence or real influence. In fact, so many new parties were formed in the early years of democracy in the 1990s that they were often disparagingly described as 'taxi-cab parties' (driving around in circles, and stopping occasionally to let old members off and new ones on), or even 'divan parties' (they were so small that all their members could fit on a single piece of furniture). Clearly, when parties cease to exist from one election to the next, it is impossible for them to be held to account. Not surprisingly, they are the least trusted public organizations in a suspicious society (Levada Centre, 2017).

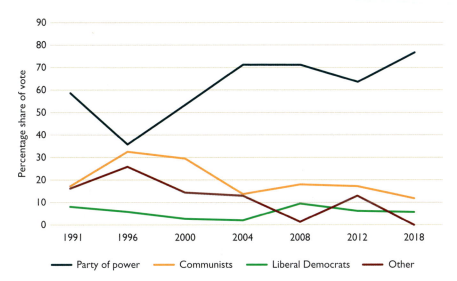

Figure 16.5 Trends in Russian presidential elections

Far more than is the case in other presidential or semi-presidential systems, voters in Russia's presidential elections are choosing between candidates, not parties. There has been an ideological line tying its three post-communist presidents (Boris Yeltsin, Vladimir Putin, and Dmitry Medvedev), and while all have formally run at elections as independents, they have mainly had the support of a single mainstream party, which has always been the vehicle rather than the driver. In the 1990s there was a modicum of competition, such that the 1996 election had to go to a second round, but since then the biggest party (first Unity, and now United Russia) has opened up a commanding position – see Figure 16.5. United Russia is what Russians term a 'party of power', meaning that the Kremlin uses threats and bribes to ensure it is supported by powerful ministers, regional governors, and large companies.

Given the weak position of Russia's parties, it is not surprising that they are poorly organized, with a small membership and minimal capacity to integrate a large and diverse country. In a manner typical of authoritarian regimes, the rules concerning the registration of parties, the nomination of candidates, and the receipt of state funding are skewed in favour of larger parties. Minor parties are trapped: they cannot grow until they become more significant but their importance cannot increase until they are larger (Kulik, 2007).

Party weakness of another kind is found in Haiti, also ranked as an authoritarian regime in the Democracy Index. A country that suffers at least as much from natural disasters as from political problems, Haiti is currently working off its 23rd constitution since becoming independent in 1804. Such changeability is both a cause and an effect of Haiti's political difficulties, and its political parties suffer even less consistency than its formal political institutions. It has elections, but they are rarely fair or efficient. It has a long history of political party activity, but has never developed durable parties with deep social roots. Party activity is at its greatest during presidential election seasons, when new parties emerge around the campaigns of the leading candidates. These have represented a wide range of issues, from Haitian nationalism to the interests of rural peasants, Haitian youth, communism, workers' rights, and opposition to the incumbent government. However, they rarely survive much longer than the terms in office of the leaders with whom they are associated, and so parties play only a peripheral role in Haitian politics.

DISCUSSION QUESTIONS

◆ Do we need political parties? If so, what are the most valuable functions they perform?
◆ Which is better: a two-party system, or a multi-party system?
◆ Which type of party system exists in your country? Does it reflect social divisions, voter preferences, the structure of government, or something else?
◆ Is it more democratic and effective for parties to choose leaders and candidates themselves, or for the choice to be put in the hands of voters?
◆ What is the fairest and most democratic means of financing political parties and election campaigns?
◆ Looking at the five roles of political parties in authoritarian regimes, are they all that different – except in degree – to the roles of parties in democracies?

KEY CONCEPTS

◆ Cartel party
◆ Catch-all party
◆ Closed primary
◆ Iron law of oligarchy
◆ Niche party
◆ Party system
◆ Political cleavage
◆ Political party
◆ Primary election
◆ Safe district
◆ Selectorate

FURTHER READING

Cross William P., and Richard S. Katz (eds) (2013) *The Challenges of IntraParty Democracy* (Oxford University Press). This book considers the principal issues that parties and the state must address in introducing greater democracy within parties.

Gauja, Anika (2016) *Political Parties and Elections: Legislating for Representative Democracy* (Routledge). A comparative assessment of the way in which democracies try to regulate the behaviour of political parties.

Hazan, Reuven Y., and Gideon Rahat (2010) *Democracy within Parties: Candidate Selection Methods and Their Political Consequences* (Oxford University Press). A comparative analysis of candidate selection methods.

Lawson, Kay, and Jorge Lanzaro (eds) (2010) *Political Parties and Democracy* (Praeger). A five-volume edited collection looking at political parties in the Americas, Europe, Asia, Africa, and the Arab World.

Pettit, Robin T. (2014) *Contemporary Party Politics* (Red Globe Press). An assessment of party politics in democracies, looking at different party systems, party ideologies, party members, and the future of parties.

Riedl, Rachel Beatty (2014) *Authoritarian Origins of Democratic Party Systems in Africa* (Cambridge University Press). A study of parties in Africa, looking at the challenging transitions from authoritarianism to competitive party systems.

VOTERS

17

CONTENTS
- Voters: an overview
- Party identification
- How voters choose
- Voter turnout
- Voters in authoritarian states

PREVIEW

How do voters make choices at elections? How do they decide even whether or not it is worth taking part in those elections? These are among the most intensively studied questions in political science, and yet there are no agreed answers. Media coverage of election results tends to focus on often small and short-term shifts in party support, while academic studies are focused on broader sociological and psychological questions such as social class, economic change, and party allegiance.

This chapter begins with a discussion of the long-term forces shaping electoral choice. It looks at party identification and at trends suggesting that the ties between parties and voters are eroding. It then reviews the main factors involved in helping us explain voter choice: social class (whose influence is declining), religion, political issues, the economy, and the personality of leaders. The effects of all of these are both debated and debatable.

The chapter also looks at rational choice analysis of voters and parties, a topic which gives us a case study of one of the theoretical approaches we reviewed in Chapter 2. It then discusses the more specific question of voter turnout: the declines seen in recent decades in many democracies, the reasons behind that decline, the impact of turnout on the quality of democracy, and the implications of compulsory voting. The chapter closes with a review of voting in authoritarian states, and of the different ways in which voters are limited, manipulated, and coerced.

KEY ARGUMENTS

- The habits and motivations of voters have long been a puzzle, with several different explanatory theories developed, but none offering universal answers.

- Party identification is key to understanding voters, but there are questions about exactly how it applies, particularly in light of partisan dealignment.

- The social bases of voting have mainly weakened in recent decades, although religion continues to play an important role in several countries.

- The evidence of short-term explanations for voter choice – such as issue voting, the economy, and the personality of leaders – is variable.

- Voter turnout has been on the decline in most democracies, although the reasons vary by time and place.

- Voting patterns in authoritarian states are less a matter of understanding voter motives than of understanding ruler motives.

Table 17.1 The economy and voter choice

Perception of the economy over the past 12 months	Percentage voting for the party of the incumbent president or prime minister
Has got better	46
Has stayed the same	31
Has got worse	23

Source: Adapted from Hellwig (2010: Table 9.1), rebased to 100 per cent.

about the same, or worsened. As Table 17.1 shows, the results were striking: voters who believed the economy had improved were twice as likely to vote for the party of the incumbent president or prime minister as voters who thought the state of the economy had worsened. Of course, those who already support the governing party are inclined to view the economy through rose-tinted glasses, exaggerating the real economic vote. Even so, the observed relationship between economic assessments and electoral choice is strong.

The actions of poor voters – whether they live in wealthy or poor countries – sets up an interesting paradox. Many studies have shown that a significant number often vote for parties that do not appear to stand for their material interests, and that instead seem to represent the interests of the wealthy. Huber and Stanig (2009) point out, for example, that large numbers of voters in wealthy democracies support parties that are opposed to the kind of higher taxes and redistributive policies from which such voters would benefit. This was reflected in the 2016 victory of Donald Trump: he won much of his support from voters who felt marginalized by political and economic elites, and who backed his promises to control immigration and create new jobs. Yet most of those he appointed to his administration were, like him, wealthy individuals from corporate backgrounds, and many of his policies were designed to reduce the tax burden on the wealthy and corporations, and to set up trade barriers that had the effect of raising prices on imports and undercutting exports.

Turning to voting in poorer (and flawed) democracies, which have been much less studied than in their wealthier counterparts, the evidence gathered to date points to a different kind of economic incentive: **vote buying**, or the promise of tangible vote-related material rewards. According to Schaffer (2007), these may take the form of cash, of commodities (he lists everything from cigarettes to watches, coffins, haircuts, bags of rice, birthday cakes, and TV sets), or of services.

Vote buying
The process whereby parties and candidates provide material benefits to voters in return for their support at elections.

Thachil (2014) looks at the case of India, and specifically at the curious success of the Bharatiya Janata Party (BJP) (a party usually identified with India's privileged upper castes) among poorer Indians. The explanation, he suggests, lies in the way the BJP has won over disadvantaged voters by providing them with basic social services via grass-roots affiliates. This 'outsourcing' allows the party to continue to represent the policy interests of its privileged base, while also drawing in many votes from the poor.

Brazil provides an example of vote buying operating within the political elite. A major scandal broke there in 2005, with charges that the ruling Workers' Party had paid a number of Congressional deputies a monthly stipend in return for their support for legislation supported by the party. Known as the Mensalão (big monthly stipend) scandal, it threatened to bring down the government of President Lula da Silva (in office 2003–10). Lula himself won election to a second term, but 25 of the 38 defendants in the resulting court case were found guilty of a variety of charges.

The trial came to exemplify the issue of corruption in Brazil, a problem reflected in more low-level instances of candidates paying cash to voters for their support. The problem, argues Yadav (2011) has worsened with the advent of stronger political parties able to exploit the Brazilian state as a source of funds. (In April 2018, Lula began a nine-year prison sentence after having been found guilty of money laundering and receiving bribes.)

The phenomenon of vote buying is far from limited to poorer states or communities. Governments legally and routinely 'buy' the votes of other governments in meetings of international organizations (Lockwood, 2013), for example, and almost any instance where elected representatives can point to a new factory, school, or military facility that was brought to their district through their efforts might be defined as vote buying. Is there much difference between buying a voter in, say, India and buying an electoral district in, say, the United States?

Crowds turn out in Sao Paulo, Brazil, to demonstrate against ongoing corruption scandals in the ruling Workers' Party. Voter protests helped bring about the impeachment and removal from office in 2016 of President Dilma Rousseff.
Source: iStock/Willbrasil21.

Leader personality

As we saw in Chapter 14, the most famous example of the importance of appearance, style, and likeability for political candidates came in 1960 with the first television debate involving presidential candidates in the United States, between John F. Kennedy and Richard Nixon. Personality has long been a factor in political choice and in the levels of support given to leaders, but it only become more important in the age of television. While she was prime minister of Britain, for example, Margaret Thatcher was encouraged by her advisers to lower the tone of her voice so as to sound more authoritative. In France and the US, polls found that François Hollande and Barack Obama won their respective presidential elections in 2012 at least in part because they were seen as more likeable than their competitors, Nicolas Sarkozy and Mitt Romney. Donald Trump, meanwhile, offered a different kind of personality: one who threw out much of the rulebook regarding appropriate behaviour, encouraging his supporters and often horrifying his critics.

There are many problems in suggesting that the personality of leaders is a factor in voter choice, not least being the difficulty of measuring such a subjective commodity. The effects of personality on electoral choice can cancel out, with as many voters being attracted as repelled by a particular candidate's personality, resulting in no net impact. The discussion of leaders also often reveals a selection bias, focusing on the characterful while forgetting the anonymous.

In the first comparative study of the subject, King (2002) attempted to assess the role of the personalities of leaders on the results of 52 elections held between 1960 and 2001 in Canada, France, Britain, Russia, and the United States. As to whether it had any impact, his results were as follows:

◆ No in 37 cases.
◆ Possibly in 6 cases.
◆ Probably in 5 cases.
◆ Yes in just 4 cases: Harold Wilson, Britain, 1964 and February 1974; Charles de Gaulle, France, 1965; and Pierre Trudeau, Canada, 1968.

King's general conclusion was that 'most elections remain overwhelmingly political contests, and political parties would do well to choose their leaders and candidates in light of that fact'. Much subsequent research has confirmed King's views, with a statistical study of nine democracies edited by Aarts *et al.* (2011) confirming the unimportance of the characteristics of leaders. Leader traits are only a part, and often a minor part, of the factors shaping individual votes and overall election results.

Where leader traits *do* make a difference, the key characteristics appear to be those directly linked to performance in office, such as competence and integrity. By comparison, purely personal characteristics, such as appearance and likeability, are unimportant. In their analysis of Australia, Germany, and Sweden, Ohr and Oscarsson (2011) conclude that 'politically relevant and performance-related leader traits are important criteria for voters' political judgements', but that leader evaluations 'are firmly based on politically "rational" considerations'. If personal traits matter, it is because they are judged to be relevant to government performance.

VOTER TURNOUT

Voter turnout
The number of voters who take part in an election, expressed as a percentage of the total number of eligible voters.

So far, this chapter has focused on the forces shaping voter choice. Equally important for a comparative understanding of government and politics, perhaps, is the topic of **voter turnout**. Rates vary by time and place, ranging from a high of about 90 per cent or more to a low of about 20–30 per cent, with an average in most democracies of about 50–70 per cent. Figure 17.5 offers some examples, showing little correlation between turnout levels and the quality of democracy: Turkey and Nigeria are both hybrids, for example, but Turkey has a turnout rate almost double that of Nigeria. Meanwhile, turnout rates in Australia and Sweden are more than double those in France, in spite of all three countries being democracies.

One phenomenon witnessed in many democracies in recent decades has been declining turnout. Despite improved education, turnout rates have fallen since the 1950s in most of the democratic world, as illustrated in Figure 17.6. Numbers are down by 35 percentage points in the US, for example, by 31 points in France, by 20

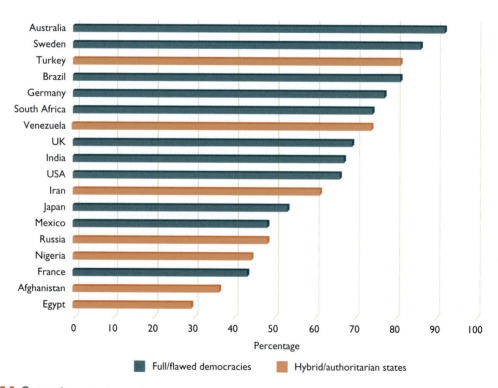

Figure 17.5 Comparing voter turnout

Source: Institute for Democracy and Electoral Assistance (2018b).

Notes: Figures are for voting-age population in most recent national legislative elections. No data for China, which does not hold national elections.

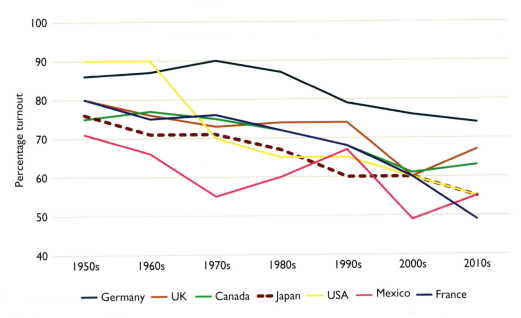

Figure 17.6 Comparing trends in voter turnout
Source: Institute for Democracy and Electoral Assistance (2018b).
Note: Figures are for voting age population in national legislative elections.

points in Japan, and by 12 points in Germany. What has caused this drop? Are there common factors involved? Should we even consider low turnout to be a problem?

On the one hand, it might be a reflection of limited engagement based on a lack of faith in government, but – on the other hand – it could also be a sign of contentment; why vote when all seems to be going well? Low turnout could also be a reflection of the diversification of participation discussed in Chapter 13; citizens may still be engaged, but through different means. Meanwhile, high turnout could be interpreted as a sign of healthy civic engagement, but it might also be a result of over-intense party competition or concern about the direction being taken by government.

In an influential analysis, Franklin (2004) linked the decline of turnout to the diminishing significance of elections. He suggested that the success of many democracies in sustaining welfare states and full employment in the post-war era (see Chapter 20) resolved long-standing conflicts between capital and labour. With class conflict on the decrease, citizens had fewer incentives to vote. As he wrote, 'elections in recent years may show lower turnout for the simple reason that these elections decide issues of lesser importance than elections did in the late 1950s'. In other words, when less is at stake, people are more likely to stay at home.

But declining satisfaction with the performance of democratic governments has also played its part. We have seen in several other chapters in this book how trust in government has fallen in many democracies; even though support for democratic principles remains strong, rising cynicism about government performance has so far encouraged more people to stay away from the polls. But there are also some very practical reasons for deflated turnout, as reflected in the recipe for higher turnout in Table 17.2. Overall, and fitting with ideas about rational choice, turnout tends to be higher in those countries where the costs or effort of voting are low and the perceived benefits are high.

On the cost side, turnout is reduced when voters are required to take the initiative in registering, as in the United States. In most European countries, by contrast, registration is the responsibility of government, helping encourage turnout. Turnout is also lower when citizens must vote in person and during a weekday, and hence higher turnout can be encouraged by allowing voting at the weekend, by proxy, by mail, by electronic means, and at convenient locations such as supermarkets. The ability to vote in advance is also helpful; the number of voters casting their ballot in advance of election day has been growing steadily in the United States, reaching a new record in 2016 of 47 million (United States Elections Project, 2016).

On the benefit side, the greater the impact of a single vote, the more willing voters are to incur the costs of voting. Thus, the closer the contest, the higher the turnout. Multiple studies over several decades have made the

Table 17.2 A recipe for higher voter turnout

Features of the political system	Features of voters
Compulsory voting	Middle aged
Automatic registration	Well educated
Voting by post and by proxy permitted	Married
Advance voting permitted	Higher income
Weekend polling	Employed
Election decides who governs	Home owner
Cohesive parties	Strong party loyalty
Proportional representation	Church-goer
Close result anticipated	Member of a labour union
Small electorate	Has not changed residences recently
Expensive campaigns	Voted in previous elections
Elections for several posts held at the same time	

Sources: Endersby et al. (2006), Geys (2006), IDEA (2018a).

Table 17.3 Countries where voting is compulsory

Compulsory voting enforced		Compulsory voting not enforced	
Argentina	Luxembourg	Bolivia	Honduras
Australia	Nauru	Bulgaria	Mexico
Belgium	Peru	Costa Rica	Paraguay
Brazil	Singapore	Dominican Republic	Thailand
Cyprus	Turkey	Egypt	
Ecuador	Uruguay	Gabon	

Source: IDEA (2018c).

Note: Voting is also compulsory in the Democratic Republic of Congo, Lebanon, and Panama, but there is no information regarding whether or not it is enforced. Countries that no longer use compulsory voting include Chile, Fiji, Italy, and Venezuela.

point that proportional representation is the most effective electoral system (see Chapter 15) in terms of encouraging turnout, in part because the benefits of voting are clearer: each vote counts because seats gained directly reflect votes won. In the single-member plurality system, by contrast, most electoral districts are secure for a particular party, meaning that individual votes are unlikely to affect the result.

Within countries, variations in turnout reflect the pattern found with other forms of political participation; the likelihood of voting is shaped by an individual's political resources and political interest (see Table 17.2, right column). Those most likely to vote are educated, affluent, married, middle-aged citizens with a job and a strong party loyalty, who belong to a church or a trade union, and are long-term residents of a community. These are the people with both resources and an interest in formal politics. By contrast, those least likely to vote have fewer resources and less reason to be committed to party politics; the archetypal non-voter is a young, poorly educated, single, unemployed man who belongs to no organizations, lacks party ties, and has recently moved home.

Attempts to boost turnout must be sensitive to political realities: while increased participation may benefit the system as a whole, it will have an unequal impact on the parties within it. Conservative parties in particular will be cautious about schemes for encouraging turnout, because abstainers would probably vote disproportionately for parties of the left. There remains one other blunt but effective tool for promoting turnout: compulsory voting (see Focus 17.2).

VOTERS IN AUTHORITARIAN STATES

So far in this chapter the focus has been on the influences that shape voter choice in democracies, the emphasis being on the noun *choice*: voters are faced with alternatives and bring multiple considerations to bear in deciding which party or leader to support, or even whether to vote at all. Looking now at authoritarian states, they almost all have elections (as we saw in Chapter 15), but the dynamics of voting are different. Although voting in authoritarian states is less well studied and understood than is the case with democracies, it is clear that understanding the motives of rulers is more important than understanding the motives of voters.

At the opposite end of the spectrum from democracies are a handful of Middle Eastern no-party states where the choices are straightforward: there are none, at least in terms of elections. People must find other and more subtle ways of making their views known to the regime, and must be careful what they say, and how they say it. Moving along the spectrum, we find a handful of communist one-party systems where voters are not given much in the way of alternatives but may still be expected to endorse the party's candidates by turning out to vote. In such systems, ruling parties cannot be meaningfully opposed or defeated, and official candidates are simply presented to voters for ritual endorsement. For an example, see Spotlight Iran.

Any opinions that voters might have about the electoral process in an authoritarian regime, or about party policies or pressing public issues, are not for expression in the voting booth. Undoubtedly voters do have such opinions, because politics in such states is more central to ordinary life than in democracies, and people are adept at distinguishing between national propaganda and local reality. With such limited choices on election day, however, such opinions are effectively suppressed. This phenomenon ties in with what we saw in Chapter 13 about mobilized participation, where the actions of voters are managed and obligatory, their involvement organized by leaders and elites in order to give the impression of support for the regime.

These no-party and one-party systems are rare, though, which means that the vast majority of authoritarian systems have two or more parties vying for the votes of citizens, in an arrangement sometimes known as **electoral authoritarianism**. Like so many concepts in

Electoral authoritarianism
An arrangement in which a regime gives the appearance of being democratic, and offering voters choice, while concealing its authoritarian qualities.

Focus 17.2
Compulsory voting: pros and cons

In the effort to encourage higher voter turnout, making it compulsory can be considered the nuclear option. Compulsory voting was first introduced in Belgium in 1892, and then in Argentina in 1914 and Australia in 1924. Although it is today used in less than 30 countries – some of which enforce it (using fines, imprisonment, or disenfranchisement as a sanction) and some of which do not (see Table 17.3) – voter turnout in these countries is about seven percentage points higher on average than in countries where voting is voluntary (Institute for Democracy and Electoral Assistance, 2018c).

The case for compulsory voting is worth making. A full turnout means the electorate is more representative and the authority of the government is enhanced, disengaged groups are drawn into the political process, more voters will lead to a more informed electorate, and parties no longer need to devote resources to encourage their supporters to vote. Most citizens acknowledge that it is their civic duty to pay taxes, serve on a jury, and perhaps even fight in a war; why, then, should they not want to invest the small amount of effort involved in voting at elections? Without it, abstainers take a free ride at the expense of the conscientious.

But the arguments against are also strong. Mandatory voting undermines the liberty which is an essential part of democracy: requiring people to participate smacks of authoritarianism rather than free choice. Also, abstention may reflect contentment, meaning that low turnout is not necessarily a problem. Most problematic of all, compulsory voting gives influence to less-informed and less-engaged voters. Brennan (2011) argues that nothing is more integral to democracy than voting, and that most people endorse the 'folk theory' that all citizens have a civic duty to vote. 'However,' he continues, 'if citizens do vote, they must vote well, on the basis of sound evidence for what is likely to promote the common good'. If they lack the 'motive, knowledge, rationality, or ability to vote well', he concludes, they should not vote at all. Clearly, compulsory voting militates against this.

In all democracies, elections still attract more than enough votes to form a decision. There is no evidence that high turnout increases the quality of the political choices made, so why not continue to rely on the natural division of labour between interested voters and indifferent abstainers?

SPOTLIGHT IRAN

Brief profile

Iran has long played a critical role in the Middle East, first because of the oil reserves that the British long sought, then because of the close strategic relationship between the United States and the regime of the Shah of Iran, and now because of the significance of the Islamic Republic created in the wake of the 1979 Iranian revolution. It has an elected president and legislature, but power is manipulated by an unelected Supreme Leader surrounded by competing cliques, candidates for public office are vetted, laws must be approved by an unelected clerical-juridical council, political rights are limited, and women are marginalized. It is a poor country that controls enormous oil and mineral wealth, and is socially diverse. Even if most Iranians are joined by a shared religion, they are still divided between those espousing conservative and reformist views. These differences are strongly structured by gender, generation, and level of education.

Form of government	Unitary Islamic Republic. Date of state formation debatable, and most recent constitution adopted 1979.
Executive	Presidential. President elected for maximum of two consecutive four-year terms, but shares power with a Supreme Leader appointed for life by an Assembly of Experts (effectively an electoral college), who must be an expert in Islamic law, and acts as head of state with considerable executive powers.
Legislature	Unicameral Majlis, with 290 members elected for renewable four-year terms.
Judiciary	Supreme Court with members appointed for five-year terms. The Iranian legal system is based on a combination of Islamic law (sharia) and civil law.
Electoral system	Single-member plurality for the legislature, simple majority for the president.
Parties	No-party system. Only Islamist parties can operate legally, but organizations that look like parties operate regardless. They are not formal political parties as conventionally understood, however, and instead operate as loose coalitions representing conservative and reformist positions.

80.3m **Population**

$439bn **Gross Domestic Product**

$5,415 **Per capita GDP**

✗ Full Democracy
✗ Flawed Democracy
✗ Hybrid Regime
✔ Authoritarian
✗ Not Rated

Democracy Index rating

✗ Free
✗ Partly Free
✔ Not Free
✗ Not Rated

Freedom House rating

✗ Very High
✔ High
✗ Medium
✗ Low
✗ Not Rated

Human Development Index rating

Voters in Iran

Iran does not fare well on comparative democratic rankings. Since the 1979 revolution that removed the Western-backed (and authoritarian) regime of the Shah of Iran, and ushered in the era of the ayatollahs (high-ranking Shi'ah clerics), Iran has possessed a pariah status in the eyes of most Western governments. It has been accused of repression at home, of efforts to support terrorist organizations such as Hezbollah in Lebanon, and of covert plans to build nuclear weapons.

It is all the more ironic, then, that it seems to have an active electorate faced with a significant number of circumscribed choices at the polls. The ruling clerics and the military still wield considerable power, many in the political opposition languish in jail, and elections are contested less by political parties than by religiously based factions. This does not mean, however, that many Iranians do not hanker after democratic choice, nor that they are unwilling to voice opposition to the regime and support reform-minded candidates at elections.

The 2009, 2013, and 2017 presidential elections, for example, provided choice among candidates opting for

Iranian voters line up at a polling station during local elections in 2017. In spite of the ban on political parties in Iran, and charges of electoral fraud, voters are presented with an array of candidates representing different policy positions.
Source: Getty Images/Majid Saeedi/Stringer.

different solutions to the country's severe economic problems. Open campaigning included debates involving the major candidates. While there is no dependable way to measure Iranian public opinion, it was clear that many citizens — particularly younger voters suffering the most from high unemployment — were willing to express themselves. Turnout in 2013 and 2017 was estimated to have exceeded 70 per cent, but charges of fraud continue to surround Iranian elections, although they are hard to verify in the absence of independent election monitoring.

With problems ranging from high population growth to unemployment, inflation, pollution, drug addiction, and poverty, Iran faces difficulties which the ruling regime has intensified rather than resolved. But there is hope in the substantial desire for change among its many young, educated voters, hinting — in the view of Brumberg and Farhi (2016) — at the possibility of multiple opportunities for change and transformation.

Further reading

Axworthy, Michael (2016) *Iran: What Everyone Needs to Know* (Oxford University Press).

Boroujerdi, Mehrzad, and Kourosh Rahimkhani (2018) *Post-revolutionary Iran: A Political Handbook* (Syracuse University Press).

Brumberg, Daniel, and Farideh Farhi (2016) *Power and Change in Iran: Politics of Contention and Conciliation* (Indiana University Press).

INTEREST GROUPS

18

PREVIEW

Where most of the institutions of government are listed in a national constitution, interest groups (like political parties) are mainly founded and operate outside these formal structures. They have evolved separately, their core purpose being to influence the shaping of policy without becoming part of government; another example of governance at work. They come in several types, and use different methods – both direct and indirect – to achieve their goals. A vibrant interest group community is generally a sign of a healthy civil society, but where the influence of different interests and the groups that support those interests is unbalanced, it can also become a barrier to the implementation of the popular will as expressed in elections.

This chapter begins with a survey of the origins and the different types of groups, and the manner in which they work. It assesses the channels of influence used by groups before looking at the ingredients of influence and asking what gives particular groups the ability to persuade. The chapter then discusses and critiques the idea of pluralism, contrasting the free marketplace of ideas with the privileged role that groups can come to play within the political process. It then looks at the distinctive qualities and effects of social movements, before assessing the global state of civil society and discussing the place of interest groups in authoritarian regimes, where they are typically seen either as a threat to the power of the regime or as a device through which the regime can maintain its control over society.

KEY ARGUMENTS

◆ Interest groups come in many shapes and sizes, with a wide variety of objectives, methods, and levels of influence.

◆ Much like political parties, interest groups are a relatively recent addition to the formal processes of government.

◆ Interest groups use a combination of direct and indirect channels of influence. Where ties with government are particularly strong, the danger arises of the emergence of sub-governments enjoying preferred access.

◆ Pluralism is closely associated with studies of interest groups, but there are reasons to question whether it describes how groups operate in practice.

◆ Interest groups are often complemented by wider social movements, whose activities challenge conventional channels of participation.

◆ Where the governments of democracies may be too heavily influenced by powerful groups, the problem can be reversed in authoritarian states.

INTEREST GROUPS: AN OVERVIEW

Interest groups are bodies which seek to influence public policy from outside the formal structures of government. They do this through a combination of direct pressure on government and the bureaucracy, and indirect pressure via the media and public opinion. They come in many different forms, including employer organizations, consumer groups, professional bodies, labour unions, and single-issue groups. They work primarily at the national level, but can also be found in local and international arenas. Like political parties, interest groups are a crucial channel of communication between society and government, especially in democracies. Unlike parties, they pursue specialized concerns, working to influence government without becoming the government. They are not election-fighting organizations; instead, they typically adopt a pragmatic approach in dealing with whatever power structure confronts them, using whatever channels are legally (and sometimes illegally) available to them.

> **Interest group**
> A body that works outside government to influence public policy. Also known as a non-governmental organization (NGO).

Although many interest groups go about their work quietly, their activity is pervasive. Their staff can be found negotiating with bureaucrats over the details of proposed laws and regulations, pressing their case in legislative committee hearings, and taking journalists out to lunch in their efforts to influence media coverage. As Finer (1966) once noted, 'their day-to-day activities pervade every sphere of domestic policy, every day, every way, at every nook and cranny of government'. Without question, interest groups are central to a system of functional representation, especially on detailed issues of policy. Even so, there are different ways of defining the relationship between interest groups and the state. Thus groups can be seen as:

- An essential component of a free society, separate from the state.
- Partners with the state in achieving a well-regulated society.
- Providers of information and watchdogs on the performance of government.
- An additional channel through which citizens can be politically engaged.
- Promoters of elitism, offering particular sectors privileged access to government.

Interest groups are also a critical part of a healthy **civil society**. In a democracy, the limited role of government leaves space for groups and movements of all kinds to emerge and address shared problems, often without government intervention. A rich civic tradition also provides the context in which interest groups can develop their capacity to influence government. Some interests can become too powerful, though, developing a privileged status with government, and compromising the principle of equal access. In authoritarian regimes, meanwhile, there are typically restrictions on the work of interest groups, because rulers see them as a potential threat, and seek either to repress them or incorporate them into the regime. As a result, civil society in authoritarian regimes is constrained.

> **Civil society**
> The arena that exists between the state and the individual, and within which groups take collective action on shared interests.

ORIGINS AND TYPES OF GROUPS

Interest groups pre-date parties, and in many ways can be seen as a more natural form of political organization: the earliest groups were created either to provide a service not yet addressed by government, or to bring together a group of people with shared interests who wanted to make a joint case to government. Individual citizens could press their case and try to influence political decisions, but to do so as part of a group always made more strategic sense, and the bigger the group, the more likely government was to listen. One of the core methods of pressing influence is **lobbying**, a concept whose origins lie in the lobby that separates the chambers of the House of Commons and the House of Lords in the British Parliament. In this space, citizens could once approach their Members of Parliament in order to plead their case or request help, and from this habit derived the terms lobbying and lobbyist (see Focus 18.1).

> **Lobbying**
> Efforts to influence the decisions made by elected officials or bureaucrats on behalf of individuals, groups, or organizations.

The earliest interest groups of the modern era date back to the industrial revolution, and include charitable organizations formed to help the poor, or bodies formed to campaign on political or social issues. In Britain, examples of the latter included the Committee for the Abolition of the Slave Trade, formed in 1787, and the Royal Society for the Prevention of Cruelty to Animals, formed in 1824. These were followed by groups formed to promote the interests of industrial and agricultural employers or workers, the latter evolving into trade unions (which had long been illegal in most industrial countries). In the early twentieth century, new associations were formed to represent the interests of professionals, such as doctors, lawyers, and teachers. Later, with the emergence after World War II of the post-material ideas discussed in Chapter 12, groups with a wider variety of agendas began to develop, promoting the rights of women and ethnic minorities, and campaigning on behalf of issues such as human rights and the environment.

Interest groups today come in many shapes and sizes, with a wide range of objectives, methods, and levels of influence. Many have been founded for practical or charitable purposes rather than for political action, but have developed a political dimension as they have worked either to modify public policy or to resist unfavourable changes. Some will have a few hundred members focusing on a short-term local issue and working with local government, while others will have millions of members and work in many different countries, targeting national governments or international organizations. Their variety, in fact, is so great, their methods so varied, and their overlap so considerable that it is not easy to develop a list of discrete types (Figure 18.1).

To help us understand this variety, it is helpful to distinguish between protective and promotional groups. **Protective groups** are the most prominent and powerful, articulating the material interests of their members: workers, employers, professionals, retirees, military veterans, and so on. Sometimes known as 'sectional' or 'functional' groups, these bodies represent clear interests, and are usually well established, well connected, and well resourced. They give priority to influencing government, and can invoke sanctions to help them achieve their goals: workers can go on strike, and business organizations can withdraw their cooperation with government.

Protective groups can also be based on local, rather than functional, interests. Geographic groups emerge when the shared interests of people living in the same location are threatened by plans for, say, a new highway, a power station, or public housing for low-income residents. Because of their negative stance, these kinds of bodies are sometimes known as **Nimby** groups, meaning 'not in my back yard'. Collectively, Nimby groups can generate a Banana outcome: 'build absolutely nothing anywhere near anyone'. Unlike permanent functional organizations, however, Nimby groups often come and go in response to particular threats and changing levels of public interest.

In contrast to the narrow interests of protective bodies (see Table 18.1), **promotional groups** are broader in outlook, which is why they are also known as advocacy, attitude, campaign or cause groups, or even public interest groups (although just how far they work in the true public interest is a matter of some debate). They do not expect to profit directly from the causes they pursue, nor do they have a material stake in how those causes are resolved. Instead, they seek broad policy

Protective group
An interest group that seeks selective benefits for its members and insider status with relevant government departments.

Nimby
An acronym for 'not in my back yard', describing the efforts of some local interest groups to block geographically focused developments.

Promotional group
An 'interest' group that promotes wider issues and causes than is the case with protective groups focused on the tangible interests of their members.

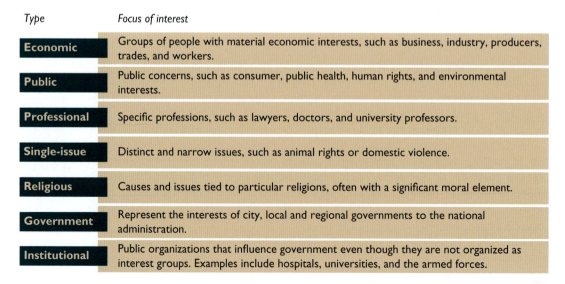

Type	Focus of interest
Economic	Groups of people with material economic interests, such as business, industry, producers, trades, and workers.
Public	Public concerns, such as consumer, public health, human rights, and environmental interests.
Professional	Specific professions, such as lawyers, doctors, and university professors.
Single-issue	Distinct and narrow issues, such as animal rights or domestic violence.
Religious	Causes and issues tied to particular religions, often with a significant moral element.
Government	Represent the interests of city, local and regional governments to the national administration.
Institutional	Public organizations that influence government even though they are not organized as interest groups. Examples include hospitals, universities, and the armed forces.

Figure 18.1 Types of interest group

Table 18.1 Comparing protective and promotional interest groups

	Protective	Promotional
Aims	Defends an interest	Promotes a cause
Membership	Closed: membership is restricted	Open: anyone can join
Status	Insider: frequently consulted by government and actively seeks this role	Outsider: consulted less often by government; targets public opinion and the media
Benefits	Selective: only group members benefit	Collective: benefits go to both members and non-members
Focus	Aim to influence national government on specific issues affecting members	Also seek to influence national and global bodies on broad policy matters

changes in the issues that interest them, which include consumer safety, women's interests, driver safety, the environment, or economic development. Their growth in recent decades constitutes a major trend in interest politics, even if many who join promotional groups are credit card affiliates only; they send donations or sign up for membership, and perhaps follow news about the issue concerned, but otherwise remain unengaged. For this reason, the effectiveness of promotional bodies as schools for democracy can easily be overstated (Maloney, 2009).

> **Peak association**
> An umbrella organization representing the broad interests of business or labour to government.

Protective interest groups representing a specific industry not only lobby government directly, but will often also join a **peak association**, or an umbrella body for like-minded organizations. Their members are not individuals but businesses, trade associations, and labour unions. For example, industrial associations and corporations may join a wider body representing business interests to government, and labour unions may do the same for wider bodies representing worker interests. Examples of peak associations include the Federal Organization of German Employers, the National Association of Manufacturers in the United States, and the Confederation of British Industry (CBI) in the UK. According to its website, membership of the CBI gives its member businesses *influence* in government, *insight* into policy trends, and *access* to political leaders (Confederation of British Industry, 2018).

Despite the widespread decline in union membership and labour militancy (see later in this chapter), many labour peak associations still speak with a powerful voice. In 2018, the German Trade Union Confederation (DGB) comprised eight unions with a total of nearly six million individual members, while Britain's Trades Union Congress had 49 affiliated unions in 2018, representing a comparable number of working people. Such numbers are usually enough to earn a seat at the policy table.

In working to influence public policy, peak associations usually succeed, because they are attuned to national government, have a strong research capacity, and represent significant economic interests. For example, the DGB (2018) describes itself as follows:

> The DGB is the political umbrella organization of the German trade unions and is the voice of working people in Germany. It unites and represents the interests of its unions and their members to politicians and other organizations at all levels: from local government to European and international bodies … The DGB and its member unions are committed to the principles of a 'general trade union'. This means they have no affiliations relating to religion, belief, ideology, and party politics, and unite workers regardless of their industry, employment relationship, political views, or beliefs.

The place of peak associations has been changing, though, because of the rise of pro-market thinking, international markets, and smaller service companies. Trade union membership has fallen, and the voice of business is now often expressed directly by leading companies. In addition, the task of influencing the government is increasingly delegated to specialist lobbying companies. In response to these trends, peak associations have tended to become policy-influencing and service-providing bodies, not just organizations negotiating collectively with government on behalf of their members.

Think-tank
A private organization that conducts research into a given area of policy with the goal of fostering public debate and political change.

Another kind of interest group is the **think-tank**, or policy institute. This is a private organization set up to undertake research with a view to influencing both the public and the political debate. Think-tanks typically publish reports, organize conferences, and host seminars, all with the goal of encouraging debate over the issues in which they are interested, and to influence government and legislators either directly or indirectly. Most are privately funded, but some are supported by governments, political parties, or corporations, and have a clear national, corporate, or ideological agenda. The work of several such bodies has been used in this book: Freedom House (United States) on democracy, Transparency International (Germany) on corruption, the Fraser Institute (Canada) on economic freedom, and Civicus (South Africa) on civil society – see later in this chapter.

CHANNELS OF INFLUENCE

Interest groups have a nose for where policy is made, and are adept at following the debate to the arenas where it is resolved. They are also adept at using different means for shaping and changing the political agenda; their methods include fund-raising (and spending), promoting public awareness, generating information, mobilizing their members, lobbying government, advising legislators, and encouraging favourable media coverage of the issues they care about. These methods can be categorized broadly into two sets: direct and indirect (summarized in Figure 18.2).

Direct influence on policy-makers

Those who make policy are the ultimate target of most groups. Direct conversations with government ministers are the ideal, and talking with ministers before specific policies have crystallized is particularly valuable because it

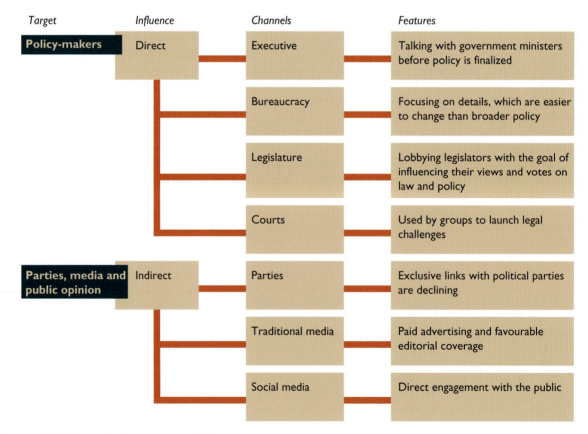

Target	Influence	Channels	Features
Policy-makers	Direct	Executive	Talking with government ministers before policy is finalized
		Bureaucracy	Focusing on details, which are easier to change than broader policy
		Legislature	Lobbying legislators with the goal of influencing their views and votes on law and policy
		Courts	Used by groups to launch legal challenges
Parties, media and public opinion	Indirect	Parties	Exclusive links with political parties are declining
		Traditional media	Paid advertising and favourable editorial coverage
		Social media	Direct engagement with the public

Figure 18.2 Channels of interest group influence

enables a group to enter the policy process at a formative stage. But such privileges are usually confined to a select few, and most interest group activity focuses in practice on the bureaucracy, the legislature, and the courts. Of these, the bureaucracy is the main pressure point: interest groups follow power and it is in the offices of bureaucrats that detailed decisions are often formed.

While the bureaucracy is invariably a crucial arena for groups, the significance of the legislature depends on its political weight. Comparing the United States and Canada illustrates the differences:

◆ The US Congress (and, especially, its committees) is a vital cog in the policy machinery. Members of Congress realize they are under constant public scrutiny, not least in the House of Representatives, where a two-year election cycle means that politicians must be continually aware of their ratings by interest groups, and are constantly looking for sources of funding for election campaigns. The ability of groups to endorse particular candidates keeps legislators sensitive to group demands, especially those which resonate in their home districts (see Cigler *et al.*, 2015).

◆ In Canada, as in most democracies, Parliament is more reactive than proactive; as a result, interest groups treat its members as opinion-formers rather than policy-makers. Party voting is entrenched in the House of Commons, extending beyond floor votes to committees and, in any case, 'committees seldom modify in more than marginal ways what is placed before them and virtually never derail any bill that the government has introduced' (Brooks and Ménard, 2017). Such a disciplined environment offers few opportunities for influence.

Lobbying is central to the idea of direct influence over policy-makers (see Focus 18.1), but it raises many troubling questions. Is lobbying just a fancy word for bribery? Is it possible for wealthy interest groups and corporations simply to pay a fee to a lobbying firm to ensure that a bill is defeated or a regulation deferred? On the whole, the answer is 'no'. Lobbyists are inclined to exaggerate their own impact for commercial reasons but, except in countries where there are particularly strong links between government and key interests (such as Japan – see later in this chapter), most can achieve little more than access to relevant politicians and, perhaps, bureaucrats. One study of lobbying in the United States, for example, found that six out of ten of the campaigns studied failed to change policy despite millions of dollars in spending (Baumgartner, *et al.*, 2009).

Despites its practical limitations, professional lobbying does contribute to effective political communication. It can focus the client's message on relevant decision-makers, ensuring that the client's voice is heard by those who need to hear it. Furthermore, lobbyists spend most time with sympathetic legislators, contributing to their pro-motion of a cause in which they already believe. Long-time Brussels-based commercial lobbyist Stanley Crossick (quoted in Thomas and Hrebenar, 2009) said that 'successful lobbying involves getting the right message over to the right people in the right form at the right time on the right issue'. In that respect, at least, it enhances the efficiency of governance.

Indirect influence through public opinion

Public opinion is a critical target for promotional interest groups, the goals being to change public perceptions and habits, and to aggregate public interest in such a way as to bring pressure for policy change on government. This wider audience can be addressed by focusing on paid advertising, by promoting favourable coverage in conventional media (public relations), and by using social media to promote ideas and bring together like-minded constituencies.

Political parties are less important as targets of influence than they once were. In Europe, for example, labour un-ions and socialist parties long had a close relationship in their efforts to promote broad working-class interests, and the environmental movement spawned both promotional interest groups dealing with specific problems (such as pollution, waste, and threats to wildlife) and green political parties. Interest groups have often since become more specialized while parties have developed broader agendas. As a result, most groups now seek to hedge their bets. Loose, pragmatic links are the norm, with interests tending to follow power, not parties.

Media, though, remain at least as important as ever, although the fragmentation discussed in Chapter 14 has meant that groups have had to develop media strategies that are both broader (using as many outlets as possible) while also being more targeted on the social media outlets in which their supporters are most likely to be interested. Either way, favourable coverage of the issues about which a given group cares is the ultimate target. Especially when groups sense that public opinion is already onside, they increasingly follow a dual strategy, appealing both to the public and to law-makers.

Focus 18.1
Lobbying

Even though it has moved far beyond its origins in the lobby of the British Parliament, lobbying remains the key means by which groups try to influence law-makers (see Godwin, *et al.*, 2013, and Bitonti and Harris, 2018). Lobbyists are usually professionals, often working for corporations or even for lobbying firms consisting of hired guns in the business of interest group communication. Such services are offered not only by specialist government relations companies, but also by divisions within law firms and management consultancies. These operations are growing in number in democracies, with some companies even operating internationally.

Lobbying is on the rise for three main reasons:

◆ Government regulation continues to grow. A specialist lobbying firm working for several interest groups can often monitor proposed laws and regulations more efficiently than would be the case if each interest group undertook the task separately.
◆ Public relations campaigns are becoming increasingly sophisticated, often seeking to influence interest group members, public opinion, and the government in one integrated project. Professional agencies come into their own in planning and delivering multifaceted campaigns, which can be too complex for an interest group client to manage directly.
◆ Many corporations now approach government directly, rather than working through their trade association. Companies, both large and small, find that using a lobbying company to help them contact a government agency or a sympathetic legislator can yield results more quickly than working through an industry body.

Revolving door
The phenomenon in which personnel move between roles as law-makers or bureaucrats and as members of industries impacted by laws and regulations.

The central feature of the lobbying business is its intensely personal character, reaching its most troubling degree in the United States where the **revolving door** is well established. Lobbying is about who you know, and a legislator is most likely to return a call from a lobbyist if the caller is a former colleague. One study of the revolving door phenomenon, however, suggests that rather than seeking privileged insider access, special interests are more focused on how lobbyists with personal experience of the political process can act as a form of insurance for their clients against a political system that is increasingly dysfunctional and unpredictable (LaPira and Thomas, 2017).

INGREDIENTS OF INFLUENCE

There is no doubt that some interest groups exert more influence over government than others. So, what is it that gives particular groups the ability to persuade? Much of the answer is to be found in four attributes ranging from the general to the specific: legitimacy, membership, resources, and sanctions.

Density
The proportion of all those eligible to join a group who actually do so. The higher the density, the stronger a group's authority and bargaining position.

First, the degree of legitimacy achieved by a particular group is important. Interests enjoying high prestige are most likely to prevail on particular issues. Groups whose members stand for social respectability can, on occasion, be as militant and as restrictive in their practices as trade unions once were, but professionals such as lawyers and doctors escape the public hostility that unions continue to attract. Similarly, the intrinsic importance of business to economic performance means that its representatives can usually be heard in government.

Second, a group's influence depends on its membership. This is a matter of **density** and commitment, as well as sheer numbers. For example, labour unions have seen their influence fall as the proportion of workers belonging to unions has fallen in nearly all democracies, especially in the private sector (see Figure 18.3). Except in Scandinavia, union members are now a minority of the workforce, weakening labour's bargaining power with government and employers alike.

New Zealand is a particular stand-out in this regard (see Edwards, 2016). In 1985, union membership reached an all-time high, with about half of the workforce being in a union. By 2016, the number had fallen to fewer than one in five. The decline began in 1991 with the passage of a law ending compulsory membership of unions, and continued with the restructuring and privatization of government services. Unions are also not well regarded, a 2016 survey revealing that they were trusted by only 30 per cent of New Zealanders, placing them in second to last place above the media. Furthermore, unions have suffered from changes in the workplace, as large sites with regular hours and low turnover have been replaced (as they have in most post-industrial societies) with smaller and more scattered workplaces with variable hours of work.

Numbers are not by themselves an indication of influence, though, as reflected in the achievements in the United States of the National Rifle Association (NRA), described by the *New York Times* as 'the most fearsome lobbying organization in America' (Draper, 2013). Although it refuses to release data, most educated guesses suggest that the NRA has a membership of about five million people, or less than 2 per cent of the US population, with a preponderance of older white men. So effective has the NRA become in its lobbying activities, though, and so willing are many of its members to contact their local and national representatives in pursuit of the group's goal of preserving the right to own guns, that the United States has some of the least restrictive gun laws in the world, resulting in by far the highest per capita rate of deaths from guns in the democratic world.

The third measure of group power is found in resources. In the European Union for example, as more decisions have been made at the EU level, so more interest groups have opened offices in Brussels, the seat of the major EU institutions (see Bitonti and Harris, 2018: Chapter 1). This has given them a greater capacity to work with those institutions, adding to the effects of their contacts with local, regional, and national government. Several cross-sectoral and multi-state federations have been created to represent wider economic interests. The latter include Business Europe (with national business federations as members), the European Consumers' Organization, the European Trade Union Confederation, and the European Roundtable of Industrialists, an informal forum of chief executives from nearly 50 major European corporations. As elsewhere, individual corporations are increasingly represented either directly or through lobbying firms.

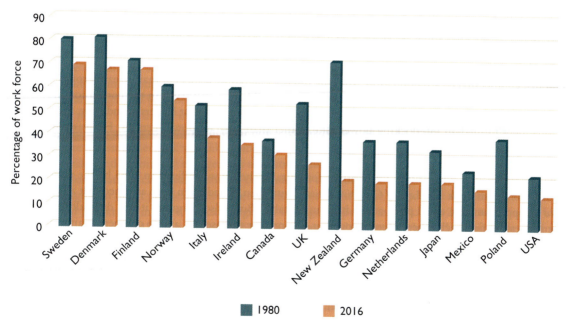

Figure 18.3 Comparing trade union membership
Source: OECD (2017b).
Note: Earlier figure for Poland is from 1990, and for Mexico from 1992.

Brief profile

Egypt has long been a major player in Middle East politics, thanks not only to its pioneering role in the promotion of Arab nationalism but also to its strategic significance in the Cold War and in the Arab–Israeli conflict. It was also at the heart of the Arab Spring, with pro-democracy demonstrations leading to the fall from power of Hosni Mubarak in 2011. Democratic elections brought Mohammed Morsi to power in 2012, but he was removed in a military coup the following year. Egyptians now face uncertainties that resulted in its recent downgrading in the Democracy Index from hybrid to authoritarian. Egypt has the second biggest economy in the Arab world, after Saudi Arabia, but is resource-poor. It relies heavily on tourism, agriculture, and remittances from Egyptian workers abroad and struggles to meet the needs of its rapidly growing population while seeking to offset the potential threat of Islamic militancy.

Form of government	Unitary semi-presidential republic. Modern state formed 1952, and most recent constitution adopted 2014.
Executive	Semi-presidential. A president directly elected for no more than two four-year terms, governing with a prime minister who leads a cabinet accountable to the People's Assembly. There is no vice-president.
Legislature	Unicameral People's Assembly (Majlis el-Shaab) with 567 members, of whom 540 are elected for renewable four-year terms and 27 can be appointed by the president.
Judiciary	Egyptian law is based on a combination of British, Italian, and Napoleonic codes. The Supreme Constitutional Court has been close to recent political changes in Egypt; it has 21 members appointed for life by the president, with mandatory retirement at age 70.
Electoral system	A two-round system is used for presidential elections, with a majority vote needed for victory in the first round, while a mixed member majoritarian system is used for People's Assembly elections; two-thirds of members are elected using party list proportional representation, and one-third in an unusual multi-member plurality system in two large districts.
Parties	Multi-party, but unsettled because of recent instability. Parties represent a wide range of positions and ideologies.

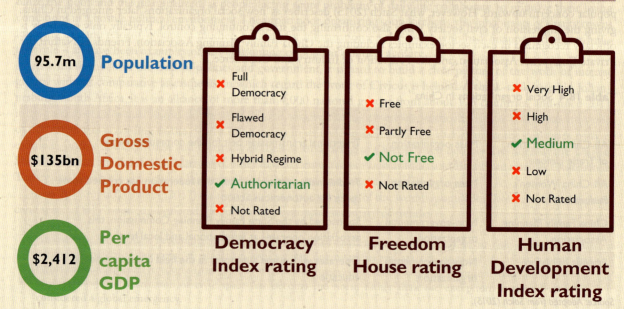

95.7m	**Population**
$135bn	**Gross Domestic Product**
$2,412	**Per capita GDP**

Democracy Index rating	Freedom House rating	Human Development Index rating
✗ Full Democracy		✗ Very High
✗ Flawed Democracy	✗ Free	✗ High
✗ Hybrid Regime	✗ Partly Free	✔ Medium
✔ Authoritarian	✔ Not Free	✗ Low
✗ Not Rated	✗ Not Rated	✗ Not Rated

Interest groups in Egypt

An Egyptian protester waves the victory sign during demonstrations in Cairo that were part of the Arab Spring, a movement that took many political scientists by surprise. *Source: Getty Images/Mosa'ab Elshamy.*

We saw in Chapter 6 how, in authoritarian political systems based on personal rule, access to policy-makers depends on patronage, clients, and contacts – proof of the adage that who you know is more important than what you know. Egypt is a case in point. It would seem to have a healthy and varied interest group community, representing business, agriculture, the professions, and religious groups, but government has long kept a close eye on access. At the same time, though, some interest groups have developed sufficient power and authority as to exert the influence usually associated with interest groups in democracies.

The number and reach of groups in Egypt grew sharply during the administration of Hosni Mubarak (1981–2011). Bodies such as the Chamber of Commerce and the Federation of Industries lobbied for economic liberalization, including the abolition of fixed prices. The leaders of professional groups such as the Journalists Syndicate, the Lawyers Syndicate, and the Engineers Syndicate used their personal contacts in government to win concessions for their members.

Interest groups became so numerous that the Mubarak government felt the need to monitor them more closely, requiring that they be officially registered, and taking the controversial step in 1999 of passing a law that gave the government considerable powers to interfere in the work of groups. It could hire and fire board members, cancel board decisions, and even dissolve a group by court order. Groups were also barred from taking part in political activity, and their members were subject to imprisonment for a variety of vague and general crimes, including 'undermining national unity'.

Egyptian civil society reached new heights during the revolution that overthrew Mubarak, and since coming to power in 2013, the administration of Abdul Fattah el-Sisi has promised to replace the 1999 law with one that would make it easier for groups to function. However, the government continues to see group activity through the narrow prism of national security concerns (Braun, 2016), and even with a change in the law, restrictions on protests and measures against terrorism and Islamic militancy continue to place limits on the activities of groups.

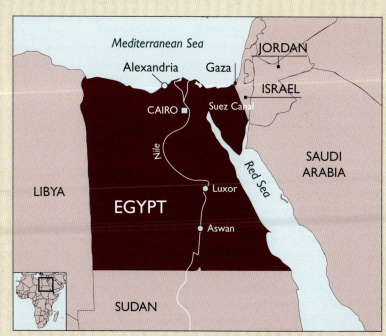

Further reading

Hassan, Abdalla F. (2015) *Media, Revolution and Politics in Egypt* (I. B. Tauris).

Ketchley, Neil (2017) *Egypt in a Time of Revolution: Contentious Politics and the Arab Spring* (Cambridge University Press).

Springborg, Robert (2018) *Egypt* (Polity Press).

In recent years, the number of NGOs in China has exploded, with several sources (including Hasmath, 2016) suggesting that there are as many as 500,000 registered bodies in China, working in areas such as education, poverty alleviation, community development, the environment, and health, and being increasingly active overseas in countries where China has commercial and investment interests. However, recent changes imposed by the administration of Xi Jinping have restricted the activities of NGOs, signalling some reversal – concludes Loeb (2017) – towards 'governance that has little tolerance for pluralism, and increased capacity for social control'.

China also stands as a leading example of the phenomenon of government-organized non-governmental organizations (GONGOs). These are bodies that are founded, funded, and staffed by governments, often to provide services that governments are unable or unwilling to provide. GONGOs are preferred over autonomous NGOs – argue Hasmath *et al.* (2016) – because 'they are more easily integrated into a government's corporatist structure, are less likely to serve as a threat to government's power … and more able to promote a certain agenda'. As well as acting as a conduit between the state and society, Hasmath *et al.* continue, GONGOs can be a safe proving ground where governments can test experimental policies, and insulate themselves from blame should the policies go wrong.

GONGOs are found in democracies, also, but are more often found in authoritarian states, where they are an outgrowth of the phenomenon of **corporatism**. This is a term with a wide variety of contested meanings, ranging from its application to fascist Italy, on the one hand, to the democratic corporatism found in Scandinavia, on the other. Here, it is used to describe political systems in which the state exerts control over a small number of interests, bringing them in to decision-making in return for their support of the governing regime. The term was long associated in particular with Latin American states such as Brazil and Mexico before they began to democratize.

One exception to the Latin American corporatist tradition is offered by Venezuela, which has seen the role of interest groups move from pluralism to confrontation as the country has become more polarized in the wake of the Chávez revolution; its civil society was rated in 2018 as Repressed. Poverty and inequality were driving forces in the work of NGOs in the 1980s, followed in the 1990s by a middle-class reaction to the declining legitimacy of political leaders (Lean, 2012). Since the 'Bolivarian' revolution instituted by Hugo Chávez after 1998, government and interest groups have come into more open conflict, taking positions based either on support for or opposition to the radical changes the country has seen. Many have had to focus on the humanitarian crisis that Venezuela has faced, and on the undermining of human rights.

Corporatism
An arrangement in which – in contrast to the competition for influence and ideas suggested by pluralism – selected interests in a society are formally involved in government, and provide support in return for access.

In hybrid regimes such as Nigeria and Turkey, the position of interest groups lies somewhere between their relative autonomy in democracies and their marginal status in authoritarian states. The borders between the public and private sectors are poorly policed, allowing presidents and their allies to intervene in the economy so as to reward friends and punish enemies. But this involvement is selective, rather than comprehensive, occasionally overriding normal business practices but not seeking to replace them.

At least in the more developed hybrid regimes, the result can be a dual system of representation, combining a role for interest groups on routine matters, with more personal relationships (nurtured by patronage) on matters that are of key importance to the president and the ruling elite. In the most sensitive economic areas (control over energy resources, for example), employer is set against employer in a competition for political influence, leaving little room for the development of influential business associations. The general point is that, even though hybrid regimes allow some interests to be expressed, interest groups are far less significant than in a liberal democracy.

In the case of Russia, with its long history of authoritarian rule (first under the tsars, then under the communists, and now under Putin), interest groups have faced the same problems as Russia's political parties in defining a place in the political system. Thousands of new organizations were created in the 1990s, and the government took steps to encourage them to be a source of assistance rather than opposition (Robertson, 2014). This included the creation of a national Civic Chamber designed to give 'citizens' a voice in public policy; it met for the first time in 2005, and was soon joined by regional equivalents in other parts of the country. Since the Chambers manage a system of federal funding for which NGOs compete, however, and since 40 of the 166 members of the national Chamber are appointed by Putin, there is clearly an element of manipulation involved. In a manner resembling China's GONGOs, the state works to collaborate with favoured groups, while condemning others to irrelevance.

The Russian government's strong nationalist tone has led to particular criticism of those groups (such as women's associations) which have depended on overseas support to survive in an unsympathetic domestic environment. Few promotional groups in Russia possess a significant mass membership; most groups operate solely at grass-roots level, working on local projects such as education or the environment. As in China, these groups operate under state supervision, so Russia's combination of an assertive state and a weak civil society continues to inhibit interest group development.

DISCUSSION QUESTIONS

◆ What do interest groups add to democracy, and what do they subtract?
◆ Is there a hierarchy of interests, giving some groups advantages over others, or does the sheer number and variety of groups result in a balancing of interests?
◆ To what extent do special interests limit the functioning of the market of political ideas?
◆ Is lobbying a natural and inevitable part of the democratic process?
◆ Does pluralism exist, or is it just a theoretical possibility that has been undermined by the unequal influence of different interests?
◆ To what extent is corporatism found in democracies as well as authoritarian regimes?

KEY CONCEPTS

◆ Civil society
◆ Corporatism
◆ Density
◆ Interest group
◆ Iron triangle
◆ Issue network
◆ Lobbying
◆ Nimby

◆ Peak association
◆ Pluralism
◆ Promotional group
◆ Protective group
◆ Revolving door
◆ Social movement
◆ Think-tank

FURTHER READING

Bitonti, Alberto, and Phil Harris (eds) (2018) *Lobbying in Europe: Public Affairs and the Lobbying Industry in 28 EU Countries* (Palgrave Macmillan). An assessment of lobbying in the European Union, including short chapters on each of its member states.

Cavatorta, Francesco (ed.) (2012) *Civil Society Activism under Authoritarian Rule: A Comparative Perspective* (Routledge). One of the few recent studies of the activities of interest groups in authoritarian settings.

Edwards, Michael (ed.) (2011) *The Oxford Handbook of Civil Society* (Oxford University Press). An edited collection of studies on civil society, including chapters on different sectors and on different parts of the world.

Staggenborg, Suzanne (2016) *Social Movements*, 2nd edn (Oxford University Press). A textbook survey of social movements, their methods, and their effects, with cases including the women's, the LGBTQ+, and the environmental movements.

Yadav, Vineeta (2011) *Political Parties, Business Groups, and Corruption in Developing Countries* (Oxford University Press). A study of the relationship between business lobbying and corruption in developing countries.

Zetter, Lionel (2014) *Lobbying: The Art of Political Persuasion*, 3rd edn (Harriman House). A global view of the dynamics of lobbying, including chapters on Europe, the United States, Asia, and the Middle East.

PUBLIC POLICY

19

CONTENTS

PREVIEW

Public policy is concerned with the outcomes of the political process: if the core purpose of government is to manage and address the needs of society, then the approaches that it adopts and the actions it takes (or avoids) collectively constitute its policies. Policies are the product of the political interactions we have reviewed throughout the preceding chapters: policy is shaped by ideology, institutions, political culture, participation by citizens, and the influence of the media, political parties, and interest groups. This chapter looks in more detail at how policy is formed and implemented, the actors involved in the process, and the influences on that process. In order to provide more focus, it uses the cases of education, health care, and environmental policy to illustrate the possibilities and limitations of policy.

The chapter begins with a review of three models of the policy process: the rational, the incremental, and the garbage-can models. It then goes on to look at the policy cycle, an artificial means for imposing some order on what is, in reality, a disorderly process. The problems experienced at each step in the cycle – initiation, formulation, implementation, evaluation, and review – give us insight into why so many public policies fall short of their goals. The chapter then looks at the related phenomena of policy diffusion and policy convergence, before ending with a review of the dynamics of policy in authoritarian systems, where – with greater centralization of power – it has its own distinctive qualities and dynamic.

KEY ARGUMENTS

- Studying public policy involves understanding what governments do (or do not do), as well as the institutional framework within which they do it.

- There is always a danger of imagining policy-making as a rational process with precise goals. The incremental and garbage-can models offer a useful dose of realism.

- There are multiple policy instruments available to governments, which can be divided broadly into sticks, carrots, and sermons.

- Breaking the policy process down into its component stages, from initiation to review, helps in analysing and comparing policies.

- The study of policy diffusion and convergence helps us explain how policies evolve in similar directions in multiple countries.

- On almost every count – ranging from the balance of power among institutions to the methods, motivations, qualifications, and priorities of policy-makers – democracies and authoritarian states differ fundamentally.

PUBLIC POLICY: AN OVERVIEW

Public policy is a collective term for the actions of government. It is more than a decision or even a set of decisions, but instead describes the approaches that rulers adopt in dealing with the demands of their office, and the actions they take (or avoid taking) to address public needs. The choices they make are driven by multiple influences, including their own priorities, their political ideology, the demands placed on them, the economic and political climate, and the available budget. Policies consist both of aims (say, to reverse climate change) and of means (switching to renewable sources of energy in order to cut carbon dioxide emissions).

> **Public policy**
> The positions adopted and the actions taken (or avoided) by governments as they address the needs of society.

When parties or candidates compete for political office, they will have a shopping list of issues they wish to address, and the positions they take in office will be their policies. These are usually expressed in the form of public statements, government programmes, laws, and actions. If policy was limited to published objectives then it might be relatively easy to understand and measure. However, government and governance are also influenced by opportunism, the ebb and flow of political and public interest, the requirement to fix unsuccessful policies, and the need to respond to new problems as they arise.

Once in office, political leaders will often find that their priorities and preferred responses will change because of circumstances. They may be diverted by other more urgent problems, or find that their proposals lack adequate political support or funding, or discover that implementation is more difficult then they anticipated. In understanding how policy is made and implemented, it is important to avoid imposing too much order on a process that is often driven by changing political considerations: policies can be contradictory, they can be nothing more than window-dressing (an attempt to be seen to be doing something, but without any realistic expectation that the objective will be achieved), and policy statements may be a cover for acting in the opposite way to the one stated.

Whatever the course taken and the eventual outcome, the actions of government (combined with their inaction) constitute their policies. These policies become the defining qualities of governments and their leaders, and the records of these policies in addressing and alleviating problems will become the reference points by which governments and leaders are assessed, and a key factor in determining whether or not they will be returned to another term in office. This is less true of authoritarian leaders, where survival usually depends less on good policy than on distributing enough patronage to allies and supporters.

The particular task of **policy analysis** is to understand what governments do, how they do it, and what difference it makes (Dye, 2012). So, the focus is on the content, instruments, impact, and evaluation of public policy, as well as on the influences that come to bear on the policy process. The emphasis is downstream (on implementation and results) as much as upstream (on the institutional sources of policy). Because analysts are concerned with improving the quality and efficacy of public policy, the subject exudes a practical air. Policy analysts want to know whether and why a policy is working, and how else its objectives might be pursued. Unfortunately, this is often easier said than done.

> **Policy analysis**
> The systematic study of the content and impact of public policy.

MODELS OF THE POLICY PROCESS

In analysing the manner in which policy is made, scholars have developed three competing models: the rational model associated with Herbert Simon (1983), the incremental model developed by Charles Lindblom (1959, 1979), and the garbage-can model, so named by Michael Cohen *et al.* (1972). Moving through each of these models in order (see Table 19.1) is, in part, a transition from ideal to reality:

◆ The rational model sets a baseline by elaborating an ideal approach to policy-making without assuming that its conclusions are reflected in what actually happens.
◆ The incremental model views policy as a compromise between actors with ill-defined or even contradictory goals, and can be seen either as an account of how politics ought to proceed (namely, peacefully reconciling different interests), or as a description of how policy is actually made.
◆ The garbage-can model highlights the many limitations of the policy-making process within many organizations, looking only at what is, not what ought to be.

The lesson is that we should recognize the different functions that these models highlight, rather than seeing them as wholly competitive.

SPOTLIGHT SWEDEN

Brief profile

Sweden ranks at or near the top of international league tables focused on democracy, political stability, economic development, education, and social equality; in this sense, it can be seen as one of the most successful countries addressed in this book. The Social Democrats have held a plurality in the Swedish parliament since 1917, Sweden has traditionally lacked significant internal divisions (other than class), and it has long followed public policies that have helped to keep economic productivity high and unemployment low. The country combines a high standard of living with a comparatively equal distribution of income, showing – with other Scandinavian states – that mass affluence and limited inequality are compatible. Meanwhile, Sweden is neutral in international affairs, remaining outside NATO but being a committed member of the European Union.

Form of government	Unitary parliamentary constitutional monarchy. Date of state formation debatable, and oldest element of constitution dates from 1810.
Executive	Parliamentary. The head of government is the prime minister, who is head of the largest party or coalition, and governs in conjunction with a cabinet. The head of state is the monarch.
Legislature	Unicameral Riksdag ('meeting of the realm') with 349 members, elected for renewable four-year terms.
Judiciary	The constitution consists of four entrenched laws: the Instrument of Government, the Act of Succession, the Freedom of the Press Act, and the Fundamental Law on Freedom of Expression. The Supreme Court (16 members appointed until retirement at the age of 67) is traditionally restrained.
Electoral system	The Riksdag is elected by party list proportional representation, with an additional tier of seats used to enhance proportionality. The national vote threshold (the share of votes needed to be awarded any seats) is 4 per cent.
Parties	Multi-party. The Social Democrats were historically the leading party, sharing their position on the left with the Left Party and the Greens. However, a centre-right coalition (led by the conservative Moderates and including the Centre Party, the Christian Democrats, and the Liberals) has recently gained ground.

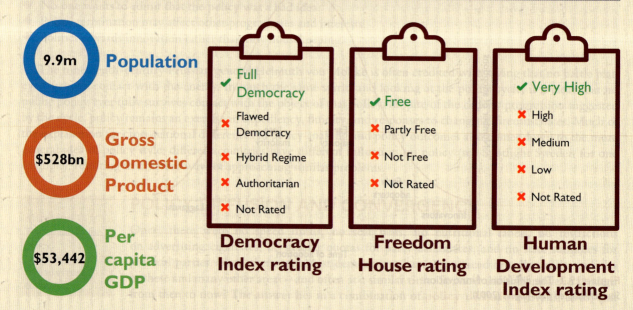

9.9m Population

$528bn Gross Domestic Product

$53,442 Per capita GDP

Democracy Index rating
- ✔ Full Democracy
- ✘ Flawed Democracy
- ✘ Hybrid Regime
- ✘ Authoritarian
- ✘ Not Rated

Freedom House rating
- ✔ Free
- ✘ Partly Free
- ✘ Not Free
- ✘ Not Rated

Human Development Index rating
- ✔ Very High
- ✘ High
- ✘ Medium
- ✘ Low
- ✘ Not Rated

Public policy in Sweden

The Riksdag in Stockholm, the national legislature that lies at the heart of Sweden's notably transparent and consensual style of policy-making. *Source: iStock/TomasSereda.*

Swedish policy-making was once described as 'open, rationalistic, consensual and extraordinarily deliberative' (Anton, 1969). Later, Richardson *et al.* (1982) characterized Sweden's policy style as anticipatory and consensus-seeking. Little has changed since then. Even in a small unitary state with sovereignty firmly based on a unicameral legislature, Sweden has avoided the potential for centralization and has developed an elaborate negotiating democracy which is culturally and institutionally secure.

One factor sustaining this policy style is the compact size and policy focus of Sweden's 11 central government departments, which together employ about 4,600 staff. The objective, as grandly outlined on the web site of the Government Offices of Sweden (2018) is 'an innovative and interactive central government administration that is legally certain and efficient, has a high degree of quality, service and accessibility, and thereby contributes to Sweden's development and effective [European Union] work'. Most technical issues, and the services provided by the extensive welfare state, are contracted out to more than 300 public agencies and to local government. This division of tasks is sustained by high levels of transparency and trust.

Committees of enquiry (also known as 'commissions') are key to the process. Typically, the government appoints a committee to research a topic and present recommendations. The commission consults with relevant interests and political parties, its recommendations are published and discussed, the relevant ministry examines the report, a government bill is drafted if needed, and the bill is then discussed in the Riksdag, where it may be modified before reaching the statute book. This procedure is slow, but it is also both rational (in that information is collected and analysed) and incremental (in that organized opponents of the proposal are given ample opportunity to voice their concerns).

There are downsides – extensive deliberation may contribute to bland rather than innovative policy, and the emphasis on policy formulation may be at the expense of insufficient focus on implementation – but the style is distinctively Swedish. It offers a useful yardstick against which to compare the less measured policy-making styles found in other liberal democracies.

Further reading

Bergh, Andreas (2014) *Sweden and the Revival of the Capitalist Welfare State* (Edward Elgar).

Miles, Lee (2015) *The New Politics of Sweden* (London: Bloomsbury Academic).

Pierre, Jon (2016) *The Oxford Handbook of Swedish Politics* (Oxford: Oxford University Press).

Table 19.6 Comparing policy in democracies and authoritarian states

Feature	Democracies	Authoritarian states
Institutions	Authority divided, with multiple motivations.	Authority focused in leadership or ruling party/elite.
Methods	Concern for inclusion and public opinion. More carrots and sermons.	A focus on leading, with more emphasis on coercion.
Motivations	To shape policy, make a difference, and secure re-election.	To stay in power as long as possible, and to exploit policy for sectional and personal gain.
Qualifications	Government leaders usually have political experience.	Government leaders often come to power with less experience or understanding of government.
Policy priorities	Wide-ranging, with a strong emphasis on social programmes and economic management.	Fewer social concerns, more focus on security matters.

is more a question of understanding internal party priorities than of understanding the wider policy landscape. Getting to grips with policy-making is in some ways easier, because the process is more focused, but also more difficult, because it is less transparent.

Second, policy methods are quite different. In democracies, we find a complex system by which information is gathered and processed, and a combination of sticks, carrots, and sermons is used to achieve policy goals. In authoritarian states, policy is accompanied – as we saw in Chapter 6 – by a higher degree of coercion, with more sticks and fewer carrots or sermons. Rulers decide what they want done (or not done) and they set out to impose their wishes, concerned less with public opinion than with keeping the supporting elite happy.

Having said that, though, one of the ironies of policy in authoritarian systems is that while policy-making institutions may be strong, this does not mean that policy is successfully implemented. As Brooker (2014) notes, the policy-implementing role of the bureaucracy in an authoritarian state tends to obscure its policy-making role; even when it is 'making' policy, it is usually doing little more than advising political leaders. Jackson and Rosberg (1982) long ago noted the gap between making and implementing policy when they noted the paradox faced by many African leaders of having the relative freedom to make policies but considerable constraints in terms of implementing or enforcing them.

The third difference between democracies and authoritarian states is that policy-makers have different motivations. The desire to control and to 'make a difference' is as much a motivation for those in democracies as it is for those in authoritarian states, and there are parallels in both situations regarding the desire to keep particular constituencies happy. Democratic leaders, though, know that their days are numbered, either by the constitutional clock or by the insecurities involved in holding on to the reins of power. They want to use the days they have to push policy in the direction they prefer while limiting the influence of the opposition. For authoritarian leaders, the motivations are quite different – see Focus 19.2.

The fourth difference between democracies and authoritarian states lies in the qualifications for office, which produce different kinds of rule. For the most part, democratic leaders have political experience before coming to office. This does not guarantee greater competence or higher quality leadership, but it usually means greater familiarity with the process of government. True enough, several modern leaders of authoritarian states had political experience before becoming president of their respective countries; this was true of Vladimir Putin of Russia, for example, as well as Mahmoud Ahmadinejad and Hassan Rouhani of Iran, and Nicolás Maduro of Venezuela. Recent Chinese leaders have all survived the cut-throat process of working their way to the top echelons of the Chinese Communist Party.

Many, though, have either come to power through the violent overthrow of their predecessors, through a military coup, or through a family dynasty. This leaves them often less experienced in administration and less knowledgeable about how to encourage supporters and to identify opponents. Such problems are especially common in military regimes whose leaders know much more about the hierarchical responsibility structures of the armed forces than they do about the more fluid kinds of decision-making found in civilian government. The generals sometimes seize power

Focus 19.2
Public policy and political survival

Public policy everywhere is impacted to a large extent by how long leaders expect to stay in office, and by the means they use to remain in office. Leaders in democracies are motivated by a complex mix of political legacies, keeping their constituents happy, and making sure that even if their terms are limited by the constitution, their parties remain in control and opposition parties stay out of office. In authoritarian regimes, by contrast, political survival has a very different meaning.

Authoritarian rulers know that their days are numbered, but they hope to give themselves as many of those days as possible. Their key priority is to play off domestic political forces against each other so as to ensure their own continuation in office, and to benefit their supporters as far as possible. Uncertain of their survival, and willing to use as many means as possible to keep the support of their constituents, they may be more tempted to enrich themselves, their family, and their supporters while they remain in control of the state's resources. Those resources, meanwhile, are diverted away from more broadly useful uses, such as investments in economic and social development. These related goals of political survival and personal enrichment are hardly conducive to orderly policy, and least of all to good economic policy.

A good example is offered by Robert Mugabe of Zimbabwe (in power 1980–2017), who governed over a country with valuable human, natural, and agricultural resources, but was too concerned with the needs of his supporters to focus on developing a broad base of policy initiatives. He may not have enriched himself as much as many other African dictators, but he instituted a policy of land grabs by which valuable farms were confiscated from their mainly white owners and given to Mugabe's supporters, many of whom were described by the government as veterans of the war of independence, even if they were far too young to have fought. Previously productive farms were driven into ruin because few of the new owners had any farming knowledge or experience.

Meanwhile, Mugabe's wife Grace – 41 years younger than him – exploited her husband's power to live a life of luxury in a country where the majority of people were either unemployed or making a living in the so-called informal sector. She earned the nickname 'Gucci Grace' for her tastes, which involved shopping trips abroad on aircraft appropriated by her husband for the purpose from the state airline, Air Zimbabwe, which was pushed into near-bankruptcy. Rumours that Mugabe was preparing the way for his wife to succeed him as president were part of the reason why he was removed from power in 2017.

in an honest attempt to improve public policy-making but then discover that good governance requires skills they do not possess.

Finally, the priorities of policy differ between democracies and authoritarian states. Governments in democracies are faced with a wide range of policy needs, and place a strong emphasis on social programme and economic management. In other words, they are incentivized by the next election to keep their people healthy, well-educated, and employed. Because authoritarian regimes are less concerned with the contentment of the broader population than they are with their supporting networks, and because they also tend to be poorer than democracies, they are less interested in – or capable of – focusing much on social policies. They take care of technical matters (such as maintaining roads, after a fashion, and building schools) and they also often have high levels of spending on the military (with an eye to internal rather than external security), but will usually spend less on social security or health care.

As always, however, it is important to distinguish between different types of authoritarian government. At one extreme, many military and personal rulers show immense concern about their own prosperity but none at all for that of their country, leading to a policy shortage. At the other extreme, modernizing regimes whose ruling elite display a clear sense of national goals and a secure hold on power follow long-term policies, especially for economic development. Such countries do not suffer from inertia, but instead find it easier to push through substantial policy change, because they can suppress the short-term demands that would arise in a more open political system.

POLITICAL ECONOMY

20

PREVIEW

This chapter focuses on the links between politics and economics, showing how important they are to each other. After decades during which they were studied in isolation, they have been reconnected since the 1960s as political scientists and economists have worked to better understand the intersection between politics and economics. Just as it is important to understand how political systems work, and how democracy and authoritarianism differ, so it is important to understand how economic systems work, as well as how and why governments take different approaches to the economy.

The chapter begins with a survey of political economy and of the kinds of questions it addresses. It then looks in turn at four major perspectives on political economy, ranging from classical liberalism to radicalism, economic nationalism, and modern liberalism, along with several of their more important sub-categories. Modern liberalism is the perspective found most often in liberal democracies today, although there are signs in several countries of a return to policies of economic nationalism.

The chapter then continues with an assessment of the dynamics of development as it applies to emerging states, and of the welfare state as it has evolved in mainly wealthier liberal democracies. It then looks at the meaning of development in a changing global environment, and at the implications of a changing global balance of economic power. The chapter ends with a review of political economy in authoritarian states, focusing particularly on how state capitalism has taken hold in countries such as China and Russia.

KEY ARGUMENTS

- The revival of the study of political economy has offered new insights into the interaction between politics and economics.
- The classical liberal emphasis on free markets offers the foundation for political economy, and continues to be found in many countries in the form of neoliberalism.
- Radicalism arose as a reaction to the weaknesses of the free market, but its analyses were hurt by the excesses of communism and state socialism.
- Most democracies today are based on modern liberal views about free markets and redistribution, with a revival of economic nationalism in some.
- There are few agreements on the best approaches to economic development, while opinions about the welfare state have been reviewed in the wake of international financial pressures.
- State capitalism is a distinctive approach to understanding political economy now found in many authoritarian states.

POLITICAL ECONOMY: AN OVERVIEW

The study of **political economy** is the study of the intersection of politics and economics. These are two fields that are impossible to fully divorce from one another: to a large degree, political decisions are driven by economic needs and pressures, while a government's economic choices are influenced by political considerations. Political economy is both a means of undertaking political analysis generally and also an approach to the study of any number of more focused topics, ranging from agriculture to communications, culture, education, the environment, finance, gender, labour, migration, trade, and war. So far in this book our attention has been focused on the political side of the relationship; in this chapter we switch to the economic perspective, referring back to the institutions and processes discussed in preceding chapters. Our interest is in how economic trends impact political decisions, and vice versa.

Political economy
A branch of the social sciences that studies the relationships between markets and the state.

Theorists as diverse as Adam Smith, John Stuart Mill, and Karl Marx studied society from the combined perspective of politics and economics, or political economy. In the latter half of the nineteenth century there was a move to divide these perspectives as economists, political scientists, and sociologists began to head in separate directions, prompted by differences in their views about the appropriate role of government and about approaches to research (economists taking a more quantitative approach than most political scientists, for example). More recently, there has been a trend back towards an integrated approach, even to the point where we often see references to **new political economy**, a term implying a combination of the original integrated approach to politics and economics, on the one hand, and the more recent research methods developed by economists, on the other.

New political economy
A resurrection of earlier approaches to economics, combining them with the tools of modern economic analysis.

This chapter offers a survey of political economy, beginning with an introduction to some of the key terms involved, and a discussion of the dimensions of different economic systems. It then compares the four major perspectives on political economy. The point of departure is the classical liberal view that individuals and societies are most likely to prosper if they are allowed to pursue their interests with minimal intervention from government. Radicals disagree, arguing that government intervention is essential in the interests of ensuring equality and justice. Economic nationalism opts for government protection of national economies, while modern liberalism believes that government should protect rights while engaging in the redistribution of wealth and opportunity. The latter point can be seen in the work of the welfare state that has been so central to thinking about political economy in wealthier democracies.

Coming to grips with political economy in authoritarian states is not just a matter of comparing dictators and democrats, or wealth and poverty, but instead of looking in more depth at the interactions between politics and economic policy. In most cases, both are used to exert control, but while it has often resulted in what is known as state capitalism, which has frequently led to inefficiency and corruption, the experiences of authoritarian systems are more complex and nuanced than the use of simple models suggests.

UNDERSTANDING POLITICAL ECONOMY

'Political economy', claims Clark (2016), 'was the original social science'. The use of the term dates back to seventeenth-century France, when it referred to the financial management of the royal household. It then expanded to describe the study of the causes of the wealth of nations (reflected in the classic work of that title by Adam Smith, 1776), assessing the policies governments should follow as they sought to build the economies of the societies they ruled. The classical liberal view of political economy was that markets worked best when left free of any government intervention short of laws aimed at protecting property rights. It was not long, though, before the costs of this approach became apparent (in the industrial world, at least) in the form of problems such as pollution, child labour, urban blight, unemployment (as workers were replaced by machines), crime, and social unrest. Clearly, argued some, governments needed to take a more radical and interventionist approach to the management of markets.

At the same time, the study of political economy fell out of favour as economists sought to divorce the study of their discipline from other related factors, including politics. They built new models based on the assumption that

Economics
The study of the theory and practice of the production, distribution, and consumption of goods and services.

Markets
The arenas within which goods and services are bought and sold, with prices determined mainly by supply and demand.

Microeconomics
The study of small-scale or individual economic decisions, and the interactions of individual economic actors.

Macroeconomics
The study of entire economic systems and their complex internal dynamics.

Economic system
The interactions and institutions through which a society chooses to manage production, distribution, and consumption, involving different degrees of interaction between governments and markets.

people made rational decisions based on calculations of costs and benefits. They also argued that economics and politics had different interests and points of departure (see Clark, 2016):

◆ Individuals drove economic choices, while political choices were collective.
◆ Economic decisions were based on a desire to achieve prosperity, while political decisions were targeted on the achievement of justice.
◆ Economic decisions took place within the market, while political decisions took place within government.

After several decades during which political scientists and economists followed different trajectories, there was an effort in the 1960s to bring them back together, since when the field of political economy has undergone a resurgence. The dominant view today is that politics and economics have close connections, and that studying one without the other will result in a failure to produce an accurate understanding of how societies function. Political economy must take into account the contrasting dynamics of different economic and political systems, the impact of globalization on domestic and international policy decisions, and a wide array of more particular questions: for example, how rising consumer demand can be balanced against the depletion of resources, how changes in patterns of production and the organization of the workplace relate to politics, and how the different priorities of democracies and authoritarian regimes are shaped.

Before going into more depth, we need to come to grips with some of the key terms used in this chapter. The first of these is **economics**. We saw in Chapter 1 that political science is the study of the theory and practice of government and politics, focusing on the structure and dynamics of institutions, political processes, and political behaviour. This is paralleled by economics, which focuses on matters such as production, the creation and distribution of wealth, the causes and effects of scarcity, the relationship between supply and demand, and the efficient use of resources. The study of economics is concerned with **markets**, finance, banking, business, and trade, the scope ranging from the study of **microeconomics** to the study of **macroeconomics**. The key actors involved range from individual consumers to small business, large business, multinational corporations, and – of course – governments.

The questions addressed by political economy include the following:

◆ How are economies structured and how do these structures vary?
◆ Why are some countries or societies wealthy while others are poor?
◆ How and when is government intervention in the economy appropriate?
◆ How should governments respond to recessions and unemployment?
◆ Why do men earn more than women for the same work?
◆ What are the implications of tax policy?

We also saw in Chapter 1 that a political system consists of the interactions and organizations through which a society reaches and successfully enforces collective decisions. As we have seen, political systems come in many different forms, beginning with the broad differences between democracies and authoritarian regimes, and moving to the more detailed differences in the way that institutions are structured, people participate in politics, and elections are organized.

For its part, an **economic system** consists of similar sets of interactions and organizations as they relate to the market, and such systems also come in many different forms. In much the same way as different political systems are identified by the extent to which citizens participate in government, and can expect government to protect their rights, so different economic systems are characterized by the manner in which citizens participate in the marketplace, and – again – can or should expect government to protect their rights. Some economic systems limit themselves to management tasks with the goal of allowing individuals to take the initiative in the creation of new businesses, or in deciding which goods or services they wish to buy or sell, and in what quantities. Others will take a more active role in shaping the marketplace, and in deciding what will be made, in what quantities it will be made, and at what price it will be sold.

Table 20.1 Five perspectives on political economy

Perspective	Main features	Application
Classical liberalism	Individuals should be allowed to pursue their interests with minimal intervention from government.	Fell out of favour following the Great Depression, but reborn in the 1980s as neoliberalism.
Radicalism	Government intervention is essential in the interests of ensuring equality and justice.	Fell out of favour after association with Marxism, Leninism, Stalinism, and Maoism.
Economic nationalism	Government should place the needs and priorities of national economies above those of others.	Mercantilism as practised once by Britain and France, and protectionism as promoted more recently by Japan and by the United States under Donald Trump.
Modern liberalism	Government should protect rights, and also redistribute wealth and opportunity.	The form of political economy found most often today in most liberal democracies.
State capitalism	Government takes responsibility for many of the functions normally left to the free market.	Recent growth in many authoritarian states, such as China and Russia.

COMPARATIVE POLITICAL ECONOMY

Coming to grips with political economy demands an appreciation of the different opinions about how markets work, about how they interact with politics and society, and about how they are best managed. A useful guide through the maze is offered by Clark (2016), who identifies several major perspectives on the confluence between politics and economics, each based on different views about the interests of individuals and societies, and of the appropriate role of government. (Another perspective, known as state capitalism, is addressed later in the chapter.) (See summary in Table 20.1.)

Classical liberalism

This is the original approach to political economy, its roots dating back to the origins of **capitalism** in the fourteenth century. The core idea here is that humans will do best, and society will most likely flourish, if individuals are allowed to pursue their own interests without the intervention of government, which should serve as little more than a **night-watchman state**.

Where medieval thinking saw individuals situated within a social hierarchy dominated by the power of the state and the church, classical liberalism was based instead on notions of individual choice and initiative, and of the importance of private property (see Brennan and Tomasi, 2012). In this view – developed by such thinkers and philosophers as Thomas Hobbes, John Locke, Adam Smith, and Friedrich Hayek – humans were seen to be self-interested and capable of identifying and pursuing the means best suited to meeting their needs. The free market was the best means for encouraging new discoveries and creative solutions to problems, and society was no more than an accumulation of individuals and their needs. Government served to protect the natural rights of individuals, to offer public services such as education, and to address inequalities created by the market, but not much more. As Thomas Jefferson once famously suggested, 'that government is best which governs least'.

Classical liberalism was dealt a severe blow with the Great Depression of the 1930s, the effects of which led many to believe that the free market was not necessarily the best means for shaping economic activities. Capitalism seemed to be unable to overcome macroeconomic fluctuations in economic activity, and the market was not a level playing field, containing – as it did – many structural problems, such as a tendency for monopolies to develop, and for powerful economic interests to exert more political influence. Classical liberalism was also (somewhat unfairly) charged with paying too little heed to the idea of community welfare: individual progress was all very well, but society and the economy itself needed good education, health care, and infrastructure, most

Capitalism
An economic principle based on leaving as many decisions as possible on production, distribution, and prices to the free market.

Night-watchman state
One which performs limited functions, such as maintaining law and order, providing national defence, enforcing contracts, and dealing with emergencies.

SPOTLIGHT TURKEY

Brief profile

Once the centre of the Ottoman Empire, Turkey is a secular republic that straddles Asia and Europe. It has long sought membership of the European Union, but its efforts have stalled over concerns about its human rights record and democratic trajectory. Matters have worsened in recent years as Recep Tayyip Erdoğan, who came to power in 2003 and spent 11 years as prime minister, was elected president in 2014 and set about converting the previously ceremonial role into an executive position with strong powers. An attempted coup in 2016 sparked a crackdown that strengthened Erdoğan's powers, and a flawed 2017 referendum narrowly approved a switch to a presidential system of government. Freedom House downgraded Turkey from Partly Free to Not Free in 2018, concerned about abuses of free expression, freedom of association, and the rule of law. It is ranked as a hybrid in the Democracy Index.

Form of government	Unitary presidential republic. State formed in 1923. The 1982 constitution was the sixth since 1876, and it has been amended nearly 20 times.
Executive	Presidential, in the process of a transition from a parliamentary system. A president directly elected for no more than two five-year terms, supported by several vice-presidents and a Council of Ministers. Office of prime minister abolished in 2017.
Legislature	Unicameral Grand National Assembly with 600 members elected for renewable five-year terms.
Judiciary	Constitutional Court with 17 members serving non-renewable 12-year terms, with three elected by the Grand National Assembly and the rest appointed by the president based on nominations from lower courts.
Electoral system	The Grand National Assembly is elected using proportional representation with a (relatively high) 10 per cent threshold. The president has been directly elected only since 2014. Presidential candidates must be nominated by at least 20 members of the Grand National Assembly and compete against each other using a majority system.
Parties	Multi-party, with the conservative and Islamist Justice and Development Party (AKP) (formed in 2001) dominating and the social democratic Republican People's Party as the major opposition.

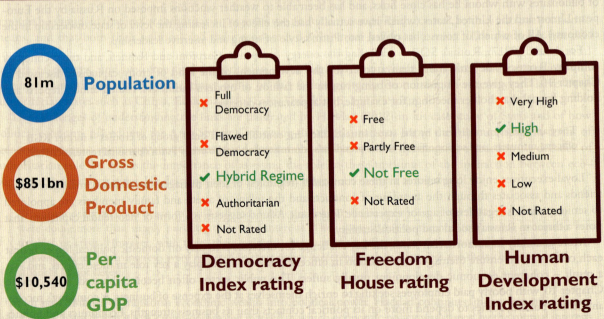

81m Population

$851bn Gross Domestic Product

$10,540 Per capita GDP

Democracy Index rating
- ✗ Full Democracy
- ✗ Flawed Democracy
- ✔ Hybrid Regime
- ✗ Authoritarian
- ✗ Not Rated

Freedom House rating
- ✗ Free
- ✗ Partly Free
- ✔ Not Free
- ✗ Not Rated

Human Development Index rating
- ✗ Very High
- ✔ High
- ✗ Medium
- ✗ Low
- ✗ Not Rated

A poster announces an election rally in Istanbul for Turkey's President Recep Tayyip Erdoğan, who has increased his grip on power since first coming to national office in 2003.
Source: Getty Images/Chris McGrath.

The political economy of Turkey

Turkey is an emerging economy that occupies an important strategic position between Europe and the Middle East. With a population almost as big as that of Germany, it has seen steady growth in recent years, quickly recovering from the effects of the global financial crisis, making significant inroads into its poverty rate, witnessing rapid urban growth, and earning a ranking by the World Bank as an upper-middle-income country (on a par with China, Brazil, and Mexico). For Önis and Kutlay (2013), Turkey is a 'near-BRIC'. The International Monetary Fund, meanwhile, classifies Turkey as an emerging market economy, or one that has some but not all of the economic features of a developed economy. In short, Turkey's economic potential is significant.

Questions hover, though, over its political economy trajectory. Turkey had been moving towards strengthening its democratic credentials, and making efforts to amend laws and regulations in the interests of its long-held hope of joining the European Union. Since coming to power in 2003, however, Recep Tayyip Erdoğan has undone many of the democratic gains, accumulating new powers for a redesigned presidency, and pursuing a policy platform that has been variously described as populist, nationalist, Islamist, conservative, and anti-Western. The political doubts

raised by his administration have raised economic doubts as well. Fuelled in part by Erdoğan's claims that he plans to take control over the setting of interest rates, and in part by growing inflation, the Turkish currency lost one-fifth of its value in early 2018.

Many have seen signs of neoliberalism in Turkey, reflected – for example – in a policy of privatization, and a move away from an already modest welfare state towards greater support for private health care and private social insurance. However, Karadag (2010) summarizes trends in Turkish political economy as a move away from state capitalism towards what he describes as 'an oligarchic form of capitalism'. He defines this as consisting of political fragmentation and the establishment of closed elite political business cartels, a trend that helps explain Turkey's persistent problems with corruption. There is, in short, an unsurprising overlap between current political and economic trends in Turkey.

Further reading

Başer, Bahar, and Ahmet Erdi Öztürk (eds) (2017) *Authoritarian Politics in Turkey: Elections, Resistance and the AKP* (I.B. Tauris).

Finkel, Andrew (2012) *Turkey: What Everyone Needs to Know* (Oxford University Press).

Genç, Kaya (2016) *Under the Shadow: Rage and Revolution in Modern Turkey* (I.B. Tauris).

do not marry well, resulting in the inefficient use of capital. Alternatively, rulers may just want to enrich themselves, their families and their ethnic or religious group by taking resources out of the economy and often out of the country. Inherent corruption, among leading officials as well as bureaucrats dealing directly with the public, is a tax on both economic growth and regime legitimacy. Such problems are particularly acute when states suffer a resource curse – see Focus 20.2.

Focus 20.2
The resource curse

Resource curse

A phenomenon by which a state that is well endowed in a particular natural resource, or a limited selection of resources, experiences lower economic growth thanks to unbalanced policy, extensive corruption, and internal conflict.

A particular problem that has skewed economic policy in several authoritarian states is the so-called **resource curse** (Auty, 1993; Collier and Bannon, 2003), or the 'paradox of plenty' as it is sometimes known. This exists when a country is well endowed in a resource that could and should be the foundation for sound economic development, but instead alters the economic and political balance such as to focus attention on a single sector, reducing economic growth below the expected level.

Several wealthy democracies, such as Canada and Norway, have faced similar risks but have been able to avoid its worst effects by pursuing careful and transparent policies, and making sure their economies were based on a broad foundation. In the case of many poorer (and often authoritarian) countries, however, their rush to develop has produced different results. Oil has turned out to be a problem, for example, for several sub-Saharan African states, such as Angola, Chad, Equatorial Guinea, Gabon, Nigeria, and Sudan. The resource curse is also a factor in countries rich in easily exploitable minerals such as copper or uranium, or in precious gems such as diamonds.

The policy element of the 'curse' stems from four main factors:

◆ Because these resources are usually relatively easy to exploit and can bring quick and often profitable returns, a state will focus its development efforts almost entirely in that sector, investing little in other sectors. This is the so-called 'Dutch disease', named for the effects of the discovery of natural gas in the North Sea off the coast of the Netherlands in the 1970s (Humphreys *et al.*, 2007). It will thereby have an imbalanced economy and will become dependent on a product whose value may be held hostage to fluctuations in its price on the international market.

◆ When a government can raise adequate revenue from simply taxing a major natural resource, it lacks incentive to improve economic performance by developing the skills of its people, thus damaging growth over the long run.

◆ The profits that come from these commodities can encourage theft and corruption, ensuring that they find their way into the bank accounts of the rich and powerful rather than being reinvested back into the economy.

◆ The effect of the curse is to encourage internal conflict, when poorer regions of the country find that they are not benefitting equally from the profits of resources found in other parts of the country. In the most extreme cases, the outcome can be violence and civil war.

One country that might have been hurt by a resource curse, but that has instead pursued coherent economic policy, is Botswana. One of the poorest countries in the world at the time of its independence in 1966, it also discovered that it was sitting on enormous diamond wealth. It could have misused this asset for a quick financial return, but it instead set up the Debswana Mining Company, a joint venture between the government of Botswana and De Beers, a company which at the time had a monopoly on the global diamond trade. Diamond mining has since fuelled the economic development of Botswana, which now ranks as a middle-income country.

Stagnation is reinforced, in many authoritarian states as well as in democracies, through a habit known as **rent-seeking** (Congleton and Hillman, 2015). This might be pursued by an individual, a company, or even an entire regime. For example, governments might take over control of valuable natural resources and charge citizens for their use, or they might require import licenses for companies bringing new products into a country, or charge visitors fees for visas. Equally, government officials might take bribes to provide a licence to a company, or a passport to a citizen. In all these cases, resources are being used unproductively to generate unearned benefits, hidden taxes are imposed on the economy and society, and no value is added to the wider marketplace. For governments reliant on rent-seeking, there is less motivation to set up the formal structures needed to collect taxes, expand the economy, and develop human capital. Rather, a stand-off of mutual distrust develops between rulers and ruled, creating a context which is incompatible with the more sophisticated policy initiatives found in many liberal democracies.

> **Rent-seeking**
> Efforts to make a profit or an income from selling a resource without using that resource to generate wealth or to benefit society.

Rent-seeking is related to the phenomenon of the **rentier state**. This label applies to countries that earn most of their revenue from exporting a natural resource. In economic terms, the rentier state makes an income from owning an asset which it exports, usually through licensing private and often foreign contractors, making a profit but adding little value to the local economy. For example, agricultural commodities may be exported raw, with processing taking place elsewhere. The authoritarian rulers of these rentier states receive a direct income from overseas, reducing their need to raise taxes, and reducing pressures for representation. A portion of the resource 'rent' can be distributed to the population as hand-outs or through providing jobs in a swollen public sector, thus buying popular acquiescence to a non-democratic regime, and delaying a transition to democracy. The phenomenon of the rentier state is one of the explanations for the lack of democracy in many states rich in key resources such as oil.

> **Rentier state**
> One which derives most or all of its national revenues from exporting raw materials or leasing natural resources to foreign companies.

Most of the major Middle Eastern oil states – including Iran, Saudi Arabia, and the Gulf States – have at various times earned the label rentier state. This has applied most obviously at times when the global price of oil has been high, though, and the long-term decline in the place of oil in the world economy may be having important implications for Saudi Arabia, among others. Its recent budget deficits have been exacerbated by the falling price of oil, encouraging the government to cut subsidies, to impose its first-ever general tax (in the form of a value added tax), and even to think about privatizing Aramco, the world's largest oil company. The long-term result, suggests Seznec (2016), might be that Saudi Arabia's political economy moves away from being 'the epitome of a rentier state' and instead begins to resemble those of more advanced industrial democracies.

DISCUSSION QUESTIONS

◆ What are the key benefits of studying the interaction between politics and economics?
◆ To what extent are classical liberal views still reflected in the modern practice of political economy in liberal democracies?
◆ To what extent are radical views still reflected in the modern practice of political economy?
◆ What is the future likely to hold for the welfare state?
◆ What are the differences between state socialism and state capitalism?
◆ Why have well-endowed liberal democracies managed to avoid the effects of the resource curse, while many authoritarian systems have not?

KEY CONCEPTS

◆ Capitalism
◆ Command economy
◆ Communism
◆ Convergence thesis
◆ Dependency theory
◆ Development
◆ Economic system
◆ Economics
◆ Externalities
◆ Fair trade
◆ Global financial crisis
◆ Macroeconomics
◆ Markets

◆ Microeconomics
◆ Neoliberalism
◆ New political economy
◆ Night-watchman state
◆ Political economy
◆ Rent-seeking
◆ Rentier state
◆ Resource curse
◆ Social security
◆ State capitalism
◆ State socialism
◆ Welfare economics

FURTHER READING

Castles, Francis C., Stephan Leibfried, Jane Lewis, Herbert Obinger, and Christopher Pierson (eds) (2010) *The Oxford Handbook of the Welfare State* (Oxford University Press). An edited collection on the welfare state, including chapters on its underlying justification, policy goals and outputs, the established welfare states of Europe, and welfare states emerging in other parts of the world.

Clark, Barry (2016) *Political Economy: A Comparative Approach*, 3rd edn (Santa Barbara, CA: Praeger). An overview of political economy, including chapters on contending perspectives, and on topics such as unemployment, inflation, trade, and the environment.

Clift, Ben (2014) *Comparative Political Economy: States, Markets and Global Capitalism* (Red Globe Press). An outline of the approaches and analytical tools used to understand contemporary capitalism.

Kurlantzick, Joshua (2016) *State Capitalism: How the Return of Statism is Transforming the World* (Oxford University Press). An assessment of the origins and effects of state capitalism, and its implications for studies of political economy.

Ravenhill, John (ed.) (2017) *Global Political Economy*, 5th edn (Oxford: Oxford University Press). A textbook on political economy as it applies to trade, finance, and development at the global level.

Ryan, Alan (2012) *The Making of Modern Liberalism* (Princeton, NJ: Princeton University Press). A detailed assessment of the origins, evolution, and contemporary features of modern liberalism.

BIBLIOGRAPHY

A

Aarts, Kees, André Blais, and Hermann Schmitt (eds) (2011) *Political Leaders and Democratic Elections* (Oxford: Oxford University Press).

Acemoglu, Daron, and James A. Robinson (2013) *Why Nations Fail: The Origins of Power, Prosperity and Poverty* (London: Profile).

Ahmad, Ahmad Atif (2017) *Islamic Law: Cases, Authorities and Worldview* (London: Bloomsbury).

Akkerman, Tjitske, Sarah L. de Lange, and Matthijs Rooduijn (eds) (2016) *Radical Right-Wing Populist Parties in Western Europe: Into the Mainstream?* (Abingdon: Routledge).

Albertus, Michael, and Victor Menaldo (2018) *Authoritarianism and the Elite Origins of Democracy* (Cambridge: Cambridge University Press).

Allen, Peter (2018) *The Political Class: Why it Matters Who our Politicians Are* (Oxford: Oxford University Press).

Allmark, Liam (2012) 'More than Rubber–Stamps: The Consequences Produced by Legislatures in Non-Democratic States beyond Latent Legitimation', in *Journal of Legislative Studies* 18:2, pp. 198–202.

Almond, Gabriel A. (1966), 'Political Theory and Political Science', in *American Political Science Review* 60:4, December, pp. 869–79.

Almond, Gabriel A., and Sidney Verba (1963) *The Civic Culture* (Princeton, NJ: Princeton University Press).

Ambrosio, Thomas (2016) *Authoritarian Backlash: Russian Resistance to Democratization in the Former Soviet Union* (Abingdon: Routledge).

Anckar, Carsten (2008) 'On the Applicability of the Most Similar Systems Design and the Most Different Systems Design in Comparative Research', in *International Journal of Social Research Methodology* 11:5, November, pp. 389–401.

Anderson, Benedict (2013) *Imagined Communities: Reflections on the Origins and Spread of Nationalism,* revised edition (London: Verso).

Andeweg, Rudy B. (2014) 'Cabinet Ministers: Leaders, Team Players, Followers?' in R. A. W. Rhodes and Paul 't Hart (eds) (2014) *The Oxford Handbook of Political Leadership* (Oxford: Oxford University Press).

Andeweg, Rudy B., and Galen A. Irwin (2014) *Governance and Politics of the Netherlands,* 4th edn (London: Red Globe Press).

Ansolabehere, Stephen (2006) 'Voters, Candidates and Parties', in Barry R. Weingast and Donald A. Wittman (eds) *The Oxford Handbook of Political Economy* (Oxford: Oxford University Press).

Anton, Thomas J. (1969) 'Policy-Making and Political Culture in Sweden', in *Scandinavian Political Studies* 4:A4, January, pp. 82–102.

Aristotle (1962 edn) *The Politics,* trans. T. A. Sinclair (Harmondsworth: Penguin).

Armitage, David (2005) 'The Contagion of Sovereignty: Declarations of Independence since 1776', in *South African Historical Journal* 52:1, pp. 1–18.

Art, David (2012) 'Review Article: What Do We Know About Authoritarianism After Ten Years?' in *Comparative Politics* 44:3, April, pp. 351–73.

Aslund, Anders (2017) 'Russia's Neo-feudal Capitalism', in Project Syndicate at www.project-syndicate.org, 27 April. Retrieved October 2018.

Auty, Richard M. (1993) *Sustaining Development in Mineral Economies: The Resource Curse Thesis* (London: Routledge).

B

Bachrach, Peter, and Morton S. Baratz (1962) 'The Two Faces of Power', in *American Political Science Review* 56:4, December, pp. 941–52.

Baek, Jieun (2016) *North Korea's Hidden Revolution: How the Information Underground Is Transforming a Closed Society* (New Haven, CT: Yale University Press).

Bagehot, Walter (1867) [2009 edn] *The English Constitution* (Oxford: Oxford University Press).

Bardach, Eugene (1976) 'Policy Termination as a Political Process', in *Policy Sciences* 7:2, June, pp. 123–31.

Bardes, Barbara A., Mack C. Shelley, and Steffen W. Schmidt (2018) *American Government and Politics Today: The Essentials,* 2017–18 edition (Boston, MA: Cengage).

Bauer, Michael W., Andrew Jordan, Christoffer Green-Pedersen, and Adrienne Héritier (eds) (2012) *Dismantling Public Policy: Preferences, Strategies, and Effects* (Oxford: Oxford University Press).

Baum, Scott (2014) 'Australia.gov.au: Development, Access, and Use of E-government', in Scott Baum and Arun Mahizhnan (eds) *E-Governance and Social Inclusion: Concepts and Cases: Concepts and Cases* (Hershey, PA: IGI Global).

Baumgartner, Frank R., Jeffrey M. Berry, Marie Hojnacki, David C. Kimball, and Beth L. Leech (2009) *Lobbying and Policy Change: Who Wins, Who Loses, and Why* (Chicago: University of Chicago Press).

Bayat, Asef (2010) *Life as Politics: How Ordinary People Change the Middle East* (Stanford, CA: Stanford University Press).

Beason, Dick, and Dennis Patterson (2004) *The Japan that Never Was: Explaining the Rise and Decline of a Misunderstood Country* (Albany, NY: State University of New York Press).

Beetham, David (2004) 'Freedom as the Foundation', in *Journal of Democracy* 15:4, October, pp. 61–75.

Bell, David S., and John Gaffney (eds) (2013) *The Presidents of the French Fifth Republic* (Basingstoke: Palgrave Macmillan).